PROGRESS IN POLITICAL GEOGRAPHY

CROOM HELM PROGRESS IN GEOGRAPHY SERIES
Edited by Michael Pacione, University of Strathclyde,
Glasgow

Progress in Urban Geography
Edited by Michael Pacione

Progress in Rural Geography
Edited by Michael Pacione

Progress in Political Geography

Edited by MICHAEL PACIONE

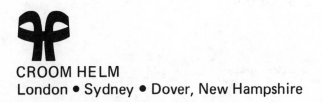

CROOM HELM
London • Sydney • Dover, New Hampshire

© 1985 M. Pacione
Croom Helm Ltd, Provident House, Burrell Row,
Beckenham, Kent BR3 1AT
Croom Helm Australia Pty Ltd, First Floor, 139 King Street,
Sydney, NSW 2001, Australia

British Library Cataloguing in Publication Data

Progress in political geography. — (Croom Helm
  progress in geography series)
  1. Geography, Political
  I. Pacione, Michael
320.1′2   JC319

ISBN O-7099-2087-3

Croom Helm, 51 Washington Street, Dover,
New Hampshire 03820, USA

Library of Congress Cataloging in Publication Data applied for.

Printed and bound in Great Britain
by Billing & Sons Limited, Worcester.

CONTENTS

FIGURES

TABLES

To Christine, Michael John and Emma Victoria

PREFACE

Political geography is an avowedly pluralist field of enquiry which spans the major disciplines of geography and politics and maintains strong links with the related social sciences of economics and sociology. For most of this century, however, political geography was essentially an empirically oriented subject which concentrated on the study of geographical aspects of contemporary political events at the macro or national-international scale. The development of a theoretical and methodological basis for the subject was a relatively neglected issue. Since the early 1970s the nature of political geography has undergone a radical transformation. Traditional areas of study have been complemented by investigations related to the exercise of power at the intra-state and intra-urban scales. New methodologies have been developed, particularly in the field of quantitative electoral geography, and a body of theory is accumulating. The range and volume of research undertaken testifies to the healthy eclecticism of modern political geography. Over the last two decades political geography has moved from being a 'moribund backwater' into the mainstream of the discipline, and the study of political issues from a spatial perspective is an integral component of modern human geography.

This collection of original essays is designed to encapsulate the major themes and recent developments in a number of areas of central importance in political geography. The volume is a response to the need for a text which reviews the progress and current state of the subject and which provides a reference point for future developments in political geography.

Michael Pacione,
University of Strathclyde,
Glasgow.

INTRODUCTION

Definitions of political geography abound, but a generally useful manifesto is that political geographers are concerned with the geographical consequences of political decisions and actions, the geographical factors which were considered during the making of any decisions, and the role of any geographical factors which influenced the outcome of political actions.

Early scholars interpreted geographical factors within an environmental-deterministic framework as witnessed by Greek models of the ideal state which sought to relate the facts of political life with the underlying physical conditions. Similarly, the development of political arithmetic in seventeenth century Europe, which entailed the cataloguing of the physical and human resources of a state, was founded on the belief that government policy should be based on a proper understanding of geography. This applied, empirical and essentially nationalistic approach was boosted by the military and strategic requirements of major wars, and remained the focus for political geography well into the present century. The period was characterised by studies of international boundaries and of ethnic and national groups, and by the emergence of theories such as Mackinder's Heartland concept. The nationalistic element was taken to a corrupt extreme in German geopolitics. Thus the core of the subject, in the view of leading practitioners like Whittlesey and Hartshorne, remained the study of the relationship between the physical environment and political organisations and activities, but the emphasis was firmly on place rather than process. It is almost anomalous to note the origins of electoral geography being laid at this time by Siegfried's (1913) study of voting behaviour in western France.

In the decades immediately following World War II political geography made relatively little progress as an academic subject. Attention continued to focus upon traditional macro-scale issues, with some consideration given to contemporary events such as the process of decolonisation. Since 1970, however, the scope and character of political geography has changed dramatically in response to a number of factors. These include (a) a growing interest in questions of public policy at the intra-state level, (b) a concern with social welfare

1

issues, such as equity and deprivation, and the working of the political systems which produce such resource distributions, (c) the development of a scientific research methodology, and (d) the emergence of new theoretical models including the political-economy perspective.

Conflict arising from the pursuit of self-interest by states, interest groups or individuals is a fundamental element of society, and therefore of political geography and the twin concepts of power and conflict continue to underlie political geography at all scales. Since the state is one of the most powerful institutions in the contemporary world the role of the modern state and how it affects the life chances of the citizens is of particular concern to political geographers. For much of the subject's history, the focus has been on the state and its relationships within the international community. Currently, however, more research effort is being directed to the relationship between political and geographical factors within the state. Neither of these perspectives, however, is of greater importance than the other; both are essential to the development of political geography. Indeed, adoption of a world economy perspective to further understanding of political processes, activities and outcomes would suggest that the division between macro- and micro-scale investigations in political geography may be more illusory than real.

Investigations in political geography, as in other scientific fields of enquiry, should ideally be embedded in a theoretical structure in order to achieve a full understanding of the processes operating. Critical examination of the methodology employed to derive and test theory is equally important. In Chapter 1 Clark Archer and Fred Shelley provide an overview of the changing nature and role of theory and methodology in political geography. The early theoretical foundations of the subject are located in nineteenth century German 'political arithmetic' and Ratzel's organic theory of the state. By the late nineteenth century, however, the dilemma which faced political geography was 'its wealth of data contrasting with its poverty of theory'. Despite contributions by Mackinder and Hartshorne the early decades of the twentieth century represented something of a Dark Age for the development of theory in political geography and it was not until after World War II that significant moves were made towards the pluralistic structure of modern political geography. Two stimuli were of particular importance. The first was the advent of the quantitative revolution in geography which in turn promoted a methodological revolution in political-geographical thought with the introduction of a logical-positivist stance which challenged the traditional chorographic methodology. The second was the introduction of a political-economy perspective in which the central question is the role of the state in society. The latter has been particularly influential over the last decade and questions of equity, conflict of interest, and the locational implications of political processes have assumed increasing importance. Particular concern with the distributional effects of public policy has created a strong interest in the geography of public service provision which is clearly related to theories of social justice. Most current research on the role of the state is based on either a liberal neo-classical or public choice approach, or a radical or structuralist viewpoint. Although these perspectives have become dominant paradigms in contemporary political geography, other important themes and theoretical developments are related to concepts of political culture, the geographical impacts of legal structures, and geographical perspectives on international systems. As Archer and Shelley emphasise, in discussing the most important theoretical developments in political geography it is necessary to consider the influence of geographic scale. At the level of the state, theoretical analysis revolves around the question of the nature and purpose of the state and its activities; while local level analysis focuses upon the response of individuals, communities and interest groups to state power, policy formation and implementation. At the international scale attention is directed toward the political-economic ramifications of global interdependence and upon international conflicts. The succeeding chapters in this volume provide discussions on each of these themes.

Geopolitics provided an early focus for students of political geography and, despite the excesses of the German geopolitik school, study of the relationship between geographic information and state power has remained an important area of enquiry. In Chapter 2 Stanley Brunn and Karen Mingst review the field. They first examine the origins of geopolitics in the work of Ratzel, Kjellen, Haushofer and Mackinder. Consideration is then given to the various definitions of the subject, and it is suggested that the essence of the post-war discipline lies in the relationship between geography and foreign policy. A bibliographic review is then employed to identify the major themes and study areas over the last century. These range from the early work of Mahan and Spykman to the more recent introduction of an ecological perspective, seen especially in the concern over resource distributions and their relationship to international conflict. An examination of the major concepts used in geopolitical studies identifies the fundamental role of power as well as a number of related concepts including polarity, stratification, partitioning, and ecological and dynamic equilibrium, but concludes that, as yet, there is no generally agreed geopolitical theory that specifies the relationship among the various concepts. The subject is also characterised by a variety of methodologies, ranging from philosophical speculation and case study approaches to sophisticated quantitative techniques, such as path analysis; and from use of maps to transactional analysis. Brunn and Mingst then identify some of the areas of continuing controversy in geopolitics, including the degree of permanence of geopolitical factors, and the relationship between geopolitics and political behaviour. In conclusion, the importance of geo-strategic studies in the modern world is stressed and a number of topics for future research are suggested. These include (a) the changing definition of the key concept of power; (b) the relative importance of the traditional factors of distance and location with the growth of 'world-shrinking' technologies; (c) the geopolitics of differing ideologies; (d) the geopolitical components of strategic studies; (e) the role of geopolitics in contemporary foreign policy; and (f) the future of the state.

Conflicts of interest are inevitable given the interdependence of states within the global political community. In Chapter 3 Neville Douglas first provides a brief account of the evolution of the modern nation state, then considers the nature and causes of inter-state conflict. These include the existence of cultural minority groups, boundary disputes, questions over resource ownership and exploitation, and a state's perceived strategic and logistical requirements, such as access to the open sea. The suggestion that the focus of contemporary territorial conflict is moving from land to sea underlines the significance of the Law of the Sea. The complex web of causal factors is such that those seeking to explain international conflict must search for state goals that are hidden as well as studying those that are made explicit. The remainder of the chapter reviews the contribution that political geography has made towards this objective. It is recognised that whereas the growth of a welfare approach to contemporary geographic problems and critical approaches to the nature and role of the state have focused attention on conflict arbitration at the intra-urban scale, study of conflict generators at the inter-state level has been marked by a lack of detailed investigation. Douglas proposes a three-fold organising structure for the geographical investigation of inter-state conflict based on consideration of the human, physical and institutional environments. Among the most important areas identified for future research within the realm of the physical environment are (a) the mapping of world 'hot-spots' and the development of the theoretical underpinnings of conflict zones, (b) the role of physical distance and proximity in conflict, (c) the diffusion of conflict, and (d) resource studies focusing, in particular, on the distribution of strategic minerals and the logistics of international transport and supply of raw materials. The basic premise for research on the human environment of conflict is that understanding of conflict behaviour can be advanced by analysis of the values, perceptions and attitudes of different groups. Finally, with reference to the institutional environment, the growing interest in the field of policy studies suggests that three types of institutions — the State, international government organisations and multinational corporations — merit particular attention. Careful investigation of these 'environments of conflict' will permit the testing of hypotheses and refinement of models, and so advance understanding of a phenomenon which is of increasing concern in the modern world.

Chapter 4 examines the geography of ethnic and minority groups in the modern state. In this, Colin Williams discusses the major themes of core-periphery interaction and state formation; uneven development and nationalism; territoriality and group perception; border regions and national identity; and ethno-regional inequality. The role of the state as an 'ethnic-defining instrument' is first underlined and the development of the West European state is examined via the key concept of core-periphery interaction, as operationalised in the nation-building models of Rokkan. A complementary approach which seeks to isolate the structural preconditions for autonomist nationalism from the triggering factors and to locate the phenomenon within certain identifiable socio-political milieux is then considered. The fact that nation-states have often incorporated internal ethnic enclaves, as well as overseas colonies, within their territory underlies the important concept of internal colonialism. This viewpoint provided the basis for Hechter's general theory of the development and maintenance of ethnic boundaries in advanced industrial states, and the characteristics and limitations of this proposition are examined. The perceptual or subjective approach to the relationship between people and places is illustrated with particular reference to the identification of 'homelands' in Canada and Wales. Attention is then focused on Northern Ireland as a prime example of the problems and prospects inherent in the theme of cultural integration and division. The question of ethno-regional inequality is considered with empirical evidence drawn from several states in Southeast Asia. This is followed by an examination of the position of minority groups in states (such as South Africa) which have institutionalised discrimination within their constitutional and economic framework. In conclusion a clear recommendation is made for greater research on the role of the state in its interaction with minority communities for, as Williams observes, it is this relationship which forms the basis of ethnic politics.

In Chapter 5 Ron Johnston addresses the key question of the relationship between central state and local government. The fundamental distinction between the two levels of government is that the subordinate authorities lack any sovereign status or existence independent of central government. Geographers have paid particular attention to variations between local authorities in the levels of services provided or functions performed, and to intra-authority spatial variations in service provision. With reference to the former, general models of the determinants of spending patterns have been proposed, normally including as independent variables indices of need, resources available, and political inclinations. Studies of the spatial allocation of services within local authorities have also employed a modification of the inter-government variations model to analyse the determinants of spatial allocation policies. The difficulty of operationalising and testing these models is considered. More generally, the limitations of a positivist approach with its implicit deterministic element are exposed and the deficiencies illustrated by two case studies of 'local fiscal crisis'. Johnston then discusses the role of the state in society, identifies the concepts of accumulation, legitimation and regulation, and applies these principles to explain the rationale for local government within the capitalist mode of production. The position of local governments in the USA and the UK are then compared, before attention is given to the special purpose authorities which operate in many countries. The dominance of central state over local government conditions all discussion of the latter. Nevertheless local government remains a subject worthy of detailed study as there is great variation in how it interprets and performs its assigned role. As Johnston concludes, full appreciation of the workings of local government must be grounded in a theoretical understanding of the role of the state in society. Since the mid 1970s political geographers have begun to balance an earlier interest in empirical and methodological issues with concern over theoretical and philosophical questions in the search to explain observed patterns. Clearly, both approaches are required to illuminate the complex relationship that exists between central state and local government.

Spatial variations in public service provision have formed a major focus of recent research in urban political geography with a central question being identification of the causal mechanisms underlying unequal patterns of resource allocation. Generally, inter-authority variations have been analysed by means of an ecological statistical methodology which seeks to correlate environmental socioeconomic and political characteristics of local authorities with levels of public expenditure or service provision. Intra-urban studies have more often employed a process-oriented case study approach with emphasis on the decision-making procedure. In Chapter 6 Alan Burnett adopts the latter perspective in examining political process and resource allocation at the metropolitan level. The basic premise is that some patterns of urban service provision can best be explained by the workings of the urban political system which represents the crucial intervening 'black-box' between the environment and resource outputs. The key question, therefore, is one of power — who makes decisions and how and why municipal spending and provision in the form of services and facilities are decided. Burnett first considers the scope and content of 'output' studies and identifies as a major deficiency their inability to elucidate the decision-making processes and so fully explain revealed resource patterns. The causal links between political process and resource distribution are then examined and the roles of key actors, such as the public, elected representatives and officials, discussed. Several models which contribute to an explanation of urban policy-making are reviewed including pork-barrel, incrementalism and bureaucratic decision rules. Finally a process-oriented perspective, which focusses on how political demands from outside the political system are processed and converted into distributive policy decisions, is applied to an empirical analysis of the making of traffic regulation orders in Portsmouth. In conclusion it is suggested that aggregate-area output studies are more important in overcoming the technical problems of analysing spatial variations in resource allocation than probing the political processes behind them. A pluralist approach which incorporates several theoretical perspectives, including ecological, behavioural and political economy models, is essential in order to improve our knowledge of who gets what, where and how in the context of urban resource distribution.

The apportionment of power is at the heart of recent demands for greater public involvement in decision-making. In Chapter 7 Ronan Paddison considers the question of local democracy within the modern city. In theory, the concept of democracy refers to the means by which the outputs of the political process are determined by popular will. It is suggested that part of the mismatch which occurs between theory and practice is attributable to the problem of scale of government. The contradiction between democracy and scale is clearly exposed by the difficulty of reconciling the need for effective administration with the need for maximum accountability. Attempts to promote local democracy in the city have sought to decentralise the decision-making process so that the separate communities have a greater role in policy-making. Basic questions to be addressed in analysing the phenomenon of neighbourhood political movements and citizen participation include, (a) the reasons underlying the emergence of such movements, (b) the implementation of local democracy, focusing on the types of administrative and political machinery aimed at meeting the objective of fuller citizen participation, and (c) the impact of the movement, measured by the extent to which local action alters the urban fabric and contributes to the solving of conflicts. In examining the different types of local political action found in western cities, Paddison emphasises the basic distinction between bodies generated spontaneously from the 'grass roots' and those deliberately fostered by a higher level of government. Analysis of the complex of reasons behind the growth of neighbourhood democracy underlines the tendency towards centralisation in the modern state, the divisibility of many public services, and the unresponsiveness of city government to local needs. Various strategies of implementing local democracy are then considered including neighbourhood councils, area management schemes and community-activism strategies. The fundamental importance of a politically mobilised community is stressed and the pre-conditions to achieve this are discussed. Finally, the impact of community-based participation is evaluated with reference to particular examples from Spain, Australia and England. It is concluded that rather than being a transitory phenomenon the demand for greater local democracy in its various guises is likely to be a permanent feature of urban society in response to the increasing power of the state to affect the life-chances of its citizens.

Study of the geography of elections is one of the most distinctive sub-branches of political geography. In Chapter 8 Peter Taylor provides an overview of the field that first examines recent research on the geography of voting, on geographical influences on voting, and on the geography of representation, before considering the wider framework for a re-oriented electoral geography. The geography of voting remains a major theme in electoral geography. Studies of voting behaviour have traditionally identified regional patterns as well as examining the processes producing observed distributions. Recent research has moved towards longitudinal studies of electoral change involving, for example, identification of electoral regions via factor analytic techniques and the application of entropy-maximising to estimate intra-constituency vote changes. Specifically geographical influences on voting include the neighbourhood, candidate voting and campaign effects and the explanatory power of each is examined. Interest in the geography of representation has centred upon electoral districting and the twin abuses of malapportionment and gerrymandering. Work on each of these topics is assessed with reference to an international selection of case studies. In the second part of the chapter Taylor emphasises the need to develop an electoral geography which counters the criticism that 'elections are often studied as ends in themselves'. The use of a systems framework to structure the components of electoral geography is considered an unsatisfactory vehicle in which to make any real advance in our understanding of elections. It is suggested that the simple geography of elections needs to be supplemented with the more subtle geography of power. Furthermore, it is stressed that technical advances in the use of sophisticated quantitative methodologies are, in themselves, insufficient. What is required is a revolution in thinking to take electoral geography beyond interesting case studies and simplistic adherence to the tenets of liberal democracy, to which a minority of world states adheres. Adopting a global political-economy perspective emphasises that the power of political parties in a state is not absolute but is relative to the position of their state within the capitalist world economy, and that changes in the world economy govern the politics within any state. It follows that a major task for a new electoral geography is to investigate the electoral processes and patterns characteristic of the different socio-political realms in the modern world.

1 THEORY AND METHODOLOGY IN POLITICAL GEOGRAPHY

J. C. Archer and F. M. Shelley

Introduction

Political geography had been defined as 'the science of political areas' (Hartshorne, 1935a, p. 804), 'the study of geographical area and political process' (Ackerman, *et al.,* 1965, p. 32), 'the spatial analysis of political phenomena' (Kasperson and Minghi, 1969, p. xi), a set of 'locational approaches to power and conflict' (Cox, Reynolds and Rokkan, 1974), and simply 'political studies from spatial perspectives' (Burnett and Taylor, 1981). Each of these definitions has served as a guide to research undertaken under the general heading of political geography. Yet a recent review likens political geography to a metaphorical Los Angeles: 'all sprawling neighbourhoods and no centre' (Short, 1983, p. 122). Like neighbourhoods in a changing and growing metropolis, theories and methodologies in political geography have changed through the years, with some once fashionable areas becoming run down as new areas develop and attain prominence. But theoretical and methodological changes rarely occur without friction, for methodologies, like neighbourhoods, involve a marking out of territory and a defence of existing property rights, such as access to publication and academic prestige.

Johnston (1983, p. 1) has noted that, 'A discipline is brought into existence because those propagating it are able to show potential sponsors that its topical content is worthy of study and that its means of study are valid.' Such demonstration is particularly difficult in the case of political geography and its diverse subcentres. Wright (1944, p. 190) perceived that 'Political geography is perhaps the most "human" phase of geography, since it deals so largely with the strengths, weaknesses and ambitions of men.' Because of this, a wholly neutral, wholly value-free approach is unattainable. While many political geographers would like to appear objective and 'scientific', they cannot escape the denotation of the adjective 'political': 'of or pertaining to the state or its government' (Stern, 1979, p. 1113). Attempts to develop theory in political geography must involve ideological implications, whether these are explicit or not.

Contempory political geography is avowedly pluralistic, with unprecedented cross-fertilisation of scholarly ideas within the political geography community and between political geographers and other students of political processes in political science, economics, sociology and law. The current pluralism of political geography stands in rather sharp contrast with the isolationism of the discipline during much of its intellectual history, in which periods of theoretical advance alternated with periods of explicit retreat from theoretical innovation. Yet in order to gain appreciation for contemporary theoretical and methodological developments in political geography, to review recent research advancing these developments, and to consider possible coming trends in the field, it is important to set the stage from a long-run perspective. This is the intent of the first part of this essay, in which theoretical developments in political geography were often undertaken via direct or indirect analogy with models from the life or physical sciences. In contrast, contemporary theoretical and methodological advances — to which Short (1983) alluded in describing the discipline as in a state of intellectual gentrification — have more often reflected models developed in the social sciences, and notably in economics. The pluralism which now characterises political geography represents a form of maturity which was earlier absent, though this pluralism could be misinterpreted as an eclectic admixture of mutual inconsistencies representing opposed ideological vantage points.

Early Theoretical Foundations of Political Geography

It is perhaps rare that the genesis of a subject of study can be traced to a single seminal work, but this is often regarded as true of political geography (Fawcett, 1957, p. 418; Fisher, 1968, p. 1). In English language discussions of the matter, this view appears traceable to Hartshorne's (1953a, p. 789) survey, in which he wrote that 'the foundations were laid by Friedrich Ratzel, whose *Politische Geographie*, published in 1897, is universally recognised as the first systematic treatment of the subject.' But Hartshorne was vague about the nature of the foundations laid down by Ratzel, who in turn was scarcely the first to use the phrase, 'political geography'.

Political geographic description had long been undertaken as an extension of historical or commercial geography. Early in the nineteenth century in Germany, for example, a research tradition known as 'political arithmetic' had arisen. With strong ties to regional geography, political arithmetic endeavoured to assemble and systematise information regarding countries throughout the world (Lazarsfeld, 1961). The approach was reminiscent of what is now labelled the 'power analysis' school of political geography with its links to military geography (Cohen, 1973, p. 7). Political arithmeticians organised information in large systematic arrays which included both numerical and verbal data; in concept, these data arrays were analogous to what Berry (1964) much more recently termed 'geographic matrices'.

Judging by Mackinder's remarks to the Royal Geographical Society in 1887, the phrase 'political geography' was common currency in England well before the turn of the century. Its intellectual role was seen as one of imparting to 'future statesmen a full grasp of geographical conditions' (Mackinder, 1962, p. 213). But Mackinder was quite critical of the subject as he surveyed it (Mackinder, 1962, p. 214):

At the present moment we are suffering under the effects of an irrational political geography, one, that is, whose main function is not to trace causal relations, and which must therefore remain a body of isolated data to be committed to memory. Such a geography can never be a discipline.

The dilemma which faced political geography during the late nineteenth century was its wealth of data contrasting with its poverty of theory. Perhaps this is why Hartshorne later pointed to Ratzel for the first *systematic* treatment of the subject. But what form did his theories take — and why have they failed to retain their earlier prominence?

Like other social scientists and social philosophers of the late nineteenth century, Ratzel was inspired by the publication of Darwin's *On the Origin of Species* in 1859. Darwin's theory of natural selection exerted an enormous impact upon biological sciences as a result of its potential for reconciling what had until then seemed disparate and contradictory facts. Although the theory rested upon careful inductive observation of nature, it is important to recall that it also rested upon analogy with human society. In Darwin's (1970, p. 196) own words, the theory of natural selection 'is the doctrine of Malthus applied with manifold force to the whole animal and vegetable kingdoms'. The impetus to natural selection was viewed as reproductive potential exceeding resources, creating competition for sustenance as populations expanded. From Adam Smith Darwin drew additional insight into the form of natural selection: a species was regarded as a natural counterpart to a specialised occupation, with such specialisation promoting efficient use of resources. Darwin's major contribution was thus to reveal nature as a competitive, interdependent community regulated by principles of political economy.

The sweeping success of Darwin's theory led others to adopt his methods, directly or by analogy, to account for seemingly contradictory facts on the basis of unifying principles. Ratzel, himself schooled in zoology and geology, looked to the biological sciences for inspiration in the study of human society. He proposed what was perhaps the first political-geographic model, in which the state is regarded as 'an organic entity increasingly attached to the land on which it lives' (Kasperson and Minghi, 1969, p. 8). Ratzel's views regarding the concept of 'laws' and the character of states were complex, and he cautioned against simple, direct 'analogy between an aggregate of men and the structure of an organic creature' (Kasperson and Minghi, 1969, p.8). A new translation of his work on 'The Laws of the Spatial Growth of States' (Ratzel, 1969, pp.17-18) reads in part:

> Inventories of states which depict the territory of the state as a stable, fully fixed object come to this dogmatic and sterile conception primarily through disregard of such ruptures. Consideration of them can only strengthen the single correct conclusion: that in the state we are dealing with an organic nature. . . . Some number of people are joined to the area of the state. These live on its soil, draw their sustenance from it, and are otherwise attached to it by spiritual relationships. Together with this piece of earth they form the state.

While sceptical of viewing the state as an individual organic creature, Ratzel none the less asserted its organic character, a distinction which was perhaps too subtle for some of his critics, and doubtless for some of his later followers as well. One of Ratzel's goals was to provide a framework within which to integrate seemingly disparate geographical facts and, given the intellectual tenor of the times, the organic theory of the state 'provided a simple and powerful model in analytical political geography' (Stoddart, 1966, p. 694). In some respects, this model presaged later systems-theory-based frameworks of political analysis.

The Retreat from Theory

It has been said that 'American academic geography reached its pinnacle of respect and achievement under the leadership of William Morris Davis', who, like Ratzel, employed Darwinian thinking to derive a theoretical framework (Herbst, 1961, p. 540). At this time, early in the twentieth century, a unity of purpose linked physical and human geography, as did, in substantial measure, a unity of theory which placed nature in a paramount position with respect to human endeavours. Sorokin's (1928) well-documented survey of socio- logical theory, for example, devoted considerable space — 93 pages — to the 'geographical school'. Sorokin (1928, p. 193) concluded that:

> Any analysis of social phenomena, which does not take into consideration geographical factors, is incomplete. We are grateful to the school for these valuable contributions. This, however, does not oblige us to accept its fallacious theories, its fictitious correlations, or finally, its overestimation of the role of geographical environment. We must separate the wheat from the chaff.

One may suspect that the harsh criticism levelled at the 'geo- graphical school' by Sorokin was motivated partly by a desire to define the search for correlations between social and natural phenomena as within the domain of sociology rather than that of geography (Sorokin, 1928, p. 760). Such an interpretation can be reinforced by noting that Park and Burgess (1970, p. 123) claimed that the study of 'Land as a basis for social contacts' was the foun- dation of the human ecology subdivision of sociological research. But, whereas human ecologists continued to seek correlations between spatial relations and social relations, human geographers, rather than trying to separate the 'wheat from the chaff', instead retreated from search for causation into chorography. Among other consequences, this meant that 'Both natural and human geography were now bereft of a causal explanatory principle that could give independence and unity to geography as a science in its own right' (Herbst, 1961, p. 542). Most 'American geographers went back to Kant, Ritter, and Hettner, and rediscovered geography as 'the science of areal differentiation of the earth's surface' (Herbst, 1961, p. 542).

If human geography in general was edged into retreat, political geography was plunged into chaos. Hartshorne's (1953a; 1935b) survey avoided mention of Darwin. Ratzel received but brief and enigmatic mention in the second instalment, and neither instalment sharply outlined Ratzel's theoretical stance or drew attention to the search for a scientific explanation of causation. Indeed, Hartshorne (1935a, pp. 790–1) distanced political geography from the possibility of such 'misinterpretation' when he wrote that:

> many geographers have changed their concept of 'historical geography' . . . and have classified studies of geographic influences in history as 'geographic history,' i.e rather a part of the field of history than of geography. Nevertheless, it was the work of the geographers that brought this subject to the attention of historians like Turner and Vogel, and geographers trust to see other historians, adequately trained in geography, make use of geographical methods and concepts in their historical studies.

Later in the same article, he averred, though with some qualifications, that 'the geographer feels justified in turning over the question of Geopolitik to the students of political science' (Hartshorne, 1935b, p. 963). Following such major amputations what remained? In Hartshorne's (1935b, p. 944) words:

> The analysis, or interpretive description, of the nature and content of the area of the state constitutes the major portion of the field of political geography.

In short, the core of the subject was to be political chorography. 'The primary facts in political geography, 'Hartshorne (1954, p. 177) later observed, 'are presented in the common political map.' As before the turn of the century, students and researchers began to suffer under an 'irrational' political geography, to recall Mackinder's phrase. The subject reverted to the status of a verbal and cartographic political arithmetic whose matrix of cells was partitioned along the boundaries between sovereign states, political dependencies or unorganised areas.

Countercurrents to the Retreat from Theory

In general, the evolution of political geography to the mid-twentieth century can be characterised as a main channel leading initially towards, and later away from, Ratzel's organic theory of the state. However, countercurrents deviating from these general trends can be observed. In England, the chief figure in political geography during the interwar era was Mackinder, who, like Ratzel, focused upon the expansion and international relationships of states and empires. However, Mackinder's debt to German scholars was modest (Hartshorne, 1935a, p. 795); he explicitly rejected the Darwinian approach under which (Mackinder, 1962, p. 2)

> men came to think that those forms of organisation would sur-
> vive which adapted themselves best to their natural environment.
> Today we realize . . . that human victory consists in our rising
> superior to such mere fatalism.

Mackinder is well remembered for the Heartland theory; what is less well known is that he relied upon analogy with Newtonian laws of motion in its derivation (Pearce, 1962, p. xvi). The Heartland concept was based upon a 'theory of political motion' rooted in two major principles: the principle that fertility and strategic opportunity are unevenly distributed across the globe so that there is 'no such thing as equality of opportunity for the nations; and the principle that 'A great and advanced society has a powerful momentum' (Mackinder, 1962, p. 2). Mackinder identified the world as for the first time constituting a closed system because of technological advancement (Mackinder, 1962, p. 29). Accordingly, he warned that a single world empire might emerge with its core in the Eurasian Heartland as transport improvements replaced the military dominance of the 'seaman's point of view' with that of the 'lands-man's point of view' (Mackinder, 1962, p. 2 and *passim*). Iron-ically, Mackinder's basic thesis exerted its greatest impact upon foreign policy not in England but in America, and not until both of these views were eclipsed by the airman's point of view. Since World War II, Mackinder's Heartland theory has been a keystone tenet of the concept of the nuclear deterrent, developed in order to counter the assumed Soviet geopolitical advantage (Walters, 1974, p. 8 and *passim*).

Reliance upon biological or physical analogies was hardly universal among Mackinder's contemporaries. For example, Bowman (1922), Chief Territorial Specialist at the Paris Peace Conference in 1919, shortly thereafter published *The New World* in which the attempt was 'made to avoid all but the most necessary expressions of editorial opinion, leaving the facts on the two sides of a given question to speak for themselves' (Bowman, 1922, p. v). The work was an exhaustive and knowledgeable, yet ultimately chorological treatise on 'major problems', ordered by region. A similarly intended, albeit less magisterial, effort was undertaken following World War II to 'rub up' knowledge of the geopolitical circumstances at that time (East and Moodie, 1956).

However, Whittlesey (1939) acknowledged links to organic theory as a framework for *The Earth and the State*. While rejecting dogmatic, ethnocentric Geopolitics, which he distinguished by capitalising, Whittlesey wrote that (1939, p. 1):

> This book, in treating Political Geography, is bound to give attention to the degree of correspondence between the pattern of states and the patterns of the national environment. . . . It must further inquire into the geographic structure of states and the organic relation between political and natural phenomena. In brief, the subject is geopolitical patterns and structures.

One theme advanced by Whittlesey (1939, p. 585) is that 'Every political unit describes an areal pattern of nuclear core, constituent or administrative regions, problem areas, vulnerable zones, capitals, strategic spots, and boundaries.' Unfortunately, later work following up on this theme often focused 'upon case studies rather than general principles' (House, 1968, p. 327). In Kasperson and Minghi's (1969, p. 70) pointedly phrased evaluation:

> the approach to political geography through structure has tended to emphasize the purely formal aspects of landscape . . . thereby tending to divert attention away from these other aspects of the system such as political processes and behaviour without due consideration of which the functional aspects of structure cannot, in the final analysis, be fully understood.

Once again, political geographers began to acknowledge that they were suffering under the effects of an 'irrational' political geography. At first, there were two major responses to this. One looked within political geography's own traditions back toward the turn of the century; the other looked beyond geography into other disciplines for escape from the retreat from theory. Both of these responses found solace in partially disguised organic analogies.

Hartshorne (1950) endeavoured to fill the lacunae left in political geography by cession of the study of geographical influences to political history and of geopolitics to political science by proposing a 'functional' approach to geographic study of the sovereign state. The major goal was to ground political chorography upon the notion of a state-idea, or *raison d'être*, specific to each such union of land and people. A corollary objective was perhaps to maintain the pre-eminence of regional methodology, which had been challenged by recognition of the fact that most cultural, as well as most physical divides, are zonal rather than linear features. In proposing this concept, Hartshorne appealed to German sources, including Ratzel. In Hartshorne's (1950, p. 112) words:

> We must discover and establish the unique distinctive idea under which a particular section of area and of humanity is organized into a unit state.

The notion of *raison d'être* is almost reminiscent of the doctrine of biological vitalism, whereby organisms are regarded as possessing intrinsic properties apart from chemical or physical forces. Perhaps surprisingly in light of the then close ties between historical and political geography, Hartshorne (1950, p. 113) admonished that in order to identify the *raison d'être* for specific states, 'we must study the current situation, rather than the remote past'. Yet this would seemingly exclude study of the Declaration of Independence, the Constitution, or the *Federalist Papers* to account for the *raison d'être* of the United States, to give an example. Like the earlier tradition of biological vitalism itself, the 'functional' tradition in political geography failed to exert a significant impact upon research beyond the first decade or two after it appeared.

The work of Kasperson and Minghi (1969), which provided an overview of both historical and contemporary research, looked beyond political geography for theoretical guidance. Their introduction of structural-functionalist methodology, most directly from anthropology, political science and sociology, illustrates the process whereby theory in political geography has sometimes been borrowed indirectly from the life or physical sciences. Many of the concepts underpinning the structural-functionalist approach derive from systems theory, which in turn draws inspiration from biology, physics, and electronics. For example, the notion of a self-regulating homeostatic system parallels that of a thermostatically controlled heating and cooling system; both of these maintain dynamic equilibrium using input resources. In turn, the idea of 'pattern maintenance' by social systems is analogous to these nonsocial counterparts. A variant form of structural-functional analysis was introduced into political science by Easton (1965a; 1965b).

In short, the structural-functional approach, like its predecessors which endeavoured to advance political-geographical theory on the basis of analogies with physical or biological systems, proved too abstract and too distant from the world of daily political antagonisms. However, the structural-functional approach, with its often explicit appeal for general theoretical propositions, helped to lower the barriers which had previously separated political geography from other social sciences concerned with the behaviour of human beings as political actors.

The Quantitative Revolution and Political Geography

By the time Kasperson and Minghi's *The Structure of Political Geography* was published in 1969, political geography, like other branches of the discipline, had been exposed to the quantitative revolution. During the 1950s and 1960s, geographers developed expertise in mathematical and statistical techniques and applied these to a variety of geographical problems. More importantly, the quantitative revolution also involved a *methodological* revolution in geographic thought (e.g. Abler *et al.*, 1971). Chorographic description as an objective was replaced by the search for verifiable law-like statements and causal explanations. This shift was promoted by Schaefer (1953), who distinguished idiographic (i.e. descriptive) and nomothetic (i.e. law-seeking) approaches to the discipline. Heavily influenced by philosopher Gustav Bergman and the Vienna School, the early 'quantifiers' introduced logical positivism into geographical thinking (Johnston, 1983, pp. 11–51).

Although Schaefer was a political geographer (Bunge, 1979), the subject was slow to adopt the technical and methodological innovations associated with quantification for several reasons. One was the strength of chorographic methodology in political geography, which directly opposed the search for geographic regularities. Another factor was that 'nuts and bolts' aspects of quantitative tools were often given precedence over the objectives of quantitative-positivistic research. For example, an early response to quantification in political geography focused upon whether traditional subjects of study were measurable. It was implied that some, such as the lengths of boundaries or the areas of administrative units, could be measured with accuracy, but that many others, such as 'the evolution of states, the acquisition of colonies . . . (or) . . . the breakdown of empires' could not be; thus, 'Political geographers would be well advised to avoid mathematical analysis of subjects like this' (Prescott, 1972, pp. 50 and 53). Conclusions of this nature rested upon limited understanding of the potential scope of mathematical models. And this limited understanding was itself an impediment to quantification, for it raised fears that 'There is so much ignorance of mathematical techniques, that there is a real danger that some papers will appear sound to the untutored' (Prescott, 1972, p. 52). Finally, because of unpleasant experiences involving earlier transformation of the organic theory of the state into Axis power geopolitics prior to World War II, there was a general apprehension even toward verbal models which reinforced the suspicion of quantitative techniques.

The barriers against positivist and quantitative approaches led some observers to predict the imminent demise of political geography (e.g. Berry, 1969). Many of the critics were young urban or economic geographers who recognised the importance of political processes to their own subjects of study, who had become well schooled in model building and mathematical methods, but who on turning to traditional work in political geography found little of relevance to their own endeavours (Johnston, 1980a). To offer illustrations: Soja (1974) adopted Berry's (1964) geographic matrix for use in political geography; Hudson (1974) explored some of the legislative apportionment implications of Christaller's (1966) central place theory; and Reynolds (1974) drew upon spatial diffusion theory to explain electoral processes. During the past decade quantification has come to characterise a broad range of research in political geography, as indicated in reviews by Bennett (1981), Johnston (1981a), and Taylor and Gudgin (1981).

Political Economy and Political Geography

The quantitative revolution brought to political geography, as it did to other branches of human geography, a renewed awareness of the importance of relatively general and empirically verifiable theory in explaining observations in causal fashion. Neither of the major historical trends previously recognised in political geography — the rise of organically based formulations or the retreat from theoretical investigations — provided a satisfactory foundation for the development of causative thought. The former proved a difficult base for the extraction of empirically testable propositions, and the latter was not oriented toward search for theory at all. Since the early 1970s, however, political geography has witnessed unprecedented theoretical development. But the theories from which political geographers have more recently drawn inspiration have come not from physical or biological sciences but from *social* sciences, and especially from the realm of political economy.

The term political economy is sometimes regarded as synonymous with economics (Stern, 1979, p. 1113). However political economy is more broadly focused upon matters of equity as well as upon matters of efficiency, and hence straddles the standard division between economics and political science. Indeed, political economists of liberal (e.g. Tullock, 1983) as well as of radical (e.g. Dear and Clark, 1981) persuasions tend to stress that their perspectives are overarching and cross-disciplinary. This helps to re-emphasise the impossibility of a 'value-free' political geography. Political geography concerns politics, and politics is often, though not always, about zero-sum competition.

Rather than in roundabout fashion via Darwinian analogies, political geographers have come to examine the locational implications of political processes directly in terms of the methodologies of political economy, both liberal and Marxian. Christaller (1966, p. 83), whose influence upon economic and urban geography was substantial, foresaw such a trend a half century ago; in his words: 'A theoretical political-geography is just as possible and may be as approximately 'exact' as a theoretical economic geography.' Pertinently, Christaller used both neoclassical and Marxian tools of analysis in developing his theory of central places, whose roles are economic and administrative. Thus, the intellectual mentors of modern political geography can be regarded as Schaefer (1953), who pointed toward logical positivism, and Christaller (1966), who pointed toward political economy.

In considering the most important theoretical developments in contemporary political geography, it is relevant to note the importance of geographical scale, since the questions considered often differ in relation to variations in geographical scale. A three-fold division — international, national, and subnational or local and regional — is frequently adopted in political-geographic research as well as in textbooks (e.g., Cox, 1979). For example, Taylor (1982) refered to global, state and urban scales of analysis in presenting his adaptation of Wallerstein's (1979) world systems framework as a viable perspective for political geographers concerned with integrating these various scales. At the level of the state, theoretical analysis revolves around the question of the nature and purpose of the state and its activities. Local-level analysis focuses upon the responses of individuals, communities, interest groups, and other individual or collective actors to state power, policy formation and implementation. At the international scale, attention is directed toward the political-economic ramifications of global interdependence, and upon international conflicts which range from peaceful competition to armed confrontation.

Consideration of the nature of the political state is fundamental to political-geographic research (Dear and Clark, 1978; Johnston, 1980a; Reynolds, 1981). With Ratzel's organic theory of the state and Hartshorne's *raison d'être* thesis having retired into historical roles, contemporary analysts have needed new frameworks for viewing the state's power, authority, legitimacy, and functions. Broadly speaking, two trends can be identified: neoclassical and structural political economy perspectives. Liberal neoclassical or public choice approaches were inspired by Adam Smith's *laissez-faire* depiction of individual-utility-based private market behaviour, in which unfettered economic competition is seen to generate stable, welfare-maximising social equilibria. Radical or structural approaches were inspired by Karl Marx and other social philosophers who argued that the dynamic tensions inherent in capitalist economic organisation lead not to stable equilibria, but instead toward continued and collective struggle between class-based groupings.

These two general themes were expanded by Dear and Clark (1978), who identified five basic theories of the state. Three of these — the state as supplier of public services, the state as regulator and facilitator of the marketplace, and the state as social engineer — correspond to the allocational, stabilisation, and distributional branches of the neoclassical theory of public finance (Musgrave, 1959) and represent the liberal approach to political economy. Alternatively, the state can be viewed as an arbiter of inter-group conflict or as an active, perhaps self-interested, agent in the struggle between capital and labour. In similar fashion, Johnston (1980a) differentiated *laissez-faire*, welfare-state, mediator, pluralist, and associate-of-capitalism theories of the state. He also noted that these are not always sharply separable. For example, Marxian classes are sometimes discussed in pluralist writings, and individual motivations are sometimes examined as impediments to collective action in structuralist discussions.

Much of the recent neoclassical oriented literature in political geography, which was reviewed by Archer (1981) and Shelley (1983a), has been devoted to tracing the impacts of space and location on the structure and operation of political markets. For example, public choice theory applies the behavioural assumptions of neoclassical microeconomics directly to non-market, collective decision contexts (Mueller, 1979). Public choice theory views the state's primary functions as allocational and regulatory; the purpose of organised government is seen as enabling the provision of public goods and services which are demanded by citizens yet which would not be efficiently provided through private market arrangements.

The application of utility maximisation postulates can provide insight into relationships between governmental institutions, geographic distributions, and policy outcomes. For example, analysis of electoral districting has shown that the geographic distribution of partisan support influences the relative ability of competing parties to elect candidates to legislatures. In representative democracies, these spatial biases affect the likelihood with which a party given a majority of popular votes will obtain a majority of legislative seats (Gudgin and Taylor, 1980). Theoretical knowledge of the impacts of space on voting processes is also under development. For example, the voting power of individual members of the electorate to influence the direction of public policy has been shown to vary systematically in geographical space (Shelley, 1983b). Rushton *et al.* (1981), and Shelley and Goodchild (1983) revealed conditions under which the paradox of majority voting arises during balloting over the locations of salutary public facilities. From a different standpoint, game-theoretic voting power indices have been applied to such situations as the European Parliament (Johnston, 1977; Taylor and Johnston, 1978), and weighted voting in the state of New York (Grofman and Scarrow, 1981).

Despite its potential in explaining relationships between power, policy outcomes, institutional design, and location, the public choice approach offers but a partial guide to public formation since it tends to overlook distributional questions. However, most political geographers recognize in some fashion the state's authority to establish and strive to attain goals of societal redistribution. While neoclassical principles can aid in the assessment of the efficiency of alternative redistributional schemes, they are much less effective for choosing among alternative redistributional goals. Hence, formal consideration of such goals requires integration of microeconomic analysis with philosophical issues of social justice. Distributional questions, which involve explicit political and philosophical considerations ignored in the technical, efficiency oriented approach of public choice theory, must be resolved if issues of justice and equity are to be understood from a theoretical perspective (Harvey, 1973; Papageorgiou, 1977; Reynolds, 1981).

The recent literature on public service provision illustrates the role of distribution-oriented theory in political geography. Early geographical analyses of public service delivery, while recognizing conceptual distinctions between choices of locations for private and collective facilities (Teitz, 1968), emphasised spatial efficiency without explicit theoretical consideration of the social and economic equity consequences of alternative public facility locations. However, spatial constraints influence the relative accessibility of low-, medium-, and high-income groups to many public services, which can be conceptualised as impure public goods since they vary in quantity or quality from place to place. Simulation and analysis has shown that the location of such services is affected by the spatial distribution of income groups (McLafferty, 1982; McLafferty and Ghosh, 1982). That the spatial structure of urban areas affects the likelihood of progressivity was determined by statistical comparison of distributions of correlation coefficients between incomes and distances to public facilities — a methodology pioneered in this context by Hodge and Gatrell (1976), and also applied to the identification of electoral biases by Taylor and Gudgin (1976), as well as to the identification of racially motivated constituency gerrymandering (O'Loughlin, 1982). Such cross-fertilisation of purpose and technique across separate substantive issues illustrates the broad explanatory power of political-geographical research undertaken under political economy methodology using quantitative tools of analysis.

Identification of locational progressivity or regressivity cannot guarantee income redistribution. Thus, attempts to develop public facility location theory have also focused upon relationships between facility location and socioeconomic processes (Kirby, 1983). No more is mere physical distance regarded as a naive surrogate for accessibility and consequently for equity in service delivery (Dear, 1978; Jones and Kirby, 1982). Underlying efforts to reformulate public facility location theory in terms of social and political processes are explicit or implicit notions concerning government's role in redistribution. One line of research, derived from welfare economics, emphasises the geography of human welfare: optimal service location is regarded as that best promoting improvements in the quality of life (Smith, 1977). Still other research has examined the broad geographic implications of public theory and public finance economics (Bennett, 1980; Lea, 1979).

Concern with the definitions and implications of equity and justice and their application has led political geographers to consider more formal theories of social justice. The influential theory of Rawls (1971) has been employed as a referent for such investigation. However, as Pirie (1983) has pointed out, the extent to which there might exist a fundamentally *geographic* theory of social justice — one which can be analysed and applied independently of social aspects of justice — remains unresolved.

Most non-Marxian studies have focused on distributive aspects of social justice. However, dissatisfaction with the *distributional* emphasis of these approaches led Reynolds (1981) to call for an approach to the geographical analysis of social justice based upon *procedural* considerations, in which the evaluation of social justice emphasises the fairness of the procedures used in the resolution of conflicts rather than the outcomes. This approach draws theoretical inspiration not only from the distributive and procedural theory of social justice (e.g. Nozick, 1974; Rawls, 1971), but also from contractarian theories within public choice economics (e.g. Buchanan and Tullock, 1962; Olson, 1965). Empirical research has indicated that such an approach has potential for the development and reform of locally based and decentralised social choice institutions (Reynolds, 1983; Shelley, 1983c). However, its application to large scale conflicts and to conflicts with predominant distributional overtones remains problematic.

The neoclassical perspective on the nature of the state has also been influenced by sociological and political perspectives within political geography, particularly those reflecting a pluralist methodology. For example, logrolling, or vote trading, is often engaged in by legislators anxious to secure the approval of projects such as highways or dams whose benefits primarily accrue to local areas. Political geographers have devoted considerable attention to achieving an understanding of geographical aspects of logrolling. The success of a locational logrolling strategy in obtaining support for a series of municipal bond issues in the city of St. Louis was investigated by Archer and Reynolds (1976). Archer (1980) sought relationships between the geographical pattern of federal outlays and the re-election prospects of US House incumbents. Johnston (1979a) looked at the influences of Congressional committee membership on the geography of Federal spending, and Archer (1983a) examined the effects of Presidential politics on the same distribution. Archer (1983b) and Johnston (1979b; 1980b) have provided comprehensive reviews of the literature on the geography of Federal spending in the United States of America.

The influence of sociological and political theory on political geography is also evident in the contemporary literature on locational conflict resolution. Although some attention has been paid to conflicts concerning the locations of desirable, salutary facilities (Reynolds and Honey, 1978; Shelley and Goodchild, 1983), most attention has been directed toward conflicts concerning the locations of noxious facilities (Wolpert *et al.,* 1972; Mumphrey and Wolpert, 1973; Ley and Mercer, 1980). Recent studies have more formally integrated the analysis of locational conflicts and conflict patterns with social and political theory in political economy. Cox (1981; 1983), for example, analysed the distribution of locational conflicts in terms of community response to proposals to locate particular facilities. The concept of 'turf politics', formulated by Cox, traces the development of neighbourhood and civic organisations which organise and act to promote salutary or to restrict noxious land uses.

In neoclassical political-economic analysis, the state is viewed as a means of regulating external effects generated by private initiatives, while facilitating market transactions and using public policy as a vehicle to guide societal progress toward collectively desired goals of distributive justice. This approach has been criticised as overly consensual in character, though it does serve as a rich source of empirically testable propositions in instances in which political behaviour is ultimately inspired by individualistic motivations. Contrasting with, though not exclusive of, the neoclassical perspective is the growing body of literature arising from structuralist premises. Such perspectives emphasise collective, or class-based, motivations and generally explicitly reject any contention of the feasibility of a value-neutral spatial analysis in political geography (e.g. Soja, 1980).

Dear and Clark's (1978) typology reveals Marxian political-geographic research as beginning with the premise that the state in advanced capitalist societies is an active agent of capital's interests in its struggle with labour to appropriate rents accruing to productive endeavours. Such rents are often referred to as 'surplus value' in Marxian analysis, and as 'profit' in neoclassical analysis. Perhaps as a result of government growth there has been an expansion in the level of attention given to the state in Marxian analysis (Miliband, 1973; Poulantzas, 1973; Harvey, 1976). Some recent reviews have traced Marxian contributions to an understanding of the role of the sovereign state in its internal social, economic, and political affairs (Jessop, 1977; Wolfe, 1977).

Political geographers working from the standpoint of structuralist premises have been especially concerned with defining the nature of the local or subnational state and in charting its geographical behaviour (e.g. Dear and Clark, 1981). For example, Dear (1981) and Fincher (1981a) have attempted development of an outline for a theory of the local state, citing Cockburn's (1977) distinction between the national state's contribution to capitalist production and the local jurisdiction's emphasis on reproduction. Clark and Dear (1981) used this framework to investigate the extent to which the local state is autonomous of the central state as an agent of capital. They argued that the existence of legitimated local government is contingent on avoiding capital-labour conflicts at local levels, and that structures of local government enable coordinated conflict avoidance and management in large heterogeneous societies. Such an argument parallels some neoclassical discussions of governance within federal systems (e.g. Elazar, 1972). However, Fincher (1981a) cautioned that the study of the functions and structures of

local states should be undertaken only with reference to the historically specific development of contradictions inherent in the capitalist
mode of production. Others have reviewed tensions created in
Marxian analysis by recognition of the geographical non-uniformity
of labour-capital conflicts and public benefit allocations (e.g. Soja,
1980). Lauria (1982) modelled the process of locational conflict
development from the standpoint of structuralist premises. The
influence of the local state on land development processes was
traced by Wolch and Gabriel (1981) in southern California, and by
Fincher (1981b) in Boston.

As Johnston (1983, p. 132) noted, 'the empirical discipline of
political geography needs a methodology for understanding state
actions'. At long last, political geographers have at least two such
methodologies: liberal political economy predicated upon the self-
interests of individuals; and structural political economy predicated
upon the group-interests of classes. Each is an enormous step beyond
the organic theory of the turn of the century, or the more recent, and
more elusive, concept of *raison d'être*. Unlike their predecessors,
each of the two variant strains of political economy now inspiring
work in political geography is capable of addressing political outcomes which are zero-sum as well as those which are positive-sum in
character. The older paradigms lacked such flexibility.

Contemporary Countercurrents

Although neoclassical and structuralist perspectives on political
economy have become dominant in contemporary political geography, other trends have emerged as countercurrents. Of particular
interest are concepts of political culture, analyses of the geographic
impacts of legal structures, and geographic perspectives on
international systems. While ties to economic theory can sometimes
be discerned, these countercurrents draw inspiration from other
intellectual traditions as well.

The geography of political culture has emerged as an influential
trend in recent years. The concept of political culture refers to individual and community views regarding the nature of organised
government and political decision processes. In the United States
political culture theory can be traced to the frontier thesis investigations of Turner (1908; 1924) and Webb (1931). Elazar (1972) drew
upon Turner's work in particular to posit the existence of three

major political traditions in the United States: the moralistic, individualistic, and traditionalistic political cultures. Because each was associated with a particular area of the origin in colonial times, and particular paths of expansion since then, Elazar's formulation contains considerable geographic content (Brunn, 1974).

In contrast to the work of early historians such as Turner, political scientists and contemporary historians working in the area of political culture have tended to focus upon non-political and non-economic factors such as those of ethnicity, religion, or migration to identify political culture areas. Yet, recent work by political geographers has shown that the older Turnerian tradition focusing upon the analysis of electoral data, though using modern multivariate techniques as well as cartographic tools, remains capable of generating insights. Third party voting patterns have been recognised as indicators of the contemporary geographical patterns of the moralistic and traditionalistic political cultures (Shelley *et al.*, 1984). Also, the identification of longstanding electoral cleavages has been accomplished for the United States through the use of S-mode factor analysis. This methodology was employed by Archer and Taylor (1981) to divide the 48 contiguous states into Northern, Southern and Western regions on the basis of similar time trajectories of popular voting for Presidential candidates between 1872 and 1980. The three factor solution accounted for over 90 per cent of the electoral variance among states. Since then, factorial techniques have been successfully applied to the regionalisation of American gubernatorial and Federal Senatorial elections (Johnston, 1982), the regionalisation of county-level Presidental election data in Arkansas, Kansas, Missouri and Oklahoma (Shelley and Archer, 1983), and the identification of electoral epochs for the Netherlands (Johnston *et al.*, 1983).

Although linkages to the traditional study of political regions can be discerned in contemporary efforts to examine political culture regions, there are two important differences. First, whereas *raison d'être*-inspired research focused upon the national state, political culture research focuses upon substate divisions. Second, contemporary works view politics as a generalisable process, drawing directly on political science for inspiration, rather than stressing the uniqueness of specific cases.

What Cox (1979) referred to as the juridical context, or the legal structure constraining political behaviour, has become increasingly recognised as an important consideration among political geographers in recent years. Law can be seen both as an outcome of political processes and as a set of rules and standards with which political actors must comply (Clark, 1981). For example, the development of American legal institutions exerted a considerable effect upon the spatial evolution and spatial integration of the United States; Clark (1981) has argued that the American legal system's development contributed to spatial homogeneity at the expense of diversity. However, Elazar (1972) noted that the American legal system can be characterised as a dual legal system in which Federal Constitutional Law and statutory law is interstitial, filling in the gaps left by common law traditions which, while originally derived from British common law, are specific to and variable among state jurisdictions. Since, subject to juridical interpretation, the US Constitution reserves for the states those powers not explicitly granted to the Federal Government, this means, for example, that there can be no direct federal regulation of land use in the United States. This is not among the powers explicitly granted to the Federal Government, and hence is within state jurisdiction. None the less, state land-use regulations must comply with the standards of the 'unreasonable searches and seizures' clause of the Fourth Amendment, and the 'due process' and 'just compensation' clauses of the Fifth Amendment to the US Constitution. Johnston (1981b) examined the role of the American judiciary in spatial organization, using Supreme Court decisions regarding school desegregation as a focus. Harries and Brunn (1978) focused upon the geography of the American criminal justice system.

Others have looked at the spatial implications of specific laws or court rulings. O'Loughlin and Taylor (1982), for example, focused upon the impacts of multi-member districting systems on the electoral power of black residents of Mobile, Alabama, following the Supreme Court's ruling in *City of Mobile* v. *Bolden* (446 US 5). Employing Taylor and Gudgin's (1976) method of statistical analysis, they were able to dispute the Court's contention that multi-member districting did not unduly disenfranchise minority voters in this instance. Templer (1978, 1981) traced disparities between the development of water law in the State of Texas and groundwater management in that state. Shelley (1983d) used voter power analysis to examine the weighted voting scheme used in California water management districts, in which policies require a majority vote of both landowners and acres owned for approval.

The international scale has not been a conspicuous focus of recent theoretical development in political geography. However, while the interwar German Geopolitik tradition may have impeded the development of theory at this scale for some years after the conclusion of World War II (Claval, 1980), a revival of international political geography with theoretical influences from the study of international relations and international economics can be discerned. In part, this resurgence reflects unavoidable general perceptions of such recent events as the development and later near collapse of OPEC, the emergence of multi-national corporations, and the increasing convergence of business cycle fluctuations at world scale (Brunn, 1981). In political geography, two major trends seem apparent: an integration of political geography with world systems theory, and application of models of international conflict in geographic context.

The relevance of the structuralist world systems viewpoint to political-geographical study has been explored by Taylor (1981; 1982). The basic premises of this approach, as originally articulated by Wallerstein (1979), is that national states are interrelated components within a global division of labour. Class cleavages within societies are mirrored, yet compounded in complexity, by cleavages between the core, semiperiphery and periphery of the global economy. As Taylor (1982, p. 16) has argued, the essential virtue of the perspective is:

> its holism — the tight integration of the historical with the social, economic, and political in a single framework, so that the traditional divisions of social science are not recognized as separate bodies of knowledge.

The structuralist world systems viewpoint has also been explored by other political geographers such as Agnew (1982) who recently (Agnew, 1983) investigated the development of American foreign policy in terms of global economic development. However, the neoclassical approach can also be employed to 'look at specific patterns of growth within jurisdictions as well as across them' (Olson, 1982, p. 121). Thus, the explanatory effectiveness of the global systems perspective may arise less from its normative objectives than from its common positive basis in political economy, which includes both neoclassical and structural branches.

O'Loughlin (1983) reviewed several approaches to the application of international relations theory to geographical analysis. He identified four key perspectives: the geopolitical tradition, the analysis of power relationships between national states, economic analyses of international relationships, and ideological conflicts and controversies. O'Sullivan (1982) used spatial analysis to suggest that the so-called domino theory, sometimes propounded by American statesmen, lacks reasonable geographical predictability. And in a later analysis. O'Sullivan (1983) looked at local, colonial, and civil insurrections to conclude that the success of guerrilla tactics varies in relation to force-to-space ratios and population densities.

Further quantitative analysis of international conflicts has been undertaken through the interdisciplinary perspective of peace science. For example, Weede (1981) has modelled the effectiveness of detente and the deterrence strategy in preventing nuclear war. Isard and Smith (1980) have identified sets of structural properties underlying systems characterising conflict participants, using those to account for conflict development and to estimate the potential effectiveness of alternative conflict resolution procedures in different categories of international conflict. From another perspective, the recently concluded Law of the Sea negotiations — whose results the Reagan administration regrettably chose not to submit to the US Senate for ratification — have been investigated using public goods theory at an international scale (Amacher and Tollison, 1978), in a manner surprisingly parallel to that developed by Tiebout (1956) for the case of American metropolitan areas. Hirschman (1978) has extended Tiebout's mobility hypotheses, which the former first developed to explain the behaviour of corporations, to account for the competitive behaviour of national states.

Conclusions

Are we yet 'suffering under the effects of an irrational political geography . . . whose main function is not to trace causal relations, and which must therefore remain a body of isolated data' as Mackinder (1962, p. 214) once suggested? This review of theory and methodology in political geography has endeavoured to show that Mackinder's charge has been of variable validity over the last century, but that it remains valid no longer.

At the time Mackinder's charge was levelled, political geography was still a form of political arithmetic, a loose aggregation of qualitative and quantitative date hopefully of value to future statesmen.

Around the turn of the century, Ratzel's organic theory of the state, grounded upon analogies with natural evolution, and Mackinder's Heartland theory, grounded upon analogies with Newtonian laws of motion, for a time served to give the subject organising rigor. But in the interwar period political geographers, especially in the English-speaking world, explicitly rejected these organizing concepts and sought to reassert political chorography as the central focus.

The reintroduction of a process orientation came from two principal directions. First, Schaefer's (1953) positivist challenge to chorography, with its initial impacts upon economic and urban geography, eventually stimulated quantitative research focused upon political matters by geographers often trained in other subareas of the discipline. Second, political geographers rediscovered political economy, and its central question of the role of the state in society. Once again, as at the turn of the century, political geographers possess a theory of the state — rather, twin closely related theories reflecting neoclassical or structuralist premises — with which to guide their research investigations.

Whether the academic gentrification of the subject will continue, or whether political geographers will again retreat from theory, as they have done in the past, remains to be seen. But, there is justification for optimism. As Grofman (1982, p. 885) concluded in his review of recent books by Bennett (1980), Burnett and Taylor (1981), and Taylor and Johnston (1979) for the *American Political Science Review:*

> Contemporary geographers doing political or economic geography are very familiar with the research and disciplinary tools that they seek to adapt and extend from economics or politics. Given the high level of theoretical and empirical sophistication of the recent work in political geography . . . it would behoove political scientists to become familiar with the renaissance that has been taking place in political geography, work directly relevant to central questions of political science, public administration, and political theory.

This is a far cry from once expressed fears that in venturing from descriptive to quantitative and theoretical work, political geographers 'will be abandoning a road of proven reliability for a track which may lead into regions of sociology where they are ill-equipped to survive' (Prescott, 1972, pp. 86–7). Not only have they survived, but some have excelled at what Burnett and Taylor (1981) called, simply and appropriately, 'political studies from spatial perspectives'. Once again, political geographers may, with some confidence, anticipate the attentions of others who are not self-proclaimed political geographers but who, like political geographers, are also interested in achieving an understanding of locational aspects of human political behaviour.

References

Abler, R., Adams, J.S. and Gould, P. (1971), *Spatial Organization: The Geographer's View of the World*, Prentice-Hall, Englewood Cliffs, New Jersey

Ackerman, E.A., Berry, B.J.L., Bryson, R.A., Cohen, S.B., Taaffe, E.J., Thomas, W.L., and Wolman, M.G. (1965) *The Science of Geography*, National Academy of Sciences — National Research Council, Washington, DC

Agnew, J.A. (1982) 'Sociologizing the Geographical Imagination: Spatial Concepts in the World-System Perspective', *Political Geography Quarterly, 1* 159-66

—— (1983) 'An Excess of "National Exceptionalism": Towards a New Political Geography of American Foreign Policy', *Political Geography Quarterly, 2,* 151-66

Amacher, R.C., and Tollison, R.D. (1978) 'Analyzing International Externalities: the Case of the Law of the Sea Negotiations', in W. Loehv and T. Sandler (eds.) *Public Goods and Public Policy,* Sage, Beverly Hills, pp. 191-206

Archer, J.C. (1980) 'Congressional Incumbent Re-election Success and Federal Outlays Distribution: A Test of the Electoral Connection Hypothesis', *Environment and Planning A, 12,* 263-78

—— (1981) 'Public Choice Paradigms in Political Geography', in A.D. Burnett and P.J. Taylor (eds.) *Political Studies from Spatial Perspectives,* Wiley, Chichester, pp. 73-90

—— (1983a) 'The Spatial Allocation of Federal Outlays and Presidential Politics: A Vote-Buying Linkage?' in A.M. Kirby, P.L. Knox and S.E. Pinch (eds.) *Public Provision and Urban Development,* Croom Helm, London

—— (1983b) 'The Geography of Federal Fiscal Politics in the United States: An Exploration', *Government and Policy, 1,*

—— and Reynolds, D.R. (1976) 'Locational Logrolling and Citizen Support of Municipal Bond Proposals: The Example of St. Louis', *Public Choice, 27,* 22-70

—— and Taylor, P.J. (1981) *Section and Party: A Political Geography of American Presidential Elections, from Andrew Jackson to Ronald Reagan,* John Wiley, Chichester

Bennett, R.J. (1980) *The Geography of Public Finance,* Methuen, London

—— (1981) 'Quantitative Geography and Public Policy', in N. Wrigley and R.J. Bennett (eds.) *Quantitative Geography: A British View,* Routledge and Kegan Paul, London pp. 387-96

Berry, B.J.L. (1964) 'Approaches to Regional Analysis: A Synthesis', *Annals, Association of American Geographers, 54,* 73-94

—— (1969) '*Review of International Regions and the International System,* by B.M. Russett,' *Geographical Review, 59,* 450-1

Bowman, I. (1922) *The New World: Problems in Political Geography,* World Book Company, New York

Brunn, S.D. (1974) *Geography and Politics in America,* Harper and Row, New York

36   *Theory and Methodology in Political Geography*

Buchanan, J.M., and Tullock, G. (1962) *The Calculus of Consent*, University of Michigan Press, Ann Arbor, Michigan
Bunge, W. (1979) 'Fred K. Schaefer and the Science of Geography', *Annals, Association of American Geographers, 69,* 128–32
Burnett, A.D., and P.J. Taylor (eds.) (1981) *Political Studies from Spatial Perspectives,* John Wiley, Chichester
Christaller, W. (1966) *Central Places in Southern Germany,* Prentice-Hall, Englewood Cliffs, New Jersey
Clark, G.L. (1981), 'Law, the State, and the Spatial Integration of the United States', *Environment and Planning, A, 13,* 1197–232
—— and Dear, M.J. (1981) 'The State in Capitalism and the Capitalist State', in M.J. Dear and A.J. Scott (eds.), *Urbanization and Urban Planning in Capitalist Societies,* Methuen, London pp. 45–61
Claval, P. (1980) 'Centre-Periphery and Space: Models of Political Geography', in J. Gottmann (ed.) *Centre and Periphery: Spatial Variations in Politics,* Sage, Beverly Hills pp. 63–72
Cockburn, C. (1977) *The Local State,* Pluto Press, London
Cohen, S.B. (1973) *Geography and Politics in a World Divided,* Oxford University Press, New York
Cox, K.R. (1979), *Location and Public Problems,* Maaroufa Press, Chicago
—— (1981) 'Capitalism and Conflict Around the Communal Living Space', in M.J. Dear and A.J. Scott (eds.), *Urbanization and Urban Planning in Capitalist Societies,* Maaroufa Press, Chicago pp. 431–55
—— (1983) 'Social Change, Turf Politics and Concepts of Turf Politics', in A.M. Kirby, P.L. Knox, and S.E. Pinch (eds.) Croom Helm, London
—— Reynolds, D.R. and Rokkan, S. (eds.) (1974) *Locational Approaches to Power and Conflict,* John Wiley, New York
Darwin, C.L. (1970) 'Competition and Natural Selection', in R.E. Park and E.W. Burgess (eds.) *Introduction to the Science of Sociology,* University of Chicago Press, Chicago pp. 195–9
Dear, M. (1978) 'Planning for Mental Health Care: A Reconsideration of Public Facility Location Theory', *International Regional Science Review, 3,* 93–111
—— (1981) 'A Theory of the Local State', in A.D. Burnett and P.J. Taylor (eds.) *Political Studies from Spatial Perspectives,* John Wiley, Chichester pp. 183–200
—— and Clark, G. (1978) 'The State and Geographic Process: A Critical Review', *Environment and Planning, A, 10,* 173–83
—— (1981) 'Dimensions of Local State Autonomy', *Environment and Planning, A, 13,* 1277–94
East, W.G., and Moodie, A.E. (1956) *The Changing World: Studies in Political Geography,* World Book Company, New York
Easton, D. (1965a) *A Framework for Political* Analysis Prentice-Hall, Englewood, Cliffs, New Jersey
—— (1965b) *A Systems Analysis of Political Life,* John Wiley, New York
Elazar, D.J. (1972) *American Federalism: A View from the States,* 2nd edn, Crowell, New York
Fawcett, C.B. (1957) 'Geography and Empire', in G. Taylor (ed.) *Geography in the Twentieth Century,* Methuen, London pp. 418–32
Fincher, R. (1981a) 'Analysis of the Local Level Capitalist State', *Antipode, 13,* 25–31
—— (1981b) 'Local Implementation Strategies in the Urban Built Environment', *Environment and Planning, A, 13,* 1233–52
Fisher, C.A. (1968), 'Introduction', in C.A. Fisher (ed.) *Essays in Political Geography,* Methuen, London, pp. 1–10
Grofman, B. (1982) 'Review Essay on Political Geography', *American Political Science Review, 74,* pp. 883–5

—— and Scarrow, H. (1981) 'Weighted Voting in New York', *Legislative Studies Quarterly, 6,* 287-304

Gudgin, G., and Taylor, P.J. (1980) 'The Decomposition of Electoral Bias in a Plurality Election', *British Journal of Political Science, 10,* 515-22

Harries, K.D., and Brunn, S.D. (1978) *The Geography of Laws and Justice: Spatial Perspectives on the Criminal Justice System*, Praeger, New York

Hartshorne, R. (1935a) 'Recent Developments in Political Geography, I', *American Political Science Review, 29,* 785-804

—— (1935b) 'Recent Developments in Political Geography, II', *American Political Science Review, 29,* 943-66

—— (1950) 'The Functional Approach in Political Geography', *Annals, Association of American Geographers, 40,* 95-130

—— (1954) 'Political Geography', in P.E. James and C.F. Jones (eds.) *American Geography: Inventory and Prospect*, Syracuse University Press, Syracuse, New York pp. 167-225

Harvey, D. (1973) *Social Justice and the City*, Johns Hopkins University Press, Baltimore

—— (1976) 'The Marxian Theory of the State,' *Antipode, 8,* 80-98

Herbst, J. (1961) 'Social Darwinism and the History of American Geography,' *Proceedings of the American Philosophical Society, 105,* 538-44

Hirschman, A.O. (1978) 'Exit, Voice, and the State', *World Politics, 31,* 90-107

Hodge, D., and Gatrell, A. (1976) 'Spatial Constraint and the Location of Urban Public Facilities', *Environment and Planning, A, 8,* 215-31

House, J. W. (1968) 'A Local Perspective on Boundaries and the Frontier Zone,' in C.A. Fisher (ed.) *Essays in Political Geography*, Methuen, London pp. 327-44

Hudson, J.C. (1974) 'Apportionment of the Central Place Legislature', in K.R. Cox, D. R. Reynolds and S. Rokkan (eds.) *Locational Approaches to Power and Conflict*, John Wiley, New York pp. 173-86

Isard, W., and Smith, C. (1980) 'Matching Conflict Situations and Conflict Management Procedures', *Conflict Management and Peace Science, 5,* pp. 1-25

Jessop, B. (1977) 'Recent Theories of the Capitalist State', *Cambridge Journal of Economics, 1,* 353-74

Johnston, R.J. (1977) 'National Power in the European Parliament as Mediated through the Party System', *Environment and Planning, A, 9,* 1055-66

—— (1979a) 'Congressional Committees and Department Spending: The Political Influence on the Geography of Federal Expenditure in the United States', *Transactions, Institute of British Geographers, 4,* 373-84

—— (1979b) *Political, Electoral, and Spatial Systems*, Oxford University Press, Oxford

—— (1980a) 'Political Geography Without Politics', *Progress in Human Geography, 4,* 439-46

—— (1980b) *The Geography of Federal Spending in the United States of America*, John Wiley, Chichester

—— (1981a) 'Political Geography', in N. Wrigley and R.J. Bennett (eds.) *Quantitative Geography: A British View*, Routledge and Kegan Paul, London, pp. 374-81

—— (1981b) 'The Management and Autonomy of the Local State: The Role of the Judiciary in the United States', *Environment and Planning, A, 13,* 1305-15

—— (1982) 'The Changing Geography of Voting in the United States: 1946-1980', *Transactions, Institute of British Geographers, 7,* 187-204

—— (1983) *Philosophy and Human Geography: An Introduction to Contemporary Analysis*, Edward Arnold, London

—— O'Neill, A.B. and Taylor, P.J. (1983) 'The Changing Electoral Geography of the Netherlands: 1946-1981', *Tijdschrift voor Economische en Sociale Geografie, 74,* 185-95

Jones, K., and Kirby, A.M. (1982) 'Provision and Wellbeing: An Agenda for Public Services Research', *Environment and Planning, A, 14,* 297-310

38   *Theory and Methodology in Political Geography*

Kasperson, R.E., and Minghi, J.V. (eds.) (1969) *The Structure of Political Geography*, Aldine, Chicago
Kirby, A. (1983) 'Neglected Factors in Public Services Research: A Comment on Urban Structure and Geographical Access of Public Services', *Annals, Association of American Geographers, 73*, 289-95
Lauria, M. (1982) 'Toward a Political-Economic Scheme of Locational Conflict Resolution in Advanced Capitalist Societies', *Working Paper 49*, Institute of Urban and Regional Research, University of Iowa, Iowa City, Iowa
Lazarsfeld, P.F. (1961) 'Notes on the History of Quantification in Sociology — Trends, Sources, and Problems', *Isis, 52*, 277-333
Lea, A.C. (1979) 'Welfare Theory, Public Goods, and Public Facility Location', *Geographical Analysis, 11*, 217-39
Ley, D., and Mercer, J. (1980) 'Locational Conflict and the Politics of Consumption', *Economic Geography, 56*, 89-109
Mackinder, H.J. (1962) *Democratic Ideals and Reality*, Norton, New York
McLafferty, S. (1982) 'Urban Structure and Geographical Access to Public Services', *Annals, Association of American Geographers, 72*, 347-54
—— and Ghosh, A. (1982) 'Issues in Measuring Differential Access to Public Services', *Urban Studies, 19*, 383-9
Miliband, R. (1973) *The State in Capitalist Society*, Basic Books, New York
Mueller, D.C. (1979) *Public Choice*, Cambridge University Press, New York
Mumphrey, A. J., and Wolpert, J. (1973) 'Equity Considerations and Concessions in the Siting of Public Facilities', *Economic Geography, 44*, 109-21
Musgrave, R.A. (1959) *The Theory of Public Finance*, McGraw-Hill, New York
Nozick, R. (1974) *Anarchy, State, and Utopia*, Basic Books, New York
O'Loughlin, J. (1982) 'The Identification and Evaluation of Racial Gerrymandering', *Annals, Association of American Geographers, 72*, 165-84
—— (1983) 'Geographic Models of International Conflicts', paper presented to the International Conference of Political Geographers, Oxford University, Oxford, England
—— and Taylor, A.M. (1982) 'Choices in Redistricting and Electoral Outcomes: The Case of Mobile, Alabama', *Political Geography Quarterly, 1*, 317-40
Olson, M. (1965) *The Logic of Collective Action*, Harvard University Press, Cambridge, Massachusetts
—— (1982) *The Rise and Decline of Nations: Economic Growth, Stagflation, and Social Rigidities*, Yale University Press New Haven, Connecticut
O'Sullivan, P. (1982) 'Antidomino', *Political Geography Quarterly, 1*, 57-64
—— (1983) 'A Geographical Analysis of Guerrilla Warfare', *Political Geography Quarterly, 2*, 139-50
Papageorgiou, G.J. (1977) 'Fundamental Problems of Theoretical Planning', *Environment and Planning, A, 9*, 1329-56
Park, R.E., and Burgess, E.W. (1970) *Introduction to the Science of Sociology*, University of Chicago Press, Chicago
Pearce, A.J. (1962) 'Introduction', in H.J. Mackinder (ed.) *Democratic Ideals and Reality*, Norton, New York, pp. ix-xxiv
Pirie, G.H. (1983) 'On Spatial Justice', *Environment and Planning, A, 15*, 465-73
Poulantzas, N. (1973) *Political Power and Social Classes*, New Left Press, London
Prescott, J.V.R. (1972) *Political Geography*, Methuen, London
Ratzel, F. (1969) 'The Laws of the Spatial Growth of States', in R.E. Kasperson and J.V. Minghi (eds.) *The Structure of Political Geography*, Aldine, Chicago, pp. 17-28
Rawls, J. (1971) *A Theory of Justice*, Harvard University Press, Cambridge, Massachusetts
Reynolds, D.R. (1974) 'Spatial Contagion in Political Influence Processes', in K.R.

Cox, D.R. Reynolds and S. Rokkan (eds.) *Locational Approaches to Power and Conflict,* John Wiley, New York pp. 233–73
—— New York (1981) 'The Geography of Social Choice', in A.D. Burnett and P.J. Taylor (eds.) *Political Studies from Spatial Perspectives,* John Wiley, Chichester pp. 91–100
—— (1983) 'School Budget Retrenchment and Locational Conflict: Crisis in Local Democracy', in *Public Provision and Urban Development,* edited by A.M. Kirby, P.L. Knox and S.E. Pinch, Croom Helm, London
—— and Honey, R. (1978) 'Conflict in the Location of Salutary Facilities', in K.R. Cox (ed.) *Urbanization and Conflict in Market Societies,* Maaroufa Press, Chicago pp. 144–60
Rushton, G., McLafferty, S.L. and Ghosh, A. (1981) 'Equilibrium Locations for Public Services: Individual Preferences and Social Choice', *Geographical Analysis, 13,* 196–202
Schaefer, F.K. (1953) 'Exceptionalism in Geography', *Annals, Association of American Geographers, 43,* 226–49.
Shelley, F.M. (1983a) 'The Public Choice Perspective in Contemporary Political Geography', in A.M. Kirby, P.L. Knox and S.E. Pinch (eds.) *Public Provision and Urban Development,* Croom Helm, London
—— (1983b) 'Spatial Effects on Voting Power in Representative Democracies', *Environment and Planning, A, 15,*
—— (1983c) 'Groundwater Supply Depletion Problems and Options in West Texas: The Farmer's Perspective', *Texas Business Review, 57,*
—— (1983d) 'Voting Power in a System of Compound Majority Rule', unpublished paper, Department of Geography, University of Oklahoma, Norman, Oklahoma
—— and Archer, J.C. (1983) 'Political Habit, Political Culture, and the Electoral Mosaic of a Border Region', unpublished paper presented to the Annual Fall Meeting of the Southwest Division of the Association of American Geographers, Norman, Oklahoma
—— Archer, J.C. and White, E.R. (1984) 'Rednecks and Quiche Eaters: A Cartographic Analysis of Recent Third Party Voting', *Journal of Geography,* forthcoming
—— and Goodchild M.F. (1983) 'Majority Voting and the Location of Salutary Public Facilities', *Geographical Analysis, 15,* 205–11
Short, J.R. (1983) 'Political Geography', *Progress in Human Geography, 7,* 122–5
Smith, D.M. (1977) *Human Geography — A Welfare Approach,* Edward Arnold, London
Soja, E.W. (1974) 'A Paradigm for the Geographic Analysis of Political Systems', in K.R. Cox, D.R. Reynolds and S. Rokkan (eds.) *Locational Approaches to Power and Conflict,* John Wiley, New York, pp. 43–72
—— (1980) 'The Socio-Spatial Dialectic', *Annals, Association of American Geographers, 70,* 207–25
Sorokin, P.A. (1928) *Contemporary Sociological Theories,* Harper and Brothers, New York
Stern, J., (ed), (1979) *The Random House Dictionary of the English Language,* Random House, New York
Stoddart, D.R. (1966) 'Darwin's Impact on Geography', *Annals, Association of American Geographers, 56,* 683–98
Taylor, P.J. (1981) 'Political Geography and the World Economy', in A.D. Burnett and P.J. Taylor (eds.) *Political Studies from Spatial Perspectives,* John Wiley, Chichester pp. 157–72
—— (1982) 'A Materialist Framework for Political Geography', *Transactions, Institute of British Geographers, 7,* 15–34
—— and Gudgin G. (1976) 'The Statistical Basis of Decisionmaking in Electoral Districting', *Environment and Planning, A, 8,* 43–58

——— (1981) 'Geography of Elections', in N. Wrigley and R.J. Bennett, *Quantitative Geography: A British View,* Routledge and Kegan Paul, London pp. 382–6

—— and Johnston, R.J. (1978) 'Population Distributions and Political Power in the European Parliament', *Regional Studies, 2,* 61–8

——— (1979) *Geography of Elections,* Penguin Books, Harmondsworth, Middlesex.

Teitz, M.B. (1968) 'Toward a Theory of Urban Public Facility Location', *Papers and Proceedings, Regional Science Association, 21,* 35–51

Templer, O.W. (1978) 'Texas Ground Water Law: Inflexible Institutions and Resource Realities', *Ecumene, 10,* 6–15

—— (1981) 'Conjunctive Management of Water Resources in the Context of Texas Water Law', *Water Resources Bulletin, 16,* 305–11

Tiebout, C.M (1956) 'A Pure Theory of Local Expenditures', *Journal of Political Economy, 64,* 416–24

Tullock, G. (1983) 'Our 40th. Volume', *Public Choice, 40,* 3

Turner, F.J. (1908) 'Is Sectionalism is America Dying Away?' *American Journal of Sociology, 13,* 661–76

—— (1924) *The Significance of the Frontier in American History,* Henry Holt, New York

Wallerstein, I. (1979) *The Capitalist World Economy,* Cambridge University Press, London

Walters, R.E. (1974) *The Nuclear Trap,* Penguin Books, Harmondsworth, Middlesex

Webb, W.P. (1931) *The Great Plains,* Ginn and Company, New York

Weede, E. (1981) 'Preventing War by Nuclear Deterrence or by Detente', *Conflict Management and Peace Science, 6,* 1–18

Westhoff, F (1977) 'Existence of Equilibria in Economies with a Local Public Good', *Journal of Economic Theory, 14,* 84–112

Whittlesey, D. (1939) *The Earth and The State: A Study of Political Geography,* Henry Holt and Company, New York

Wolch, J., and S. Gabriel (1981) 'Urban Housing Prices and Land Development Behaviour of the Local State', *Environment and Planning, A, 13,* 1253–76

Wolfe, A. (1977) *The Limits of Legitimacy: Political Contradictions of Contemporary Capitalism,* The Free Press, New York

Wolpert, J., A.J. Mumphrey, and J. Seley (1972) 'Metropolitan Neighborhoods: Participation and Conflict Over Change', *Resource Paper 16, Commission on College Geography,* Association of American Geographers, Washington, DC

Wright, J.K. (1944) 'Training for Research in Political Geography', *Annals, Association of American Geographers, 34,* 190–201

2 GEOPOLITICS

S. D. Brunn and K. A. Mingst

Of all the topics of study in political geography, probably none has attracted as much controversy as geopolitics. In large part, the manipulation of the concept by German geographers and Nazi military strategists during World War II to promote overt expansionist policies not only besmirched the term but tarnished political geography itself as a legitimate area of scholarly investigation for the following two decades. Nevertheless the application of geographic information, whether relating to resources, power, diplomacy, or military strategy, continued to be recognised, even though the term geopolitics was avoided. Within the past decade, the term has crept back into the literature and vocabulary of the scholarly and governmental community, even though it never had lost its appeal to military and defence analysts.

The purposes of this paper are sixfold:

(1) to examine the origins of geopolitics in the political geography literature
(2) to assess the literature on the subject in the past century by identifying major themes and regions
(3) to ferret out the major concepts that have been used in studies on geopolitics by geographers, political scientists, and others
(4) to discuss the methodologies employed in studies on geopolitics on a global scale and on individual regions and selected topics
(5) to identify some of the persistent controversies that perplex students of geopolitics
(6) to present an agenda for research on geopolitics in the 1980s and 1990s.

Origins of Geopolitics

Friedrich Ratzel (1844–1904), who is usually recognised as the founder and father of modern political geography because of his ideas on state formation and features, is also often credited with the earliest thinking about geopolitics. His thesis on the theory of the organic growth of the state, included in his *Politische Geographie* (1896), was based in part on evolutionary biological and environmental determinism of the late nineteenth century. While Ratzel postulated seven 'laws' of state growth, he did not coin the term geopolitics or Geopolitik; that credit is given to Rudolph Kjellen (1864–1922), a Swedish political scientist. His ideas on territorial expansion (*Lebensraum* or living space according to Ratzel) as a legitimate goal for a state influenced the writings of a number of German and other European geographers, historians, and political scientists. Kjellen (1916) argues that:

> Vitally strong states with a limited area of sovereignty are dominated by the categorical imperative to enlarge their area by colonisation, union with other states, or conquests of different types . . . it is not the raw material of conquest, but the natural and necessary trend towards expansion as a means of self-preservation.

It was out of such thinking that geopolitics became associated with a state's territorial expansion. The state, according to Kjellen, was behaving like a biological organism, the same theory advocated by Ratzel. Large states would survive, be powerful, and influence continental and global politics. Only a few of these were likely to persist.

The third individual who had a major influence in the thinking about world politics early this century was Sir Halford Mackinder (1861–1947). Mackinder, a Member of Parliament and student of geography, history, biology, and military affairs, was concerned with the changes he saw occurring among warring Eurasian powers and the expansive colonial systems. He believed (in 1904) that the 'pivot region' of world politics, which later was termed Heartland by Fairgrieve (1915, 1922), was in continental Eurasia. That area was critical to world power and domination, for whoever controlled it would dominate the world. Beyond Mackinder's pivot area, he identified and mapped inner and outer crescents. Interestingly, Mackinder's Pivotal Area of 1904 had expanded to his Heartland of 1919. His famous (1919, p. 150) dictum is:

> Who rules East Europe commands the Heartland; Who rules the Heartland commands the World-Island;
> Who rules the World-Island commands the World.

Mackinder in 1904 was writing during Britain's decline; Germany, Russia, and Japan were about to emerge as dominant continental powers. According to Short (1982, p. 30):

Mackinder was giving a strategic rationale to the British presence overseas, sanctified by the need to save world democracy and legitimated by the course of historical development in the post-Columbus era.

It was primarily the ideas and writings of Kjellen and Mackinder that influenced European political and military thinking in Europe in the pre- and post-World War I periods. One individual who became concerned about Germany's position after World War I was Karl Haushofer (1896–1946). He was attracted to the concept of geopolitics and its application, as interpreted from Kjellen. Haushofer had served both in the Bavarian and German armies. He also had served in Japan and witnessed how Japan had become a powerful state by expanding its territory through conflict. Space for expansion was deemed necessary and an appropriate goal for a state. He was also impressed by Britain's successful imperialism in the peripheries not in the Eurasian core. Haushofer was disappointed and disillusioned by Germany's loss in World War I; he attributed the loss to poor strategic and military planning by the state's leaders and generals. In his mind, Germany could become a powerful state if it could capture the Eurasian Heartland and form an alliance with Russia.

To promote Germany's expansionist policies, Haushofer seized on the notion of geopolitics and made it a legitimate area for academic inquiry. He founded the Institute für Geopolitik in Munich where geopolitics became a subject of intensive research by some major German geographers (Gottman, 1942; Crone; 1948; Troll, 1949). He also founded the *Zeitschrift für Geopolitik* in 1924, a monthly journal devoted to the 'science' of geopolitics. Both the institute and magazine thrust Haushofer into a position as the leading supporter and proponent of Nazi expansion. Haushofer's brand of geopolitics coincided with the Third Reich's expansionist policies. The extent to which Haushofer had any direct influence on Hitler and Nazi strategy is debatable, but there is no doubt about the contributions his numerous publications, public presentations, use of propaganda maps and training of journalists and students had on German political and military strategies during World War II.

Haushofer, according to Hartshorne (1954, p. 172), was instrumental in 'supplying a pseudo-scientific rationalisation for the Nazi policy of expansion'. Haring and Norris (1980, p. 46) commenting on German geopolitics write:

> The analysis of the geographical basis of national and international power became a pseudo-science; the early theories were shrewdly manipulated to further German nationalism, and to rationalise German territorial expansion.

Haushofer's thinking and indeed that of the German School of Geopolitics is reported in *Zeitschrift für Geopolitik* (Weigert, 1942, p. 14):

> [Geopolitics] should suggest the future course of political action, and, like the still, small voice of conscience, keep reminding politicians of what they should do in the best interests of their country. Yet geopolitics was something more than strategy because it helped to formulate the objective of policy as well as being the means by which that objective might ultimately be reached.

Glassner and de Blij (1980, pp. 268–70) in discussing the origin of *Geopolitik* succinctly summarise Haushofer's views:

> Haushofer and his group blended together the organic state theory of Ratzel, its refinements and elaborations by Kjellen, and the geostrategic principles of Mahan and Mackinder, added a heavy dose of German chauvinism, wilful ambiguity, and mysticism, and created a case for a German policy of expansionism. They used not only maps but slogans and pictographs to influence people.

According to Busteed (1983, pp. 36–7) the German School of Geopolitics espoused certain views. These included (1) the primacy of the state over the individual; (2) the state as an organism (following Ratzel and Kjellen); (3) the adoption of Kjellen's use of the term Geopolitik; and (4) the endorsement of Kjellen's notion of national self-sufficiency (autarky). Considering that the School and *Zeitschrift* emerged in importance in defeated World War I Germany, it was little wonder that geopolitical ideas and thought came to influence policy.

Three other individuals who are credited with promoting geopolitical applications are Admiral Thomas Mahan (1840–1914), Nicholas Spykman (1893–1943), and Major Alexander P. de Seversky (1894–1974). Mahan, an historian in the US Navy, was writing before Mackinder about the importance of seapower in a state's military strategies and international relations. Among his books are *The Influence of Seapower Upon History, 1660–1783* (1890), *The Influence of Seapower upon the French Revolution and Empire, 1793–1812* (1892), *The Interest of America in Sea Power, Present and Future* (1897), and *The Problem of Asia and its Effect upon International Politics* (1900). Mahan was an advocate of a large and strong navy to contain the expansionist policies of Russia in particular. His ideas exerted substantial influence on US, British, Japanese, and German foreign policies at the turn of this century.

Spykman, a political scientist, writing after Mackinder's ideas had been publicised, revised, and criticised, is credited with stressing the geopolitical importance of Mackinder's 'Inner or Marginal Crescent' or the Rimland. Spykman believed that powerful states are those that forged alliances between land and sea powers, i.e., those in the Rimland. Their survival and power were derived from their strategic Rimland location, hence his dictum:

Who controls the Rimland rules Eurasia;
Who rules Eurasia controls the destinies of the world

Spykman's major books were *America's Strategy in World Politics* (1942a) and *The Geography of the Peace* (1944). A timely review of the former book is by Bowman (1942). Spykman, according to Hartshorne (1954) used geopolitics to show the Rimland's importance to the US *vis-à-vis* the rest of the world. Prescott (1968, p. 40) believes Spykman deserves credit for:

putting international politics at the centre of international relations, for awakening American political scientists of the interwar period to the importance of understanding geographical facts, and for convincingly destroying the arguments of those who would advocate a policy of isolation for America.

Unfortunately Spykman neither acknowledged previous writings on geopolitics by political geographers and political scientists nor benefited from previous constructive criticisms of the concept (Prescott, 1968, pp. 29–40).

De Seversky contended that air power represented a new and challenging dimension for a state's defence and security. He was influential in alerting the government and public to the importance of developing air warfare. His books included *Victory Through Air Power* (1941) and *Air Power: Key to Survival* (1950); he also wrote in popular magazines during World War II. In addition to stressing the need for the US to develop air power superiority, he also introduced an azimuthal equidistant projection centred on the North Pole. It showed a pilot's view of the world. Glassner and de Blij (1980, p. 272) remark that his 1949 map:

> performed a most useful function by tearing us away from our Mercator-view of the world, by developing an interim defence system, and by emphasizing defence instead of expansion as the prime goal of geostrategy.

The ideas of de Seversky, while considered revolutionary at the time, were responsible for traditional and emerging European, Asian, and North American powers rethinking their political relations *vis-à-vis* other states and their own military strengths, treaty agreements, and defence systems.

The defeat of the Nazis brought an end to the term *Geopolitik*, as used by its German supporters, but not an end to writings about geopolitics in military/strategic thinking. According to East (1965, p. 417),

> Geopolitics, despite the ill-famed *Geopolitik* of the inter-war years, remains a valid field for the political geographer in search of a difficult and ûseful exercise; it remains one of the few fields where the geographer still dares to look the whole world squarely in the face.

Futhermore, as Sprout (1968; p. 121) reports,

> Time has blurred the odious policy connotations of geopolitics, perhaps more so in America than in Europe. The term has even acquired some respectability, especially in the context of military-defence analysis.

Today, much of what might be included under the rubric of geopolitics deals with economic and military ties, state security, power influences, and military/defence strategies.

Cohen (1973) is a major user of the the term geopolitics in interpreting contemporary international relations. He defines (p. 30) the components of a geopolitical study as:

(1) description of geographical settings as they relate to political power, and
(2) laying out of spatial frameworks that embrace interacting power units. It is much more difficult to attempt such analysis today than in the past. Because of the hierarchical spatial overlap that exists among great power blocs and the process of constant political realignment, sharply defined global political divisions cannot be easily rationalized. Moreover, the exercise of political power may be the measure of a man's daring or a people's desperation, rather than the result of the cultural and physical setting.

Cohen (1982, 1983) uses geopolitical considerations in assessing the contemporary political scene and in identifying 27 states that he believes have, or aspire to, regional power status. Glassner and de Blij (1980) discuss in some detail 'Geopolitics on a Smaller Scale' by focusing on the decay of the buffer zone in southern Africa since 1960 and the geostrategic importance of the Indian Ocean. Finally, McColl (1983, p. 284) comments on the current use and acceptance of the term geopolitics:

. . . in recent years, there has been a reintroduction of the term in pronouncements from the United States Government. Geopolitics is a perfectly legitimate and useful word with explicit meaning and simply refers to geographic factors that lie behind political decisions.

In summary, geopolitics represents one of the major thrusts of political geography investigation during the past century whether or not the term has been specifically identified.

Definitions of Geopolitics

Hartshorne (1954, pp. 171-2) stated in his detailed examination of 'Political Geography' in *American Geography: Inventory and Prospect* that at the turn of the century it was difficult analytically to separate political geography from geopolitics.

But for Hartshorne (1935, pp. 960-5) geopolitics had a specific meaning:

> the application of the knowledge and techniques of political geography to the problems of international relations.

Similarly, Sprout (1968) in his discussion of political geography in the *International Encyclopedia of the Social Sciences* recognises the association geopolitics had with political geography. Much of the confusion came from the adjective 'geopolitical'. He states (p. 120)

> This word entered the English language as a loose translation of *Geopolitik,* which came, in the interwar period (1919-1939), to denote mobilisation of a real Knowledge for purposes of state — in short, *geo-policy.*

Not all scholars agree, so in this section we observe how geopolitics was defined by the earliest practitioners and determine its current usage by geographers and political scientists.

Ratzel did not coin the term nor is he given credit for introducing it into political geography. That credit is given to Kjellen who used Ratzel's ideas and theories of the state as a living organism to develop the 'science of geopolitics'. Kjellen (1914) defined geopolitics as:

> The theory of the state as a geographic organism or phenomenon in space, i.e., land, territory, area, or most especially, as country.

States, according to Kjellen, were regarded more as competing powers than legal units. With this view it is easy to see that the inevitable result would be a few large and powerful units devouring the smaller, weaker ones. Kasperson and Minghi (1969, p. 8) wrote about Kjellen and his ideas:

> He [Kjellen] viewed this process as a perpetual interchange among 'country, people, and government.' This process of

human occupation of a region gave it, in causal sequence, continuity, solidarity, interaction, loyalty, and nationality; that is, the creation of a nation with what Kjellen called a 'geopolitical instinct.'

Mackinder also did not use the term geopolitics, but in his writings he discussed the emerging strategic importance of pivotal areas in Eurasia, later called the Heartland. His ideas about position, power, dominance, and influences in the rapidly changing military and political world of the early twentieth century influenced Haushofer personally and the German School of Geopolitics.

Haushofer saw in the writings of Ratzel, Kjellen, and Mackinder the basis for a theory to explain state growth. To make geopolitics a science, he had to search for 'laws' that could explain and justify the organic growth of a state. He and his disciples even developed a vocabulary to fit their science. An organism (viz., the state) needed living space (*Lebensraum*), to retain power (*Grossmachte*), to define military boundaries (*Wehrgrenze*), to define an ethnically homogeneous population (*Kultur*), and to become economically self-sufficient (*Autarky*). One of Haushofer's students Otto Maull (1936, p. 31) provides a concise definition of German *Geopolitik*.

Geopolitik concerns itself with the state, not as a static concept, but as a living being. Geopolitik investigates the state primarily in relation to its environment — its space — and attempts to solve all problems resulting from spatial relationships. . . . Geopolitik is concerned with the space *requirements* of a state while political geography examines only its space *conditions*. In putting geography at the service of space-conscious politics, Geopolitik devoted itself to questions of the future. Are the space needs of a state met? If not, how can they be brought into accord with geographical conditions? In what direction should any change be made? The extent to which these questions are answered determines a state's national and economic structure and influences its foreign relations. . . . Geopolitik . . . is a discipline that weighs and evaluates a given situation and by its conclusions seeks to guide practical politics.

Definitions during the 1940s by non-German political geographers reflected the emotional and propaganda connotations associated with geopolitics.

Others, such as Fifield and Pearcy (1944) and East and Moodie (1956) related geopolitics directly to foreign policy. Later theoreticians, including Hartshorne (1954) and Russell (1954), in their assessments of political geography and military geography were mindful of how geopolitics was related to power and strategic studies. Hartshorne writes (1954, p. 126) that:

It would seem well to identify this area [national power] of joint interest with a clear and simple name, such as 'power analysis,' rather than to obscure it with the all-embracing term, geopolitics, the origin of which is steeped in error, exaggeration, and intellectual poison.

More recently, Sprout (1968, p. 121) suggests that geopolitics is:

the areal aspect of any political pattern and, in particular, hypotheses that purport to explain or to predict area distributions and patterns of political potential in the society of nations.

Cohen (1973, p. 29) adds a dynamic dimension in his observation that,

The essence of geopolitical analysis is the relation of international political power to the geographical setting. Geopolitical views vary with the changing geographical setting and with man's interpretation of the nature of this change.

Sen (1975, p. 6) sees geopolitics in a much broader context, stating (pp. 14–15) that:

. . . the scope of geopolitics is wider than that of political geography; it also includes a study of military, naval, and air strategies. Moreover, geopolitics has a double function. Like political geography, it represents facts as they are, but unlike political and other departments of geography, it analyzes and interprets the national situations of a country and the global scene on the basis of facts presented and formulates the internal and external policies of that country.

Finally, Glassner and de Blij (1980, p. 263) write that geopolitics:

is concerned basically with the application of geographic information and geographic perspectives to the development of a State's foreign policies. It has been called, with some justification, 'applied political geography.'

Hence, post-war geopolitical writers all focus their inquiry on the relationship between geography and foreign policy in a changing international environment. All seek to play down the negative connotations associated with the term during the war years.

The Literature on Geopolitics

A recent bibliography by Enggass (1984) entitled *Geopolitics: A Bibliography of Applied Political Geography,* includes 501 titles in twelve categories. Following a brief two-page introduction to the subject of geopolitics, Enggass organised his entries into these categories: General Titles; Sea Power Advocates and Detractors; Mackinder's 'Heartland' Theory; Fairgrieve's 'Crush Zone' Theory; Spykman's 'Rimland' Theory; Airpower Advocates; German 'Geopolitik', 1924–1945; Maps as Tools of Propaganda: Contemporary Geopolitical Theories; Geopolitics of Resources; Arms and Geopolitics; and Foreign Titles. We use this recent and comprehensive bibliography, and supplement it with additional items to identify major trends, topics, and regions that have been studied within a geopolitical framework. The entries include articles in scholarly geography, political science, history, and military journals as well as weekly news magazines. All items in the Enggass bibliography are in English, save the 49 'Foreign Titles', most of which are in German.

While the earliest references to geopolitics and geopolitical actions and thought are by List (1856) and Ratzel (1896; 1897), the terms, as we have noted, did not become popular until the decades of World War I and II. The two periods with the largest number of studies listed by Enggass were before and during World War II (175 between 1930 and 1945) and 1970 to the present (144). There has been a small but steady stream of publications on geopolitics and geopolitical subjects since the late 1800s; the fewest were during the first two decades this century. More studies were completed during the 1950–83 span (250) than in the first five decades of this century, which demonstrates the currency of the term and subject in the scholarly and lay literature.

The major topics, according to the entries in the Enggass bibliography, are in his General category (85), German 'Geopolitik' (81), and Resources (67). The next most numerous entries were Foreign Titles (49), Mackinder (44), Airpower (42), and Arms and Geopolitics (33). He included only 15 entries on Spykman's 'Rimland' Theory and two on Fairgrieve's 'Crush Zone' theory.

The earliest studies, while few in number, represent significant contributions to the concept and development of geopolitics as a scholarly and pseudo-scholarly area of investigation. The major early works that are cited most frequently are those by Ratzel (1896, 1897) on the organic growth of the state, by Mahan (1890, 1892; 1897) on seapower, by Mackinder (1890; 1902; 1904) on the emerging political order at the beginning of the century, and by Kjellen (1914; 1916; 1924) on geopolitics as applied to power and wars. Much of this early thinking on the organic growth of states (Atwood, 1935), power and space, nationalism, boundaries and frontiers was reflected in subsequent books and articles by Karl Haushofer and by Otto Maull during the 1920s and 1930s (Enggass, 1984).

If we examine the major categories by major time frames, we can discern some distinct patterns. During the 1930–45 period, there were 65 titles dealing with German 'Geopolitik', 23 on airpower, 19 on maps as tools of propaganda and 14 foreign titles. These four categories illustrate the major thinking, writing, and activities of the German strategists before and during World War II. From 1970 to the present, there were 46 in the resources category and 28 dealing with arms and geopolitics. The categories with the next largest number of entries were contemporary geopolitical theories and seapower with 15 each.

Early studies this century dealt with a variety of topics including general international relations (Colby, 1938; Means, 1935), the emergence of nationalism (Broek and Junis, 1945), and the increasing influence of airpower in European and global theatres (Mitchell, 1925; Warner, 1944). Another favourite theme was Germany and her relations with European neigbours (Whittlesey *et al.*, 1942), the emergence of *Geopolitik* (Mattern, 1942; Gyorgy, 1944). *Lebensraum* was examined in some detail by Kruszewski (1940) and Dickinson (1943) and the role of geopolitics in Hitler's foreign policies by Raup (1943). During World War II the uses of maps for propaganda purposes and in military campaigns were discussed by

Weigert (1941), Quam (1943), and Boggs (1946). The books and articles on resources during the Second World War dealt with the subject in general (Orchard, 1942), with food and national power (Brandt, 1939), the distribution and availability of raw materials (Behre, 1940), the availability of strategic minerals (Leith *et al.,* 1943; Hessell *et al.,* 1942), shatter zones (Hartshorne, 1944), and the role of technology (Turner, 1943). The importance of coal as a vital resource in assessing political power was discussed by Voskuil (1942). Resources for victory was a theme examined by Orchard (1942). In general, a content analysis of the geopolitical studies published before and during World War II reveals that they addressed, for the most part, impending security, military, and resource questions facing Europe.

The research conducted from 1970 to the present reflects a decidedly different flavour from the topics and themes addressed during the war and the immediate post-war period. In general, these works focus beyond the unidimensional theme of geopolitics to the multi-dimensional theme of an environmental or ecological perspective. As Sprout and Sprout (1971: p. 14) suggest, works should examine the relationship among interdependent earth-related communities that share a crowded planet. The emphasis should thus be on change and the sources of change (Pirages, 1978, 1983). Changes in technology in general are one of the recent prominent themes (Ashley, 1980). One of the most important changes in technology has occurred in armaments and arms sales (Pierre, 1982). How change in military technology affects geopolitical calculations is explored in Steinbruner (1978), Gray (1977), and Freedman (1983). Some of the diverse implications of these changes are reviewed in Deudney (1983), McColl (1975), O'Sullivan (1982, 1983a, 1983b) as the changes affect peace, revolution, and warfare, respectively.

Another series of themes examined in the post-1970 literature deals with the uneven distribution of natural resources and limits on resources and their implications. These recent studies emphasise mineral dependence (Wu, 1973; Eckes, 1979), critical strategic minerals (Jordan and Kilmarx, 1979), and more general global resources (Glassner, 1983). Not surprisingly, the politics of energy in all its diverse forms dominates the resource-related themes (Odell, 1979; Conant and Gold, 1978; Levy, 1982). The oceans have been examined as a resource with implications for geopolitics (Prescott, 1975; Oxman *et al.,* 1983; House, 1984). Finally, how information changes affect geopolitics is a relatively new and intriguing theme

Boulding (1983); Segal (1983).

Geopolitical writers have progressed further than just cataloguing these sources of change; a critical theme that has emerged is the relationship between these changes (be they technological, resource, or information) and conflict. For example, Choucri and North (1975) look at the impact of population change and resource inadequacies on eco-conflict. Hveem (1979) examines what control over strategic resources means for peace; Most and Starr (1980) try to correlate spread of war to diffusion patterns. Castro (1977) assesses hunger and its conflictual consequences. House (1983, 1984) examines the political and strategic importance of conflict in the South Atlantic (Falkland Islands or Malvinas) and Indian Ocean. In both regions he places recent events within a systems context, an approach Cohen and Rosenthal (1971) use in discussing the law-landscape processes in Venezuelan nationalism and social democracy and that Cohen (1983) also uses to examine recent global political changes.

In terms of regions and countries studied, pre-1930 publications focused mainly on Britain, the US and their roles in the political worlds. From 1930–45 articles appeared on Germany, Japan, Europe, Asia, Pacific Ocean, as well as on Britain and North America. Since World War II, a number of items have appeared with specific reference to individual countries or regions. Notable exceptions are those that specifically examine the geopolitics of the major superpowers (US and USSR). The Third World or individual countries include Brazil (Pittman, 1981), India (Karan, 1953), Mexico (Philip, 1980) Afghanistan and Pakistan (Quddus, 1982); strategic areas include the Indian Ocean (Adie, 1975), Middle East (Panda, 1959), Persian Gulf (Blake, 1980, 1981), Antarctica (Mitchell and Kimball, 1979; Zumberge, 1979), East Africa (Odingo, 1966), the South China Sea (Joo-Dock, 1979), and southern South America (Child, 1983).

Core Concepts/Scales of Inquiry

While the geopolitical literature may lack discipline, as Gray (1977) states, there exists a group of core concepts which inform the analysis. These concepts may be best organised according to the scales of inquiry chosen by the authors; in other words, some concepts are most relevant to discussion of the state level, others to the regional level, and still others to the international level (Taylor, 1984). Besides introducing these concepts at each of the different scales of inquiry, we suggest the dominant trends in the literature and show how the concepts apply to these trends.

The geopolitical theorist at the outset selects his scale of inquiry. Focusing at the state/national level means that the author is more likely to emphasise detailed description of his subject matter, with some attempts at explaining the findings. However, such a micro-analysis provides very poor predictive capability. In contrast, if the author focuses his inquiry at the international level, then descriptive material is often superficial while theoretical explanations may be emphasised. Finally, by focusing on macro-level trends, predictive capability should improve. Good theory should be able to describe, explain, and predict. Yet most social scientists are confronted with selecting a scale of inquiry which best suits their purposes and geopolitical theorists are no exception.

Traditional geopolitical studies have confined their analysis to the state level. Organising via the core concept of national *territory* and *boundaries*, scholars have devoted their inquiry to analysing geographic power factors, such as climate, location, raw materials, size, topography, population, shape and economic zones of a specific country. Usually these concepts are treated as bases of national power ingredients separately or, in few cases, treated as aggregated national attributes (Ferris, 1973; Sawyer, 1967). Other authors examine the state, without name, in mere dynamic terms, its growth (Deutsch, 1953), and its rise and demise (Herz, 1957).

An examination of some recent geopolitical studies using the state scale suggests that the traditional trends continue. The authors are concerned with the historic basis of geopolitics (Wesson, 1974). After analysing these national bases of power, the authors inevitably examine that particular state's relationship with at least one, if not both, Great Powers in the international system (Rupen, 1982 on Mongolia; Overholt, 1980 on Afghanistan). Or the systemic factors will be analysed more generally (Gorman, 1982 on Peru; Ewell, 1982 on Venezuela; Roett, 1975 on Brazil). In most of these studies, geopolitical theory really does not inform the analysis. Rather geopolitical factors are utilised as a framework or a typology to organise the country study. As a framework, geopolitical concepts are useful, but geopolitical *theory* is not advanced significantly by the plethora of the state idiographic studies.

Authors who turn to the regional scale of analysis sacrifice the descriptive detail present in the state analysis in favour of attempting to explain regional trends. They focus on key concepts applicable to the region, including explanations of how political areas are formed, expand, disintegrate, or integrate and how balance of power and spheres of influence operate. In addition, terms such as satellites, shatter-belts, and containment are also explored. The authors utilising these concepts seem to operate under the assumption voiced by Jay (1980: 45) 'Good regionalism is good geopolitics; and bad regionalism is bad geopolitics.'

Many of the regional studies are general (Russett, 1967; Jay, 1980; Vayrynen, 1979) without reference to more systematic study of regional power centres. Other studies, and these tend to dominate the literature, focus on a specific region. Western Europe remains a favourite area of inquiry, although recent literature goes beyond traditional description and strives for sophisticated models. Rokkan's (1980) model of differentiation is an example. Most importantly, regionalism outside Europe has become a favourite subject of inquiry. Such studies as Roucek (1978) on the Horn of Africa, Sander (1981) on the Caribbean, Tambs (1979) on South America, and Vanhollen (1980) on South Asia are pertinent examples. Finally, water bodies have become an important organising geographic unit for regional studies, ranging from the Mediterranean Sea (Muller, 1979), South Atlantic (House, 1983) to the Indian Ocean (Dowdy and Trood, 1983; House, 1984), and to the broader configuration of the South Atlantic 'unifying' Brazil and Africa in a regional area (Forrest, 1982).

The non-European emphasis in recent geopolitical regional studies can be succinctly explained. In geopolitical terms, the argument is that the superpowers are now 'playing' out their confrontation outside Europe proper, so it is crucial to examine these pivot points which have become part of the balance of power, the spheres of influence or shatter-belts, to use geopolitical terminology.

Examination of the international level offers the most potential for reliable prediction of general trends. To predict, authors need a group of concepts which describe and explain key systemic relations. Power is probably the key concept at this level, although how power is defined and utilised is itself a subject of extensive inquiry (Jones, 1954, 1955). In geopolitical analysis, power was traditionally viewed as distance, now it is analysed as a general relationship. The key to analysing the distribution of power in the international system is in the terms of polarity and stratification, polarity being the horizontal distribution of power (multipolar, unipolar), and stratification being the vertical distribution of power (dominance, dependency, hegemony). More specific concepts describing the power relationships include buffer zone (crush zone), political orbit, and the ubiquitious balance of power.

The traditional approach to geopolitics at the international level was to focus on competition between or among the dominant powers in the international system (Harkavy, 1982; O'Sullivan and Miller, 1983a; Kennan, 1947; Liska, 1977, Griffith, 1975). Obviously in the postwar era this was the US-Soviet Union rivalry and, more recently, the People's Republic of China created the third side of a triangle. Beyond the territorial focus, geopolitical writers have added non-territorial competition, geopolitics of the dollar (Novak, 1979), resource scarcity and population pressure (Choucri and North, 1975; Ashley, 1980), and control of media.

Other geopolitical concepts are applicable across scales of analysis, thus becoming the important integrating concepts of the theory. Among the key concepts at these scales are: partitioning (Waterman, 1984), system, power, power shifts, and ecological and dynamic equilibrium in addition to the more specialised terms of strategic points and regionalism. The difficulty with all geopolitical concepts is there is no systematic organisation; authors seem to pick and choose those concepts which are best suited to their purposes, discarding those which are inappropriate, even though they might be key components of geopolitical theory. In fact, there is no agreed-upon geopolitical theory which specifies the relationship among the various concepts. Rather, we are left with a highly eclectic list of concepts, heavily borrowed from other academic disciplines and in which there is loose agreement among geopoliticians that these terms are central.

Methodology

Geopolitical writers have utilised a variety of methodologies, ranging from philosophical speculation to the most sophisticated quantitative techniques. Philosophical speculation and case studies are the traditional methodological approaches. In the first case, writers speculated on the consequences of various geographic configurations, with little systematic reference to historical patterns. They used the tools of analytical analysis to argue their case. In the second instance, writers using history as their data points developed elaborate case studies. Each had a descriptive emphasis, often capped with some policy prescription. These idiographic efforts form the bulk of the state case studies (Brohman and Knight, 1981, on Namibia, in addition to Gorman, 1982; Ewell, 1982; Rupen, 1982). The emphasis in these idiographic studies is on description of a certain phenomenon, with the geopolitical concepts playing a rather insignificant, if not marginal, role.

Interestingly enough, philosophical analysis has recently been revived with the plethora of futurist studies in geopolitics. The thrust of this work is to speculate on future power configurations, both within and between states (Brunn, 1984), often based on adherence to normative values and taking into account cultural milieux (Kothari, 1974; Falk, 1975; Galtung, 1980). For a review of futurist literature, see Brunn (1981).

Comparativist methodologies have become increasingly prevalent in the geopolitics literature; such comparisons run across historical time periods and across different countries. Geopolitical analyses across historical time periods have recently become prominent in the world-systems literature popularised by Wallerstein (1979), Friedman (1982), and Chase-Dunn and Rubinson (1977). The emphasis is on the comparative basis of power, defined in economic terms; the analysis suggests the reasons for the rise and fall of hegemonic powers in the dominant world-systems since the sixteenth century. Specific analyses of the US contrasted with the Netherlands and the United Kingdom are offered. Geopolitical factors are critical as they are translated into economic power.

More than historical analyses, most geopolitical studies have offered cross-national comparisons, usually comparing the basic national attributes (hence geopolitical basis of power). Similar analysis is offered by Vayrynen (1979) in his assessment of national attributes of various regional power centres. When a relatively few countries are compared on a few dimensions the methodology is usually descriptive.

Most promising for the creation of a more general theory of geopolitics is the new use of aggregate data to compare national attributes of many different countries. Compilations of raw data of national attributes are available in Banks (1971) and Taylor and Hudson (1972) and recently updated in Taylor and Jodice (1983). An analysis of some of these data archives is available in Tanter and Rosenau (1970). Other authors have utilised these national-attribute data (Rummel, 1968; Ferris, 1973; O'Loughlin, 1984) and using sophisticated methodologies like path analysis (Kean and McGowan, 1973) have tried to relate geographic factors to state policies, such as foreign military interventions (Pearson, 1974). While the results are suggestive, more studies need to be conducted, particularly since the cross-national data are available. Unfortunately, many scholars schooled in geopolitical theory are less well versed in the quantitative techniques needed to conduct such analyses. And methodologies capable of authoritatively aggregating national attributes still remain primitive.

Transactional methodology offers a third approach to geo-political studies. Authors adopting the methodology first need to gather information on the flow of transactions across national borders including economic, trade, financial flows, communi-cation, mail, radio diffusion, visits, tourists. Some of these data are already available in raw form in Soja (1969) and Taylor and Jodice (1983). But beyond compilation, scholars need to relate these trans-actions to political and strategic outcomes. The two areas most explored are transactions between frontier or bordering countries (House, 1982, between US and Mexico); and transactions in a regional unit leading to levels of political, economic, and strategic integration (Cobb and Elder, 1970; Puchala, 1970; Lindberg and Scheingold, 1971). Obviously, work on the European Community is the most advanced. Most transactional studies utilise multiple types of transactions.

Like the methodological hurdle faced by those working with comparative national attributes, aggregation of transnational data is plagued with difficulties. How can various indicators be weighted? The theoretical position adopted by the investigator at the outset often determines relative ranking. The geopolitical theorists place utmost importance on strategic factors. They are more apt to give weight to transactions involving weaponry. Brzoska (1982) presents data sources for arms transfer most relevant to this transactional analysis; SIPRI (1975) presents specific data, while Husbands (1980) offers a geographic assessment of the weapons trade. In contrast, other theorists adopting different posi-tions will give more importance to other types of transactions, the most prominent example being the Marxist selective scrutiny of economic transactions. Hence, the methodological inadequacies of aggregation techniques for transaction data force the investigator to make choices based upon his own theoretical position.

Maps have also been a major element in geopolitical writings. Individual maps and atlases were an important instrument of the propaganda strategy used by the German School of Geopolitik to generate public support for Nazism and the Third Reich. Propaganda cartography included distorted maps of territories and countries, their sizes, shapes, orientations, etc. Aside from land areas being distorted, the appearance of air-age maps generated a fresh look at countries and continents, 'exposed' areas were now seen differently. The topic of propaganda cartography has not attracted much attention in the past two decades. It does merit study as propaganda maps are issued by governments to display strategies, ambitions, and goals of the state, military, and government agencies. The popular and colourful political and military atlases by Kidron and Segal (1981, 1983) illustrate how appealingly power strength and development can be portrayed in map form.

Continuing Controversies

Intellectual controversies have persisted among geopoliticians. One group of controversies is embedded in geopolitics itself; scholars working within the geopolitical tradition challenge other scholars working from the same theoretical framework. The second source of controversies pits the geopoliticians against scholars working outside the tradition. We want to explore the sources of these controversies and raise the important theoretical questions. It merits mention that these controversies persist; they have not been solved and we, in turn, offer no 'solution'.

Historically, scholars working within the geopolitical framework have debated the extent to which geopolitical factors can or cannot be altered or modified. The most extreme position is that geopolitical factors cannot be modified; this view tended to dominate the literature when geopolitics was narrowly defined in territorial or spatial terms. And political scientists criticised the geographic profession for this position (Dougherty and Pfaltzgraff, 1981). In the language of Morgenthau (1948), geography was viewed as a stable factor in national power (note that he did not state that it could *never* be changed). The view that geopolitical factors cannot be modified has been seriously challenged by the possibilist school, including Tatham (1951) and Spate (1957). As exemplified in Sprout (1963), and Dahlberg (1979), geopolitical factors may be substantially modified by technology and by information. As Sprout and Sprout (1971: 264) explain:

> The political value and significance of location, distance, space, distribution, and configuration — the prime geographic dimensions formerly — remain fairly static for long periods.

However, with changes in the system (technological), these relationships have become unstable and dynamic. In fact, the definitions of geopolitics presented earlier attest to the prevalence of the view that geopolitical factors are changeable. As Cohen (1973: 29) suggests:

> geopolitical views vary with the changing geographical setting and with man's interpretation of the nature of this change.

Thus, an important segment of geopolitical analysts no longer see this as a continuing source of controversy — geopolitical factors can be modified and their research agenda is crowded with discovering how and to what extent these factors have been and can be modified.

A second controversy within the field of geopolitics involves the specification of the relationship between geopolitics and political behaviour. Three contrasting views specify this relationship. The first view is that geopolitics *determines* political behaviour. German Geopolitik of the inter-war and war period comes closest to this position. By suggesting that sufficient land area and natural resources were needed to support the population of a nation, they implied that these geopolitical factors determined the policy of *Lebensraum* or living space supported by Ratzel, Kjellen, and Haushofer. The above determinism became the rationale for Nazi expansion and aggression. Presently, the deterministic view is largely eschewed. As Gray (1977, p. 11) argues, geopolitics is a framework 'without predetermining policy choice'.

Currently, the controversy revolves around whether geopolitics conditions or circumscribes political behaviour or whether geopolitics is but one factor among many that make up political behaviour. Disciplinary self-interest and parochialism seem to permeate this controversy. Those trained in geography tend to subscribe to the former position, thereby reaffirming the critical nature of the geographic, whereas political scientists adhere to the latter, asserting the primacy of political factors (Morgenthau, 1948). Few authors have achieved the balance that is sought (Sprout, 1971). As long as disciplinary 'tunnel vision' prevails, this controversy is not likely to be resolved.

A second group of controversies questions whether geopolitics is a separate viable field of study. To answer with an unequivocal 'yes', geopolitical theorists must differentiate themselves not only from the more general field of international political geography within the parent discipline, but must also differentiate themselves from power politics or political realism of political science, and from systems theory of general systems theory.

The wide variety of definitions of geopolitics suggests that the differentiation between geopolitics and political geography is not rigid. Political geography, it must be remembered, encompasses more than geopolitics or the political geographic strategies designed to influence a state's foreign policies (Hartshorne, 1960; and see other chapters in this volume). While some political geographers maý still shun the use of the term geopolitics because of the pejorative label acquired during the war years, there is no question but that macro level political geography research that focuses on military strategies, economic/political policies, and power balances does sound strikingly similar to studies that previously were termed geopolitics. The Enggass (1984) bibliography in listing a revival of studies in the past decade seems to point to the term's renewed use and acceptance.

The most serious challenge to geopolitics as a separate field of inquiry comes from political realism or power politics. Geopolitics is unquestionably an integral part of realist theory. As summarised by Dougherty and Pfaltzgraff (1981, p. 85)

> Geographic, demographic, resource, and geopolitical factors are central to realist theory of international relations.

Writers such as Morgenthau (1948) and Spykman (1942) reiterate that geography is a crucial concept to political realism. For both, the pursuit of national interest is related to geopolitics. Wright (1955), one of the fathers of political realism, attributes major importance to the geopolitical field in influencing international political behaviour. However, political realists offer a more integrated and comprehensive theory of national political behaviour. They begin with assumptions regarding the nature of man, with a group of integrated propositions linking that view to state behaviour. They extensively analyse state behaviour in terms of the concept of power — and power as a relationship is composed of a number of key ingredients, both the stable factors and the more unstable ones such as national character and morale (Morgenthau, 1948). In other words, the logic of political realism is more developed.

Interestingly enough, both geopoliticians and political realists offer similar policy prescriptions. Jay (1980: 486) defines geopolitical success as:

> . . . at a minimum of consolidating the strength and cohesion of the group of nations which form the core of one's power position, while preventing the other side from extending the area of its domination of clientele.

This statement sounds remarkably similar to the realists' call for balance of power as the major way to limit national power and prevent hegemony, although it may not be the only way (Morgenthau, 1948). Hence balance of power and power are the core concepts in both theories.

Whether geopolitics is a separate field apart from political realism seems once again to depend on one's disciplinary training. Geopoliticists within geography may argue 'yes', while political scientists suggest not. Apart from acknowledging the unique contributions of the early political writers (Mackinder, 1904; Mahan, 1897; Douhet, 1942), they tend to see geopolitics as an integral, but not separate, field within political realism.

In recent years geopolitical writers have widened their research agendas beyond the unidimensional theme of geopolitics to the multi-dimensional theme of environmental theories or an ecological perspective. As Sprout and Sprout (1971) popularised, an ecological perspective examines the relationship among interdependent earth-related communities that share a crowded planet; the focus is on the individual interacting with the environment in a system (Pirages, 1978, 1983; Dunlap, 1980). By widening their subject of inquiry in this way, geopolitical/ecological writers utilise concepts and discuss subjects very close to the concerns of systems theorists. Hence, the possibility again exists that geopolitics is not a separate field of inquiry but is part and parcel of systems theory.

Systems theory posits that there are a number of interrelated parts and that a change in one or more variables means changes in the others. Boulding (1956) identified several different levels of system, arranged according to levels of complexity: mechanistic, homeo-static, and biological; he takes the latter and has reinterpreted it in broader ecological terms (Boulding, 1983). While systems theorists differ among themselves, they share a common concern with stability of the system, analysing the adaptive controls by which equilibrium is maintained, and by examining the capacity of the system to deal with disturbances (Dougherty and Pfaltzgraff, 1981). Similarly, an ecological perspective in geopolitics is now focusing on the sources of change, be they changes in technology, armaments, population growth patterns, or distribution of natural resources. They tend to utilise the language of systems theory, the term system itself (Cohen, 1983), dynamic equilibrium and change. Hence, both of the cognate fields of inquiry in geopolitics seem to be more comprehensive alter-natives; geopolitics may be subsumed in political realism and geo-politics uses the language of system theory. Both trends tend to confirm the eclectic nature of the field of inquiry.

Research Agenda

It is our view that research into geopolitical questions is a legitimate area of scholarly inquiry by political geographers, political scien-tists, and others interested in international dimensions of a state's goals, strategies, and policies (Weigert and Stefansson, 1949). While we recognise the misuse and misapplication of the term before and during World War II, we feel that questions into the geopolitical nature of resource distribution, technology transfer, nuclear weapons and arms, and power should be investigated at state, regional, and international scales (Cole, 1981). Not to pursue such inquiries would leave potential gaps in our knowledge about how states perceive and behave with others, and, more importantly, result in cursory analysis by those in other disciplines where distri-butions, resources, and state policies are not a major focus. We also remain cognisant of some of the methodological and conceptual pitfalls previous investigators have encountered and of the criti-cisms levelled at the subject in general. While much needs to be corrected, we remain undaunted in our view that geopolitics, whether termed such or clothed in geostrategic labels, can and should become an area of even more attention in the coming decade. We support Taylor's (1982) comments on the revival of geostrategic studies as a major theme demanding our attention. He states (p. 9):

The current East-West strategic contest is superficially much like the two-power model proposed by Mackinder at the beginning of the century. However much has happened since Mackinder developed his ideas and the current situation is by no means as simple as applications of these early models would imply. In particular, the massive growth of the world economy in the twentieth century has meant that economic links between countries are much stronger and hence more important. Add to this the decolonization of the 'South' providing very many new countries on the international scene and clearly new models are required to encompass these complexities. Geostrategic considerations will now have to take into account the world distribution of key raw materials upon which the superpowers and their allies depend. The rise of multinational corporations as economic actors and developments in military technology require further consideration in the field. What is clear is that new geostrategic modelling will require an integration of economic and military considerations in ways not considered by early workers in the field.

We offer the following topics as legitimate for a research agenda on geopolitics for the 1980s and 1990s.

The changing definition of power. How is power defined in a nuclear age? In a postindustrial world? Are traditional measures of size, military prowess, and resources satisfactory? Does the accumulation of information and the ability to acquire, process, and sell it represent the newest and most effective definition of power? How is power defined in a multi-power world? We agree with Agnew (1982, p. 168) who in evaluating Taylor's (1982) research strategies for political geography in the 1980s commented regarding power that it:

> . . . is a fundamental concept for political geography. We cannot ignore it, as do some public choice theorists, or reduce it to 'fate' as do those advocates claiming a political economy mantle for their work.

While political scientists have a rich literature in power as a concept, the geographic dimensions, measurement, and significance of power await much further investigation.

Adjusting to shrinking geopolitical worlds and global interdependence. How important are traditional (absolute) locations in a time-space converging world? Has the tyranny of distance been replaced by the tyranny of time? What significance do nineteenth century notions of Heartland, Rimland, cores, peripheries, containment, and domino theories have in the tightly knit world of instant communication? Are points replacing areas in global politics? Are we witnessing the demise of distance as a barrier? Is technology (word and picture) or the acquisition of it the new barrier? As spaces between states shrink because of faster transportation and communication, so do the types, forms and scales of transaction and interaction (Brunn, 1981). We agree with Glassner and de Blij (1980, p. 275) that global interdependence ushers in the need for new ways of thinking about geopolitics and geostrategy.

> Although all these geostrategic views [Mackinder, Haushofer, Mahan, Spykman, de Seversky, Meinig, Hooson, and Cohen] have serious flaws, they do have the virtue of analyzing the world as a whole, rather than as scores of discrete political units. In view of the increasing interdependence of the world, we need a good deal more of this holistic thinking, not directed toward formulation of strategies of confrontation, but toward strategies of cooperation; not a geostrategy of war, but a geostrategy of peace.

Geopolitics of various ideologies. While most of the studies recently have avoided political philosophy and ideology, it might be worthwhile to examine how geopolitics is practised, viewed, and used by major global and regional powers. Cole's (1982, p. 170) statement on Soviet geography is tantalizing; he suggests the Soviets:

> . . . avoid political geography like the plague (haunted by Haushofer) the Soviet Union is a country in which all decisions (including those affecting geographical aspects) are political.

How are the Soviets using geopolitics in their strategies to control buffer states or access to the Indian Ocean? What are the geopolitical policies and strategies of China? Brazil? Saudi Arabia? Japan? Nigeria? India? Indonesia? or Iran? We need to move away from European, Soviet, and US studies on geopolitics to study other regions and powers.

Strategies of warfare and defence. Although we would distinguish between studies of geopolitics and military geography, with the former dealing with power, resources, information, and political strategies and the latter addressing the logistics of battles, wars, and fighting (air, land, ocean, or space), we do feel that it is worth examining the geopolitical elements in strategic studies (van der Wusten, 1984). We believe Massam (1982, p. 168) in his commentary on Taylor's (1982) agenda for political geography in the 1980s makes a valid point:

> Questions of scale spread throughout the discipline, and within the subdiscipline of political geography; we might ask questions about the patterns of defense, aggression attack and retreat behaviour of different scales.

The innovative studies by O'Sullivan (1982, 1983a, b) represent good starting points for examining the interfaces between a state's internal and external policies *vis-à-vis* military strategy. The Pepper and Jenkins (1984) effort also represents a breakthrough in our thinking. Similar investigations might be carried out in East Asia, Latin America, and the Pacific.

Geopolitics in contemporary foreign policy. To what extent can geopolitics be used to explain a state's foreign policy? What is significant about the rise of the South? of NIC (newly industrialised countries)? The appearance of emerging regional powers? The declining role of traditional powers? And the acquisition of highly sophisticated weapons technologies that influence foreign policy relations? What do the demise of distance as a barrier, the development of a global interconnected communications system, and the threats of surprise nuclear attacks by small nations contribute to how a state conducts (or fails to conduct) foreign policies? We agree with Cohen (1983, p. 307) when he states the following about US foreign policy:

> American foreign policy for the Eighties must aim at the increased involvement of the other first-order, and key regional powers as partners in search for world stability.

and (p. 309)

To envision a world of equilibrium, American foreign policy-makers should adopt a new mental map of the world. This is not a world divisible in two, along traditional seapower and landpower lines.

and his conclusion (p. 307) that the:

. . . international system is exceedingly hierarchical and regionally framed, as well as multi-polar.

Cohen also believes political geographers can contribute to an understanding of a nation's foreign policy. He states (p. 296):

Political geographers have a responsibility to contribute to their respective national foreign policy debating grounds, rather than to avoid the field of international relations.

The historical and geographical reasons behind a state's foreign policy merit much further analysis (Hoffman, 1982).

The future of the state. What is happening to the nation-state and traditional and contemporary definitions of geopolitics? Is the state being replaced by a system of states? By transnational corporations? By regionalism (Knight, 1984)? By regional federations and alliances? Or by active citizen groups with common causes? Who negotiates with whom? What roles does a state play in a world of countervailing national and international powers that sometimes work at cross-purposes? These questions are worthy of serious study (Brunn, 1984).

The postnuclear state. What configuration will exist in the aftermath of a limited or extensive nuclear war? How does one develop national and international policies? How will power be defined? Do local survival strategies replace regional and global policies and goals? Who will make decisions? How will states be organised? What will be a viable state? Are we reduced from global scales of interest and concern to the local 'state'?

Conclusion

In our examination of geopolitics within geography, political science, and the social sciences in general, we have discussed its origin, the extensive literature on the subject, the core concepts and methodologies, prevailing controversies, and also presented a research agenda of topics meriting investigating. While the subject of geopolitics has a rather chequered and tainted history, its recent emergence as a legitimate topic for social scientists signals the importance of examining the role of geopolitics in a state's or region's policies relating to resources, technology and weapons transfers, conflicts, and military strategies. We believe that legitimate advances in the study of geopolitics must incorporate concepts that are integrated into descriptive or quantitative models and that promote the development of theory. Furthermore, we believe that progress in the study of geopolitics can best be made by acknowledging and incorporating the contributions of geographers, political scientists, and others concerned with state and regional geopolitics.

References

Adie, W.A.C. (1975) *Oil, Politics and Seapower: The Indian Ocean, Vortex*, Crane, Russak, New York

Agnew, J.A. (1982) 'Comments on Research Agendas for the Nineteen Eighties', *Political Geographer Quarterly, 1*, 168

Ashley, R. (1980) *The Political Economy of War and Peace*, Nichols, New York

Atwood, W.W. (1935) 'The Increasing Significance of Geographic Conditions in the Growth of Nation-States', *Annals, Associations of American Geographers. 25*, 1–16

Banks, A. (1971) *Cross-Polity Time Series*, MIT Press, Cambridge, Massachusetts

Behre, C.H., Jr. (1940) 'Mineral Economics and World Politics', *Geographical Review, 30*, 676–8

Blake, G. (1980) 'Flash-Point Through Which Middle East Oil Must Pass', *Geographical Magazine, 53*, 50–2

—— (1981) 'Coveted Waterway of Bab el Mandeb', *Geographical Magazine, 54*, 233–5

Boggs, S.W. (1946) 'Cartohypnosis', *United States Department of State Bulletin, 15*, No. 390, 1119–1125

Boulding, K.E. (1956) *The Image: Knowledge in Life and Society*, University of Michigan Press, Ann Arbor

—— (1983) 'On Dennis Pirages' The Ecological Perspective and the Social Science', *International Studies Quarterly, 27*, 267–9

Brandt, K. (1939) 'Foodstuffs and Raw Materials as Elements of National Power', Chapter 5, in H. Speier and, Kahler (eds.). *War in Our Time*, W.W. Norton, New York, pp. 105–31

Brohman, J.A. and Knight, D.B. (1981) 'Some Geopolitical Aspects of the Conflict

70   *Geopolitics*

in Namibia/South-West Africa' in A.D. Burnett and P.J. Taylor (eds.), *Political Studies From Spatial Perspectives*, John Wiley, Chichester and New York, pp. 467–513

Brunn, S.D. (1984) 'The Future of the Nation-State System' in P. Taylor and J. House, *Political Geography: Recent Advances and Future Directions*, Croom Helm, London, pp. 149–67

—— (1981) 'Geopolitics in a Shrinking World: A Political Geography of the Twenty-First Century' in A.D. Burnett and P.J. Taylor (eds.), *Political Studies From Spatial Perspectives*, John Wiley, Chichester and New York, pp. 131–56

Broek, J.O.M. and Junis, M.A. (1945) 'Geography and Nationalism', *Geographical Review. 35*, 301–11

Brzoska, M. (1982) 'Arms Transfer Data Sources', *Journal of Conflict Resolution, 26*, 77–108

Busteed, M.A. (1983) 'The Developing Nature of Political Geography' in his *Developments in Political Geography*, Academic Press, New York and London, pp. 1–67

Castro, J.D. (1977) *The Geopolitics of Hunger*, Monthly Review Press, New York

Chase-Dunn, C. and Rubinson, R. (1977) 'Toward A Structural Perspective on the World-System', *Politics and Society, 7*, 453–76

Child, J. (1983) 'The American Southern Cone: Geopolitics and Conflict' in B. Lentnek (ed.), *Contemporary Issues in Latin America*, Muncie, Indiana, pp. 200–13

Choucri, N. and North, R. (1975) *Nations in Conflict*, W.H. Freeman, San Francisco

Cobb, R.W. and Elder, C. (1970) *International Community: A Regional and Global Study*, Holt, Rinehart and Winston, New York

Cohen, S.B. (1964 and 1973) *Geography and Politics in a World Divided*, Random House, New York

—— (1982) 'A New Map of Global Geopolitical Equilibrium: A Developmental Approach', *Political Geography Quarterly, 1*, 223–42

—— (1983) 'American Foreign Policy for the Eighties' in N. Kliot and S. Waterman (eds.), *Pluralism and Political Geography*, Croom Helm, London, pp. 295–310

Cohen, S.B. and Rosenthal, L.D. (1971) 'A Geographical Model of Political Systems Analysis', *Geography Review*, 61, 5–31

Colby, C. (ed.) (1938) *Geographic Aspects of International Relations*, University of Chicago Press, Chicago

Cole, J.P. (1981) *Geography of World Affairs*, 6th ed., Penguin Books, London and New York

—— (1982) 'Comments on Research Agendas for the Nineteen Eighties', *Political Geography Quarterly, 1*, 170

Conant, M.A. and Gold, F.R. (1978) *The Geopolitics of Energy*, Westview Press, Boulder, Colorado

Crone, G.R. (1948) 'A German View of Geopolitics', *Geographical Journal, 101*, 33–6

Dahlberg, K.A. (1979) *Beyond the Green Revolution: The Ecology and Politics of Global Agricultural Development*, Plenum, New York

deSeversky, A.D. (1941) *Victory Through Airpower*, Williams and Wilkins, Baltimore

—— (1942) 'Air Power to Rule the World', *Science Digest, 12*, (October), 33–36

—— (1950) *Air Power: Key to Survival*, Simon and Schuster, New York

Deudney, D. (1983) *Whole Earth Security: A Geopolitics of Peace*, Worldwatch Institute (Worldwatch Paper No. 55), Washington, DC

Deutsch, K.W. (1953) 'The Growth of Nations — Some Recurrent Patterns of Political and Social Integration', *World Politics. 5*, 168–95

Dickinson, R.E. (1943) *The German Lebensraum*, Routledge and Kegan Paul, London

Dougherty, J.E. and Pfaltzgraff, R.P. (1981) *Contending Theories of International Relations*, 2nd edn., Harper and Row, New York

Douhet, G. (1942) *The Command of the Air*, Translated by Dino Ferrari, Coward-McCann, New York

Dowdy, W.L. and Trood R.B. (1983) 'The Indian Ocean: An Emerging Geostrategic Region', *International Journal, 38*, 432–58

Dunlap, R. (1980) 'Paradigmatic Change in Social Science: The Decline of Human Exemptionalism and the Emergence of an Ecological Paradigm', *American Behavioral Scientist* (September-October)

East, W.G. and Moodie, A.E. (1956) *The Changing World*, World Books, Yonkers-on-Hudson, New York

—— (1965) 'Review of Geography and Politics in a World Divided', *Geographical Journal, 131*, 417–18

Eckes, A., Jr. (1979) *The United States and the Global Struggle for Minerals*, University of Texas Press, Austin, Texas

Enggass, P.M. (1984) *Geopolitics: A Bibliography of Applied Political Geography*, Vance Bibliographies, Pub. Admin. Series: #P 1438, Monticello, Illinois

Ewell, J. (1982) 'The Development of Venezuelan Geopolitical Analysis Since World War II'. *Journal of Interamerican Studies and World Affairs, 24*, 295–320

Fairgrieve, J. (1915) *Geography and World Power*, Dutton; 2nd ed. rev, 1921, University of London Press, London

—— (1922) 'Geography and World Power', *Journal of Geography, 21*, 285–94

Falk, R.A. (1975) *A Study of Future Worlds*, The Free Press, New York

Ferris, W.H. (1973) *The Power Capability of Nation-States*, Lexington Books, Lexington, Massachusetts

Fifield, R.H. and Pearcy, G.E. (1944) *Geopolitics in Principle and Practice*, Boston, Massachusetts

Forrest, T. (1982) 'Brazil and Africa: Geopolitics, Trade and Technology in the South-Atlantic', *African Affairs, 81*, no. 322, 3–20

Freedman, L. (1983) *The Evolution of Nuclear Strategy*, St. Martin's Press, New York

Friedman, E. (ed.) (1982) *Ascent and Decline in the World-System*, Sage, Beverly Hills, California

Galtung, J. (1980) *The True World. A Transnational Perspective*, The Free Press, New York

Glassner, M.I. (ed.) (1983) *Global Resources: Challenges of Interdependence*, F. Praeger, New York

—— and deBlij, Harm (1980) *Systematic Political Geography*, John Wiley, New York

Gorman, S.M. (1982) 'Geopolitics and Peruvian Foreign-Policy'. *Inter-American Economic Affairs, 36*, 65–88

Gottman, J. (1942) 'The Background of Geopolitics' *Military Affairs, 6*, 197–205

Gray, C.S. (1977) *The Geopolitics of the Nuclear Era: Heartland, Rimlands and the Technological Revolution*, Crane, Russak for the National Strategy Information Centre, New York

Griffith, W.E. (1975) *The World and the Great-Power Triangles*, MIT Press, Cambridge, Massachusetts

Gyorgy, A. (1944) *Geopolitics: The New German Science*, University of California Press, Berkeley, California

Haring, L. and Norris, R. (1980) *Political Geography*, Merrill, Columbus, Ohio

Harkavy, R.E. (1982) *Great Power Competition for Overseas Bases: The Geopolitics of Access Diplomacy*, Pergamon, Elmsford, New York

Hartshorne, R. (1935) 'Recent Developments in Political Geography', *American Political Science Review, 29*, 785–804; 943–66

—— (1944) 'The United States and the Shatter Zone of Europe', in H.W. Weigert and V. Stefansson (eds.), *Compass of the World*, Macmillan, New York, pp. 203–14

—— (1954) 'Political Geography' in P.E. James and C.F. Jones (eds.), *American Geography: Inventory and Prospect*, Syracuse University Press, Syracuse, New York, pp. 167–225

—— (1968) 'Political Geography in the Modern World', *Journal of Conflict Resolution, 4*, 52–66

Herz, J.H. (1957) 'Rise and Demise of the Territorial State', *World Politics, 9*, 473–93

Hessell, M.S., Murphy, W.J. and Hessell, F.A. (1942) *Strategic Materials in Hemispheric Defense*, Hastings House, New York

Hoffman, G.W. (1982) 'Nineteenth Century Roots of American World Power Relations: A Study in Historical Political Geography', *Political Geography Quarterly, 1*, 279–92

House, J.W. (1982) *Frontier on the Rio Grande: A Political Geography of Development and Social Deprivation*, Clarendon Press, Oxford

—— (1983) 'Unfinished Business in the South Atlantic', *Political Geography Quarterly, 2*, 233–47

—— (1984) 'War, Peace and Conflict Resolution: Towards an Indian Ocean Model', *Transactions, Institute of British Geographers*, N.S., *9*, 3–21

Husbands, J.L. (1980) 'A World in Arms: Geography of the Weapons Trade', *Focus, 30*, No. 4, 1–16

Hveem, H. (1979) 'Militarization of Nature, Conflict and Control Over Strategic Resources and Some Implications for Peace Policies', *Journal of Peace Research, XVI*, No. 1, 1–26

Jay, P. (1980) 'Regionalism as Geopolitics', *Foreign Affairs, 58*, 485–514

Jones, S.B. (1954) 'The Power Inventory and National Strategy', *World Politics, 6*, 421–52

—— (1959) 'Global Strategic Views' in *Military Aspects of World Political Geography*, US Air Force, Alabama

Joo-Dock, J. (1979) *Geo-Strategy in the South China Sea Basin*, Singapore University Press, Singapore

Jordan, A.A. and Kilmarx, R.A. (1979) *Strategic Mineral Dependence: The Stockpile Dilemma*, Sage Publications, Beverly Hills, California

Karan, P.R. (1953) 'India's Role in Geopolitics', *India Quarterly, 9*, 160–9

Kasperson, R.E. and Minghi, J.V. (eds.) (1969) *The Structure of Political Geography*, Aldine, Chicago

Kean, J.G. and McGowan, P.J. (1973) 'National Attributes and Foreign Policy Participation: A Path Analysis' in P.J. McGowan (ed.) *International Yearbook of Foreign Policy Studies*, Vol. 1., Sage Publications, Beverly Hills, California

Kennan, G.F. (1947) 'The Sources of Soviet Conduct', *Foreign Affairs, 25* (July)

Kidron, M. and Segal, R. (1981) *The State of the World Atlas*, Simon and Schuster, New York

—— and Smith, D. (1983) *The War Atlas: Armed Conflict — Armed Peace*, Pan Books, London and Sydney

Kjellen, R. (1914) *Die Grossmachte der Gegenwart*, Ubersetzt von C. Koch. B.G. Teubner, Leipzig and Berlin

—— (1916) 'Die Politische Probleme des Weltkrieges', *Ubersetzt von Dr. Friedrich Stieve*, B.G. Teubner, Leipzig

—— (1924) *Der Staat als Lebensform*. Leipzig: S. Hirzel Verlag, 1917, Kurt Vowinckel, Berlin

Knight, D.B. (1984) 'Geographical Perspectives on Self-Determination' in P. Taylor and J. House (eds.), *Political Geography: Recent Advances and Future Directions*, Croom Helm, London, pp. 168–90

Kothari, R. (1974) *Footsteps Into the Future. Diagnosis of the Present World and a Design for an Alternative*, The Free Press, New York

Kruszewski, C. (1940) Germany's Lebensraum. *The American Political Science Review, 34*, 964–75.

Leith, C.K., Furness, J.W. and Lewis, C. (1943) *World Minerals and World Peace*, The Brookings Institution, Washington, DC

Levy, W.J. (1982) *Oil Strategy and Politics, 1941–1981*, edited by Melvin A. Conant, Westview Press, Boulder, Colorado

Lindberg, L.N. and Scheingold, S.A. (eds.) (1971) *Regional Integration: Theory and Research*, Harvard University Press, Cambridge, Massachusetts

Liska, G. (1977) *Quest for Equilibrium: America and the Balance of Power on Land and Sea*, Johns Hopkins Press, Baltimore and London

List, F. (1856) *National System of Political Economy* (Translated by G.A. Matile), J.B. Lippincott, Philadelphia

Mackinder, H.J. (1890) 'The Physical Basis of Political Geography'. *Scottish Geographical Magazine, 6*, No. 2, 78–84

—— (1902) *Britain and the British Seas*, Appleton and Co., Clarendon Press, Oxford

—— (1904) 'The Geographical Pivot of History', *Geographical Journal, 23*, 421–44

—— (1919) *Democratic Ideals and Reality: A Study in the Politics of Reconstruction*, Henry Holt, London and Constable, New York

Mahan, A.T. (1890) *The Influence of Sea Power Upon History, 1660–1783*, Little Brown, Boston, Massachusetts

—— (1892) *The Influence of Sea Power Upon the French Revolution and Empire, 1793–1812*, Little Brown, Boston, Massachusetts

—— (1897) *The Interest of America in Sea Power, Present and Future*, Little Brown, Boston, Massachusetts

—— (1900) *The Problem of Asia and Its Effect Upon International Politics*, Little Brown, Boston, Massachusetts

Massam, B.H. (1982) 'Comments on Research Agendas for the Nineteen Eighties'. *Political Geography Quarterly, 1*, 168

Mattern, J. (1942) *Geopolitik — Doctrine of National Self Sufficiency and Empire*, Johns Hopkins University Studies in Historical and Political Science, Baltimore

Maull, O. (1936) *Das Wesen der Geopolitik*, B.G. Teubner, Leipzig

—— (1940) *Die Vereinigten Staaten als Grossreich*, De Gruyter, Leipzig

McColl, R.W. (1975) 'Geopolitical Themes in Contemporary Asian Revolution'. *Geographical Review, 65*, 301–10

—— (1983) 'A Geopolitical Model for International Behaviour' in N. Kliot and S. Waterman (eds.), *Pluralism and Political Geography*, Croom Helm, London, pp. 284–94

Means, M. (1935) 'International Problems: A Study in Political Geography', *Journal of Geography, 34*, No. 5, 187–92

Mitchell, B. and Kimball, L. (1979) 'Conflict Over the Cold Continent', *Foreign Policy, 35* (Summer), 124–41

Mitchell, W. (1925) *Winged Defense: The Development and Possibilities of Modern Air Power — Economic and Military*, G.P. Putnam, New York

Morgenthau, H.J. (1948) *Politics Among Nations: The Struggle for Power and Peace*, 4th edn., Alfred A. Knopf, New York

Most, B.A. and Starr, H. (1980) 'Diffusion, Reinforcement, Geopolitics, and the Spread of War', *American Political Science Review, 74*, 932–65

Muller, F.G. (1979) 'Divide-Up to Clean-Up: Geopolitical Solution to Mediterranean Pollution', *Environmental Policy and Law, 5*, 13–15

Novak, J.C. (1979) 'The Geopolitics of the Dollar', *Worldview, 22*, New York, 23–6

Odell, P.R. (1979) *Oil and World Power*, 5th ed, Penguin Books, New York

Odingo, R.S. (1966) 'Geopolitical Problems of East Africa', *East Africa Journal, 2*, no. 9, 17–24

O'Loughlin, J. (1984) 'Geographic Models of International Conflicts' in P. Taylor and J. House (eds.), *Political Geography: Recent Advances and Future Directions*, Croom Helm, London, pp. 202–26

Orchard, J.E. (1942) *Resources for Victory*, Pamphlet No. 4, Columbia University Press series, New York

O'Sullivan, P. (1982) Antidomino. *Political Geography Quarterly, 1*, 57–64

—— (1983a) 'Geopolitics and Grand Strategy' in *The Geography of Warfare*, St. Martin's Press, New York, pp. 93–109

—— (1983b) 'A Geographical Analysis of Guerilla Warfare', *Political Geography Quarterly 2*, 139–50

—— and Miller, J.W., Jr. (1983b) *The Geography of Warfare*, St. Martin's Press, New York

Overholt, W.H. (1980) 'The Geopolitics of the Afghan War', *Asian Affairs 7*, 205–17

Oxman, B.H., Caron, D.D. and Buderi, C.L.O. (eds.) (1983) *The Law of the Sea. US Policy Dilemma*, Institute for Contemporary Studies Press, San Francisco

Panda, B.P. (1959) 'Geopolitical Problems of the Middle East', *Journal of Geography* (University of Jabalpur), *1*, (November), 27–36

Pearson, F.S. (1974) 'Geographic Proximity and Foreign Military Intervention', *Journal of Conflict Resolution, 18*, 432–60

Pepper, D. and Jenkins, A. (1984) 'Reversing the Nuclear Arms Race: Geopolitical Bases for Pessimism', *Professional Geographer 36*

Philip, G. (1980) 'Mexican Oil and Gas: The Politics of a New Resource', *International Affairs, 56*, 474–81

Pierre, A.J. (1982) *The Global Politics of Arms Sales*, Princeton University Press, Princeton, New Jersey

Pirages, D. (1978) *Global Ecopolitics: The New Context for International Relations*, Duxbury Press, North Scituate, Massachusetts

—— (1983) 'The Ecological Perspective and the Social Sciences', *International Studies Quarterly, 27*, 243–56

Pittman, H.T. (1981) 'Geopolitics and Foreign Policy in Argentina, Brazil, and Chile' in E.G. Ferris and J.K. Lincoln. (eds.) *Latin American Foreign Policies*, Westview Press, Boulder, Colorado, pp. 165–78

Prescott, J.R.V. (1965) *The Geography of Frontiers and Boundaries*, Aldine, Chicago

—— (1968) *The Geography of State Policies*, Aldine, Chicago

—— (1975) *The Political Geography of the Oceans*, David and Charles, Newton Abbot, Devon

Puchala, D. (1970) 'International Transactions and Regional Integration', *International Organization. 24*, 732–63

Quam, L.O. (1943) 'The Use of Maps in Propaganda', *Journal of Geography*, 42, no. 1, 21–32

Quddus, S.A. (1982) *Afghanistan and Pakistan: A Geopolitical Study*, Ferozsons, Lahore

Ratzel, F. (1896) 'The Territorial Growth of States' (an abstract), *Scottish Geographical Magazine, 12*, 351–61

—— (1897) *Politische Geographie: oder die Geographie der Staaten, des Verkehrs, und des Krieg*, Oldenbourg, Munchen

Raup, H.F. (1943) 'Geopolitics: The Background Pattern of Hitler's Foreign Policies', *Education, 63*, 266–72

Roett, R. (1975) 'Brazil Ascendant-International Relations and Geopolitics in Late 20th Century', *Journal of International Affairs, 29*, 139–54

Rokkan, S. (1980) 'Territories, Centres and Peripheries', in J. Gotterman (ed.), *Centre and Periphery*, Sage, London, pp. 163–204

Roucek, J.S. (1952) 'The Geopolitics of the Adriatic', *American Journal of Economics and Sociology, 11*, 171–8

—— (1978) 'Horn of Africa in Geopolitics', *Revista de Politica Internacional*, no. 160, 53–100

Rummell, R.J. (1968) 'The Relationship Between National Attributes and Foreign Conflict Behavior', in J.D. Singer (ed.), *Quantitative International Politics: Insights and Evidence*, Free Press, New York

Rupen, R.A. (1982) 'Mongolia — Pawn of Geopolitics', *Current History, 81*, no. 475, 215

Russell, J.A. (1954) 'Military Geography' in P.E. James and C.F. Jones (eds.), *American Geography: Inventory and Prospect*, Syracuse University Press, Syracuse, New York, pp. 484–95

Russett, B.M. (1967) *International Regions and the International System: A Study in Political Ecology*, Rand McNally, Chicago

Sander, G. (1981) 'Regional Structures and Geopolitics in the Greater Caribbean, A Contribution to Political-Geography', *Geographische Zeitschrift, 69*, no. 1, 34–56

Sawyer, J. (1967) 'Dimensions of Nations: Size, Wealth, and Politics', *American Journal of Sociology, 73* (September), 145–72

Segal, B. (1983) 'Geopolitics of Broadcasting'. *Washington Quarterly, 6*, no. 2, 140–8

Sen, D. (1975) *Basic Principles of Geopolitics and History*, Concept, Delhi

Short, J.R. (1982) *An Introduction to Political Geography*, Routledge and Kegan Paul, London and Boston, Massachusetts

Soja, E. (1969) 'Communications and Territorial Integration in East Africa: An Introduction to Transaction Flow Analysis', *East Lakes Geographer, 4*, 39–57

Spate, O.H.K. (1957) 'How Determined is Possibilism?' *Geographical Studies, 14*, 3–8

Sprout, H.H. (1963) 'Geopolitical Hypotheses in Technological Perspective', *World Politics, 15*, 187–212

—— (1968) 'Geography: Political Geography', *International Encyclopedia of the Social Sciences*. vol. 6, pp. 116–23

—— and Sprout, M. (1971) *Toward a Politics of the Planet Earth*, Van Nostrand, Reinhold, New York

Spykman, N.J. (1942a) *America's Strategy in World Politics: The United States and the Balance of Power*, Harcourt Brace, New York

—— (1944) *The Geography of the Peace*, edited by Helen R. Nicholl, Harcourt Brace, New York

Steinbrunner, J.D. (1978) 'National Security and the Concept of Strategic Stability', *Journal of Conflict Resolution. 22*, 411–28

Stockholm International Peace Research Institute (1975) *Arms Trade Register; The Arms Trade With the Third World*, Prepared by Eva Greenback, Almquist and Wiksell, Stockholm, MIT Press, New York and Cambridge, Massachusetts

Tambs, L.A. (1979) 'The Changing Geopolitical Balance of South America', *Journal of Social and Political Studies, 4* (Spring), 17–35

Tanter, R. and Rosenau, J.N. (1970) 'Field and Environmental Approaches to World Politics: Implications for Data Archives', *Journal of Conflict Resolution, 16*, 513–26

Tatham, G. (1951) 'Environmentalism and Possibilism' in G. Taylor (ed.), *Geography in the Twentieth Century*, Philosophical Library, New York

Taylor, C.L. and Hudson, M.C. (1972) *World Handbook of Political and Social Indicators*. 2nd edn, Yale University Press, New Haven, Connecticut

—— and Jodice, D.A. (1983) *World Handbook of Political and Social Indicators*. 3rd edn, vol. I,II. Yale University Press, New Haven, Connecticut

Taylor, P. (1982) 'Editorial Essay — Research Agendas for the Nineteen Eighties', *Political Geography Quarterly, 1*, 1–18

—— (1984) 'Introduction: Geographical Scale and Political Geography' in P. Taylor and J. House (eds.), *Political Geography: Advances and Future Directions*, Croom Helm, London, pp. 1–7

Troll, C. (1949) 'Geographic Science in Germany During the Period 1933–1945; A Critique and Justification', *Annals, Association of American Geographers*, 39, no. 1, 99–137

Turner, R. (1943) 'Technology and Geo-Politics', *Military Affairs*, 7 (Spring)

Vanhollen, C. (1980) 'The Tilt Policy Revisited — Nixon-Kissinger Geopolitics and South-Asia', *Asian Survey* no. 4, 339–61

Vayrynen, R. (1979) 'Economic and Military Position of the Regional Power Centers', *Journal of Peace Research, XVI*, 349–69

Voskuil, W.H. (1942) 'Coal and Political Power in Europe', *Economic Geography*, *18*, 247–58

Wallerstein, I. (ed.) (1979) *The Capitalist World Economy: Essays by Immanuel Wallerstein*, Cambridge University Press, New York

Warner, E. (1944) 'Douhet, Mitchell, deSeversky: Theories of Air Warfare' in E.M. Earle (ed.), *Makers of Modern Strategy: Machiavelli to Hitler*, Princeton University Press, Princeton, New Jersey, pp. 485–503

Waterman, S. (1984) 'Partition — A Problem in Political Geography' in P. Taylor and J. House (eds.), *Political Geography: Recent Advances and Future Directions*, Croom Helm, London, pp. 98–116

Weigert, H.W. (1941) 'Maps are Weapons', *Survey Graphic*, No. 10 (October), 528–30

—— (1942) *Generals and Geographers: The Twilight of Geopolitics,* Oxford University Press. New York.

—— Stefansson, V. and Harrison, R.E. (eds.) (1949), *New Compass of the World*, Macmillan, New York

Wesson, R.G. (1974) *The Russian Dilemma: A Political and Geopolitical View*, Rutgers University Press, New Brunswick, New Jersey

Whittlesey, D.S. with Colby, C.C. and Hartshorne, R. (1942) *German Strategy of World Conquest*, Farrar and Rinehart, New York

Wright, Q. (1955) *The Study of International Relations*, Appleton-Century-Crofts, New York

Wu, Y. (1973) *Raw Material Supply in a Multipolar World*, Crane, Russak and Company, New York

Zumberge, J.H. (1979) 'Mineral Resources and Geopolitics in Antarctica', *American Scientist, 67*, 68–77

3 CONFLICT BETWEEN STATES

J. N. H. Douglas

The State and the World

For each of us, as inhabitants of the earth, our most immediate and accurately perceived global map is probably that of the world divided into states. The familiarity with areas and shapes and sharp lines of international boundaries reflects our recognition that in the world security, territorial integrity and political power lie enmeshed in this pattern of states. Each state, large or small, is a sovereign unit; the repository of *de jure* authority, it is by far the most vital influence upon the lives and well-being of those who live within it.

Despite their sovereignty, power and authority, however, states do not exist and function with total freedom and independence. Each state has also to be recognised as a component in an inter-dependent international world structure. While freedom of action within its territory is seldom constrained, actions of the state beyond its boundaries are fraught with economic, political and even military risks and consequences which can involve one or more of the other state components in the world structure. As no state, even the largest, is completely self-sufficient and therefore separate from all other states, continued existence means continued co-existence involving some level of international relations. The familiar map of the world of states therefore portrays but a partial reality and, for deeper truth, its precise shapes and sharp boundaries must be criss-crossed with a mass of spatial linkages and transactions and super-imposed with less familiar boundaries of economic, political and military associations. This international network encloses each state in a complex set of relationships — some equal, some dominant and others subservient — which limits its freedom of action. It is also important to note that relationships in the world of states are funda-mentally conditioned by the state of the world. With a growing population dependent upon finite resources and concentrated by technologically telescoped distances, the changing state of the world has created an increasingly competitive international structure. To achieve its aims — seen in terms of state or national interest — each state must compete with constant vigilance, and competition leads to conflict; at least, 'conflict of interest', at most, violent conflict in limited or unlimited warfare.

In the world of states not all strands in the international web are of equal significance and the construction of reality can be strengthened by identifying the most important linkages and associations. Furthermore, as the contemporary pattern of states and inter-state relations represents the culminating legacy of past processes, an evolutionary account, however brief, provides the context of state relations in the international structure.

The modern nation state, based on territorial integrity with sovereignty invested in the national community and authority in the state government, evolved in western Europe at the end of the eighteenth century and gained root and spread with the French Revolution and the ideals of 'liberty, equality and fraternity'. Throughout the nineteenth century as new states emerged to replace old feudal regimes and empires, the ideals of liberal humanitarianism were replaced by competitive nationalism with agressive exclusivism being reflected in the emphasis placed upon precise and internationally recognised boundaries (Bergman, 1975). With bounded state territories stifling economic and territorial expansion in western Europe, national energy and competition transferred from home territory to the seemingly more open lands of Africa, Asia, Australasia and the Americas. Backed by capitalist investment in the search for new wealth and underpinned by emergent technology, the nation states acquired colonies and constructed empires of territories clearly delimited on maps but seldom surveyed or demarcated on the ground. The spread of colonies and empires through the nineteenth century was paralleled by the slow emergence of one closed world growing in economic and political interdependence. In the twentieth century the nation state emerged from World War I and the Treaty of Versailles strengthened and more totally accepted as the 'national' unit of political organisation. So with decline of empire and independence of colonies the concept of the nation state spread and was implemented across the globe. A world of states became the reality — by 1982 one hundred and sixty-six states had membership of the United Nations Organisation (UNO) or of its related agencies (Statesman's Year Book, 1982–3).

The decline of colonialism created a new political equality between states and required a redefinition of inter-state relations; economic relations remained less amenable to change. The dominance-subservience relationship of former mother country with former colony often continued as entrenched patterns and flows of trade were maintained by the economic power of existing investment, promised new investment and the political persuasiveness of aid-with-strings. The failure to equalise wealth and the increasing economic inequalities between states led to the emergence and the widespread recognition of the international superstructure of the Developed and Lesser Developed Countries. As the Developed states continue to increase in wealth and the Lesser Developed states struggle to maintain their economic position, the superstructure has crystallised into a rich North-poor South dichotomy (Brandt, 1980). In a more causal and explanatory way, this same superstructure has been framed in terms of a world economic core-economic periphery (Short, 1982). In describing this superstructure the 'core' states comprise the economically and technologically advanced states of Western Europe, North America and Japan. The 'periphery' includes all other countries, a broad category including states at varied levels of development but all set apart from the core states. Because the core-periphery framework essentially describes the western capitalist world, the Soviet Union and its allies are not included. In terms of explanation the core-periphery superstructure can be viewed as both an outcome and an ally of the world capitalist system. The states of the core dominate the world economy and manipulate it to their own benefit making it difficult if not impossible to break the shackles of narrow economic bases and deficient industrial technology. The economic dominance of the core is strengthened by the economic activities of multi-national companies whose investment programmes and search for ways of maximising profits, often with political acquiescence of core states, means that new wealth usually ends up in the core states. This superstructure, whether described in terms of Developed-Lesser Developed, North-South, core-periphery or in the finer detail of core-semiperiphery-periphery (Taylor, 1982), overarches the world of states and persistently conditions competition and conflict between states.

The general dissociation of the Soviet Union and its allies from the core-periphery world economy model points to the other fundamental framework superimposed upon the world of states. This structure results from the broad dichotomy between East and West, between capitalist and socialist and between the dominant bloc leaders, namely the USA and the USSR. Interstate relations since World War II have been dominated by the east-west superstructure. The 'cold war' which attends the superstructure reflects this central human fracture and, despite the growth of China, Japan and the emerging political unity in Western Europe which threaten to break down this bipolar structure, critical competition and conflict — ideological, political and military — are still framed and implemented in the context it provides (Short, 1982).

Composing the detailed interweave between the major North-South and East-West strands of the international web are the many groupings of states with limited aims or limited regional extent. The variety of groups is bewildering and the number grows as states search for economic, political, social and military security. Most common are the trading blocs which by reducing tariffs and economic barriers bind states into regional co-operative associations. Some groups such as the European Economic Community (EEC) have longer-term aims of political integration whilst others such as the European Free Trade Association (EFTA) or the Latin American Free Trade Association (LAFTA) have purely economic and commercial objectives. On a more extensive scale the many associations of the United Nations tie states loosely together for economic, development, health, education and welfare functions (van Meerhaeghe, 1980). The emergence of state organisations aimed at achieving and benefiting from international monopolies, e.g. the Organisation of Petroleum Exporting Countries (OPEC), is a recent trend reflecting the increasing competition for key finite resources (Cox, 1979).

Competition and conflict between states is thus set within the framework of overlapping state groupings. Economic associations structure regional trade flows and condition competition between states within and outside the same association. State associations do not however remove competition and conflict between member states. As the history of the EEC shows, the search for economic advantage within the Community continues and conflicts of interest remain. Through its organisations, nevertheless, the Community does provide a forum for the resolution of conflict. While every state is bound by such international contacts, the contacts are conditioned significantly by the major North-South and East-West strands of the international superstructure. In particular, the East-West cleavage is reflected again and again in the membership of international groups. The EEC and the Council for Mutual Economic Assistance (Comecon), the North Atlantic Treaty Organisation (NATO) and the Warsaw Pact represent this cleavage in Europe. Development associations such as the Organisation for

Economic Co-operation and Development (OECD) and the Association of South East Asian Nations (ASEAN) owe much to the continued perception of an East-West bipolar world in constant conflict (van Meerhaeghe, 1980; Lee Yong Leng, 1983).

Understanding of conflict between states cannot therefore begin until the familiar map of a world of sovereign, independent states is placed beneath the international superstructure that is the maze of political, economic, social and military linkages and associations. Conflict between states, whatever the cause and whatever the intensity, is thus seldom dyadic or even triadic. In the modern world every conflict, however limited in scale, sends reverberations across the strands that link the world regions and the world itself into a closed interdependent system.

The Nature and Characteristics of Conflict

Since 1945 and the onset of 'peace' there have been throughout the world over 130 armed conflicts involving at least 90 states. Over 80 per cent of this war activity, which took place overwhelmingly in the developing world, has been anti-regime; the classical idea of all-out war between two or more states has been less frequent. This does not mean however that wars have been 'internal' or intra-national civil wars and that conflict *between* states has all but disappeared. The wars within states in most cases have involved — officially or unofficially — foreign participation from at least one other state. Border conficts have been of great frequency and intervention in local wars by West or East or latterly by states of the Developing World has been a hallmark of the age (Kende, 1978; Kidron and Smith, 1983).

Conflict between states like other forms of conflict, even in an era of peace, is very common and is perhaps an inevitable component of individual and group existence — especially in view of the fact that 60 per cent of scientific manpower in the Super-powers and 25 per cent in other countries is employed on devising more weaponry (Galtung, 1981). If we accept that 'conflict is the infra-structure of social and economic existence' (Johnston, 1981) and that 'the essence of politics is struggle' (Weber, 1968) then any satisfactory account of politics and the political must contain the element of human conflict (Thrift and Forbes, 1983). Additionally, conflict includes a strong element of location. Some conflicts are derivatively locational, most

obviously those involving boundaries, and most conflicts have locational consequences seen frequently in group or boundary relocation or both. Despite such clear spatial and environmental overtones
there is little sustained effort in the geographic literature to clarify
the nature of conflict or to define and classify the nature of conflict
behaviour. In political geography with its traditional concern for
problem regions, that is, regions containing conflicting states or
groups, few sustained insights can be found. Even papers directly
concerned with conflict, such as those in the special 'Geography of
Conflict' issue of the Journal of Conflict Resolution (1960), spend
little time considering the nature of conflict and pass on quickly to
its environmental causes and consequences. Recently, as concern
for human welfare and the allocation of scarce resources has
emerged in geography and the importance of the conflict element
has been more clearly recognised, the meaning of the term conflict
has still been taken as understood. Studies simply move on to outline
conflict causes and describe conflict outcomes in spatial or
environmental terms (Cox and Johnston, 1982). The geographical
study of conflict however cannot progress easily until the term conflict and the meanings and definitions which it encompasses are
effectively established.

Conflict refers to some form of incompatibility between the
courses of action open to two or more parties (Elliot and Hickie,
1971); conflict may thus occur when two buyers wish to purchase the
same article or when two governments want to control the same
territory. This definition has immediate value as it suggests that by
determining the precise nature of the goals of the two parties it is
possible to begin to estimate the extent to which the achievement of
the goal of one party will frustrate the other party. The extent to
which there is a basic contradiction in opposed goals will point to the
nature and likely inevitability of conflict and to possible conflict
behaviours (Rabushka and Shepsle, 1972). Deeper analysis of goals
may however point not to inevitable conflict but to a perception of
such conflict resulting from the inadequacy of information and
communication flows. The recognition of cognitive gaps in some
situations leads towards the possible development of conflict
resolution.

Conflict exists at different levels of experience and intensity which
are not always obvious. An individual smoking in a non-smoking
compartment may extinguish the cigarette in response to an objection or may ignore the objection. The intensity of conflict, the likely

duration of conflict and the consequent conflict behaviour results from the goals of the smoker. If he is smoking from habit he is likely to stop when requested; if he is smoking as a matter of principle to oppose authority, he is unlikely to stop. The individual's central values and attitudes condition the conflict. Similar conditions apply, at potentially more serious levels, when conflict involves population groups or states. For example, in a conflict over independence between a colony and the colonial power the deepest central values are involved; in such conflicts an authoritative arbiter acceptable to both sides is unlikely to be found.

Clarification of the goals involved in conflict and the likely extent of contradiction and frustration resulting in the degree of goal incompatiblity aids understanding of the type of conflict-related behaviour likely to emerge. Deep intensities and continued goal frustration encourage a movement toward *fight behaviour* in which the behaviour of each side becomes predominantly a set of reactions to the activity of the other. Self-control deteriorates, control over the conflict diminishes and on-going processes become increasingly mindless and destructive. *Game behaviour* is found in conflicts when each side attempts to maintain rational control over its own moves. Threats and actual use of force may take place but within a developed though ultimately uncertain rational plan. Formal analysis of the likely behaviour of the other side becomes particularly important. In *debate behaviour* controlled communication on an area of conflict can change each group's perceptions, cognitive images and attitudes of the other. Often such areas of conflict, perhaps better referred to as competition, do not involve contradictory goals of deep intensity. Debate behaviour in the attempt to change the other side's goals and motives lies at the heart of conflict resolution yet the debate can as easily escalate towards fight behaviour as towards removal of frustration (Rapaport, 1960).

Given the fundamental security role of the state with its emphasis upon sovereignty and its importance to its inhabitants, many conflicts between states are likely to result from, and to cause important levels of, contradiction and frustration. These conflicts will not be susceptible to resolution through goal changing and so will lead ultimately to fight behaviour. Taking care with meanings and definitions relating to the term conflict also forces more consideration of the nature of the state. The state, even when advisedly labelled the nation state, is not a constant unit unchanging from place to place and time to time. Each state is an individual mix of government, institutions, political, economic and social organisations, and a set of social classes including an elite group of decision-makers. Each of these components is likely to perceive any new situation in different conflict or competition terms and as a result responses will vary. Support for a particular form of conflict behaviour chosen by government will seldom be universal and the pattern of support and indeed opposition will change as group interaction and information flows change perceptions and attitudes. It has to be recognised therefore that the nature and course of conflict relations between states are influenced to an important degree by the social and economic conditions and differences within each state that is a party to the conflict.

Conflict is not a clear-cut concept with a sharp and singular meaning; rather, it includes a range of ideas with associated behaviours of varied intensities, all set in a dynamic milieu. When it is recalled that 'the essence of politics is struggle' and noted that 'human society is stitched together by conflicts' (Coser, 1967) so that some conflict is both necessary and remedial, then the study of conflict between states must be more than the study of problems set in a context emphasising the possibilities of conflict resolution. To study the wider role of conflict, with its positive as well as negative aspects, in the world of states must be the objective.

The Causes of Conflict Between States

As conflict results from incompatible and contradictory goals the genesis of conflict between states is to be found in the central values and goals of each state. The much-discussed questions 'What is the national interest or nation state interest?' and 'What is the fundamental function of the state; for what reason does it exist?' are concerned with precisely these values and goals. In whatever way the emergence of the state is viewed — as a cultural phenomenon (Kamenka, 1973), as an expression of economic self-interest (Nairn, 1977) or as an outcome of capitalist processes (Johnston, 1982) — the fundamental goal of the state is to achieve security; security for its political system, its economic system and for its people with their cultural characteristics and ethos. Most important, security lies in maintaining sovereignty over state territory and continued political independence. With these, the state can plan its future and control its destiny (Deutsch, 1966).

The desire for cultural security puts the emphasis upon the nation and upon the community which, through accordance of values and perceptions, provides the cement for the state and its legitimacy. Preservation of the national culture and what has been traditionally called the '*raison d'être*' of the national community in the state is a fundamental goal. It is this goal that House (1983) is referring to when he quotes Schell (1982) to note that 'National sovereignty lies at the very core of the political issues that the peril of extinction forces upon us'.

The search for economic security places rather more emphasis upon the state. The state is clearly an economic entity preserved by politics as much as by economic activity. The second fundamental goal of the state is thus to maximise its economic strength and so secure the wealth and economic well-being of its population. The Marxist would point to the naivety of this view, noting that in the capitalist world system the state acts to ensure the well-being of only a certain section of its inhabitants, that is, the capitalists. Whatever the stance taken however it is clear that the state strives persistently to achieve economic security through maximising economic strength.

To achieve its cultural and economic goals each state must inevitably to some degree compete and conflict with other states. In the history of the world of states this competition and conflict have focused most sharply upon territory. While territory for the human group takes on deep psychological and symbolic meaning and may even satisfy certain physiological imperatives (Ardrey, 1969) it is the qualities, benefits and advantages that territory and territorial control can bring that places it at the crux of conflict between states (Sack, 1981). Throughout the world there is a persistent non-accordance of state and nation. The cultural minority group in the 'wrong' state inhabits territory; to the cultural peer group in another, usually adjacent, state the redeeming of the unredeemed minority will be achieved by territorial extension and annexation. Such extension of territorial control will make the nation whole, strengthen the state and remove a cause of internal tension. No state, however voluntarily, cedes territory to another and the fundamental quality of political boundaries (the limits of state sovereignty) is that of intrenchment (Minghi, 1963). Minority and boundary disputes are therefore a common cause of interstate conflict and result in considerable frustration and aggression (Ashworth, 1977, 1978, 1980). Territory can bequeath the economic benefits of resources — natural resources of water and land for agriculture, mineral resources for industry. Territory rich in resources is prized highly by all states and competition for control and development of resources leads to winners and losers, the rich and the poor; relative economic deprivation, by generating frustration, can be a potent cause of conflict. Territory can ensure certain strategic advantages by providing vantage points, defensible positions, launching zones in time of war while preventing their use by opponents in conflict. Territory can meet logistic requirements, not just for supplying armed forces in time of war but also the imperative of access for land-locked states. The economic security and cultural survival of at least twenty nation states in the world is made possible by agreed access over land or along rivers to the open seas (Reitsma, 1982).

Historically, conflict involving territory related predominantly to land territories and geographic proximity had considerable influence upon the likelihood of conflict and upon its nature. The axiom that states are more likely to have conflicting relations with their neighbours was upset to some degree during the building of colonial empires, yet often the continued control of empires depended less upon organisation of the colonial territory than upon success in conflict relations between the colonial powers within Europe. Contemporary territorial conflict between states is moving in emphasis from land to sea. The extension of maritime control from three to twelve nautical miles and the development of an exclusive economic zone of two hundred nautical miles for every coastal state reflects the decline in the freedom of the seas and represents in the oceans the same trend towards precise territorial control and exclusive sovereignty which divided the continents in the nineteenth century. The competition for control of the sea moreover is based on the search for economic, strategic, logistic and political security which characterised the earlier scramble for land (Blake, 1982). In this competition and conflict over sea territories, however, cultural and minority group problems are much less significant. The new conflict over territorial control is primarily concerned with economically valuable resources in and under the seas and oceans. While technology has made the sea bed accessible and the potential benefits considerable, maritime law and traditional maritime practice have become even less capable of dealing with new conflict situations (Rao, 1975). Thus the new United Nations Convention on the Law of the Sea (UNCLOS III), despite its non-signatories and problems of implementation, is an important piece of legislation which will influence all future maritime conflict between states (United

Nations, 1983). In terms of future conflict the disappearance of the open sea will have most serious consequences for maritime transport and international access, while the economic and logistic implications for land-locked states are critical.

Finally in consideration of conflict and territory it is worthy of note that conflict over control may result from negative as well as from positive goals. States may desire and claim control to prevent control by competing states. The territory itself, as in Antarctica, may have little economic value and may prove costly to maintain even with a minimum presence but control prevents any possible advantage, especially strategic, accruing to any other state and with continued technological advance territory may assume new properties. The case of Antarctica is particularly informative as the economic value may be found less on land and more in adjacent seas, e.g. the rich resources of krill. Inter-state conflict in the region may hang on whether recognition of a land claim can lead to a sovereignty claim over adjacent sea territory (Auburn, 1982). In a world of declining resources and advancing technology increasing state pressures and competing goals resulting from different values may turn Antarctica into an arena of even greater conflict of interest and possibly make a renewal of the Antarctic Treaty in 1989 very difficult to achieve (Glassner and De Blij, 1979).

Conflict between states also results from contradictory goals which do not directly involve territory and its control. These conflict-generating goals are contained most often in the economic and social policies of the state, policies which can have solely intra-national goals and arenas of implementation. Thus intra-state policies concerning the treatment of minorities can result in inter-state friction as peer groups in other states note policy implications. Israel watches with considerable intensity the treatment of Jewish minorities in other states. The Arab world watches and reacts to the treatment of the Arab minority in Israel, while the introduction of internment in Northern Ireland in 1971 provoked strong reactions not just in the Irish Republic but also in the USA. Intra-state economic policies, e.g. concerned with development and subsidising of particular economic sectors, can produce inter-state reactions as can the use of resources such as rivers which are international or of industries which use pollution-spreading processes. The conflict results from the international implications and consequences of intra-state activity. International policies of the state, such as social policies concerning migration or causing forced migration, are full of conflict potential. Economic policies with international goals are increasingly significant as conflict generators; in this context the maritime resource policies specifically concerned with fisheries provide a good example. Such policies have already resulted in the so-called 'cod war' between Britain and Iceland (Jónsson, 1982) and give rise to friction between states with large fishing and whaling fleets, e.g. Japan and the USSR, who wish to exploit resources and those states who wish to use resources more conservatively. International whaling and fishing agreements do little to help reduce friction as monitoring and implementation of agreements are very difficult in practice.

In understanding conflict between states, it must be recognised that every state is more than the sum of its parts, i.e. of its territory, its people and its organisation. As the state struggles for existence and recognition, and as it acts and interacts creating history, it develops a self-concept and image. Its territory takes on an inviolable sanctity, its people an ethos built on fact and fiction and the state itself a larger-than-life importance built on collectively perceived central values and a national ego. Often the goals of states and their conflict behaviour can be understood only by reference to their subjective rationale (Lowenthal and Bowden, 1976). The history of United States foreign relations can hardly be understood without recognising Americans' strong self-image as the protectors of democracy and freedom throughout the world. Inter-state conflict resulted when this role was translated into the policy of expansion (or democracy American style) and containment (stop any opponent) (Agnew, 1983). Similarly, China's relations with other states are best viewed through the Chinese ethnocentric view of world order (Ginsberg, 1968) and Britain's international behaviour in terms of the deeply ingrained images of colonial empires and world leadership.

The causes of conflict between states are wide-ranging involving land and sea territories and soon, no doubt, outer space, as well as cultural values and perceptions and collective image of self and others. The causes are complex and interdependent. Seldom are conflicts between states based solely upon a singular, contradictory, clear-cut goal. Conflicts at whatever intensity level result from a range of incompatabilities, shaped or misshapen and forged by past events and twisted into a particular emphasis for the sake of present argument. The student of conflict between states must look for those goals which lie hidden as well as those that are made explicit.

Political Geography and the Study of Conflict between States

Consideration of the world of states and the nature and causes of conflict leads to two questions: how have political geographers viewed conflict between states? and what progress have they made in developing useful concepts and theories and in establishing methods of analysis which provide deeper explanatory insights? The remainder of this chapter attempts to answer these questions.

The nation-state has long provided the central focus for study of the relationship between geography and politics. From the Greek philosopher Aristotle (383–322 B.C.) who constructed a model of the ideal state, to Ratzel who in 1896 formulated 'Laws of the Spatial Growth of States', the growth, nature and functions of the state provided a major attraction. In the twentieth century, despite a deepening understanding of the range and complexity of politics and geographic relationships, the state remains centre stage. Jackson, in a review article in 1958, asserted that 'the state has been accepted as the central subject matter of political geography'; Taylor, in 1979, notes that 'political geography has stubbornly maintained its focus at the level of the state'; Johnston (1981) has defined political geography as 'the study of those social and economic conflicts which focus on the state'. In many respects, therefore, progress in the study of the state and its (conflicting) relationships with other states represents progress in the study of political geography. None the less, political geographers have not developed a singular concept of the state or a strongly integrative framework for its study. For some, study of the state involves the analysis of federalism, for others it can lead to a consideration of capital cities or local government or patterns of voting and representation. A variety of methods of analysis has evolved, each method related to the nature of the topic of study and the individual emphasis of approach. Amid this plurality there is no co-ordinated concentration upon the arena of geography, politics and conflict and the ongoing processes and changing intensities of conflict behaviour have seldom received prolonged or explicit attention from political geographers. Conflict rather has been noted as the phenomenon which somehow accompanies the other environmental attributes and processes such as voting patterns and behaviour, boundary locations and barrier functions, minority group distributions and government allocation policies which form the locus of political geographers' concern. Traditionally political geographers have possibly come closest to the consideration of conflict in their descriptions of ethnic and cultural diversity (Alexander, 1957) and in analyses of competing territorial and boundary claims (Burghardt, 1973). Most textbooks on political geography set out the cultural, environmental and geographic factors which can act as conflict generators at varied scales, but the generative roles of these different factors are rarely explored in depth either in general theoretical or specific example contexts. The role of conflict behaviour itself — in fight, game or debate forms — as a generator of further conflict has escaped attention. Such considerations have been left to students of international politics. Perhaps the most significant commentary on political geographers' study of conflict lies in the fact that the roles of spatial proximity and contiguity as factors influencing conflict between states have received most attention from students of international relations (Starr and Most, 1976).

With the recent growth of a welfare approach to contemporary geographic problems (Smith, 1977) and critical approaches to the nature and role of the state (Johnston, 1982) the phonemenon of conflict has become a more central concern of political geographers. The emphasis so far however has been placed upon the outcomes of conflict arbitration at the intra-state level (Cox and Johnston, 1982; Kirby, 1982). The nature and intensities of conflicts and their effects at the inter-state level, where authoritative arbiters hardly exist, have received little attention. Recent work however on the economic and political geography of multi-national companies (Taylor and Thrift, 1982; Siddayao, 1978) and Taylor's (1981, 1982) championing of Wallerstein's world economy views and designation of the international scale as the scale of reality, must generate contemporary interest among geographers in conflict between states. After a decade of much emphasis upon local state and metropolitan political geography progress in the study of inter-state relations with a new emphasis upon the role of conflict will be conditioned, especially at the outset, by geographic work already completed which establishes models for structuring and methods for analysing conflict between states. Such work can only be reviewed effectively when the nature of conflict and its milieu are clear.

Earlier sections in this chapter have established conflict as a behavioural phenomenon emerging from the values and perceptions of individuals and groups and related to contradictory goals and scarce resources — there is thus *the human environment of conflict*. Conflict in its emergence and progression is influenced by its physical setting. At many scales from the local, where the character-istics of territory and physical distance are important, to the global, where patterns, shapes and sizes of lands and oceans can be vital, there exists *the physical environment of conflict*. Finally it is clear that conflict and asssociated behaviour is set within and influenced by the web of national and international organisations outlined earlier — these provide *the institutional environment of conflict*. While the generation, progress and outcome of conflict at every scale is a consequence of the dynamic interaction of these three environments — known in traditional political geography as terri-tory, people and organisation (Pounds, 1972) — as separated entities they provide a useful classification within which work in political geography can be considered in terms of its relevance for the study of conflict between states.

The Physical Environment of Conflict

The earliest explanations in political geography were essentially deterministic. From Greek times to the twentieth century physical and climatic controls have been used to 'explain' the nature of the state, the quality of its people and its success or failure in conflict with other states. For Aristotle (383–322 B.C.) the geographic and climatic location of the Greek people explained their spirit and intel-ligence; spirit ensured continued freedom, intelligence permitted the attainment of the highest level of political development and the capacity for governing others. In the nineteenth century the concept of 'Manifest Destiny' justified the westward expansion of the United States of America. As one American Congressman put it 'the great engineer of the universe has fixed the natural limits of our country and man cannot change them' (cited in Pounds, 1972, p. 61). In the twentieth century the view of Irish leader James Connolly that 'the frontiers of Ireland are the handiwork of the Almighty and as marks of Ireland's separate nationality were not made by politicians and so cannot be unmade by them' (cited in MacAonghusa and O Réagan, 1967, p. 193) bears an uncanny resemblance to those of the American congressman and shows that environmental determinism still had its effect upon political thought and activity. Ratzel in 'Laws of the Spatial Growth of States' (1896) combined a form of locational determinism and biological analogies drawn from the work of Darwin to suggest that the state, like an organism, must grow and expand or decay and die.

In the contemporary world environmental and biological determinism no longer acceptably explain relations between states. Yet it is informative to recognise how far such deterministic theories and writings have influenced political decision-making and consequent conflict. Environmental determinism as a basis for action leads unerringly to conflict behaviour, it establishes one correct or 'natural' order with inevitable superiority-inferiority and dominance-submission relationships. The biological analogy justifies expansion and fight behaviour and excludes the possibilities of balance, debate and peaceful negotiation. Thus it is not surprising that the history of the Greek city states was one of continuous bitter conflict (Dahl, 1982); that 'Manifest Destiny' left no separate territory for the North American Indian; and that the partition of the island of Ireland led to much straight shooting in the cause of crooked thinking. Ratzel's 'Laws' were carried forward by Kjellen (1917) and by Haushofer after 1924 in the *Zeitschrift für Geopolitik* to exert an influence upon the decisions of the leaders of Nazi Germany. Such crude determinism died with the defeat of the Nazi regime but not before war had split Germany and Europe and bequeathed a new level of conflict and tension between the separated states of East and West.

Rejection of environmental determinism however must not blind geographers to the important influences which the physical environment has upon all stages of conflict, at whatever scale. While the excesses of German Geopolitik were running their course, geopolitical relationships (that is, the study of geographical factors in politics) at local, national and global scales were being studied actively and with attempted objectivity by geographers in different countries. In Britain, Dickinson in *The German Lebensraum* (1943) positively countered deterministic theories; earlier the work of the American geographer Bowman laid the foundation and set the fashion for later study. In his monumental work *The New World: Problems in Political Geography* (1922) Bowman set out to establish the importance of painstaking geopolitical analysis as a basic context for national policy making. With a largely descriptive method and an inventorial approach Bowman systematically reviewed the environment and resources of states and, with reference to their relative locations, drew conclusions as to power potential, political roles and zones of conflict. Many works such as those of Whittlesey (1944), Alexander (1957), and East and Moodie (1956) followed along similar lines covering the world region by region and state by state and amassing a wealth of factual information. Such works were voluminous, short on theory and long on individual cases. They did, however, in many instances point to the environmental component of inter-state conflict, to conflict flashpoints and to the physical environmental component of state power and its potential effect on the successful achievement of objectives through fight and game behaviour.

At the grander world scale the geopolitical theories of Mackinder (1904, 1919, 1943) and Spykman (1944) laid emphasis upon the geographic qualities and resultant heightened political significance of particular areas. Certainly Mackinder's Heartland Theory and Spykman's concept of the Rimland, which is often viewed as an American response to Mackinder, had considerable influence upon foreign policy makers. The view of Heartland supremacy together with the perception of Soviet Russia as an expansionist state encouraged an American foreign policy of containment at all points in the Rimland and led to many impossible alliances and logistically unfavourable conflicts. A more recent global geopolitical analysis by the American geographer Cohen (1973) outlined a world of cores and shatterbelts — the significant shatterbelts being in the Middle East and South East Asia — and argued that conflict was generated and resolved in the changing consolidation and fragmentation of these belts. In relation to the American foreign policy of all-points containment and 'domino' mentality Cohen concluded that complete control of shatterbelts and so complete defence was neither possible nor desirable.

As this brief review shows, the work of geographers on geopolitical analysis, while following a number of false trails, has provided useful insights at regional, national and global scales. But what of future work with an emphasis upon inter-state conflict? The theoretical structures of Mackinder, Spykman and Cohen provide an effective starting point for renewed global geopolitical analysis. The mapping of world 'hot spots' and the development of the theoretical underpinnings of conflict zones is a most important task. In this context the work of McColl (1983) is valuable; he builds a model of conflict behaviour based upon the perceived significance of different territories for the maintenance of national security. McColl's concepts of fight zones, critical zones and flight zones and the associated predicted levels of conflict intensity build upon earlier work of Boulding (1962) to provide a basis for progress in the study of conflict between states.

The role of physical distance and proximity in conflict has been neglected by geographers but could prove a useful field for future study. A basis for such study is to be found in the analyses of transactions and interaction already carried out by geographers but not specifically related to conflict (see section on the Human Environment of Conflict). The examination of relationships between boundaries and inter-state alliances, boundaries and war, and the diffusion of war by Starr and Most (1976) — students of international politics — has also theoretical and methodological value for the geographic study of conflict. Such analyses have clear practical significance as for example in relation to American political leaders' persistent espousal of the Domino Theory of international relations. Refutation of the theory depends not only upon a clear understanding of the nature of geographic space and distance but also upon an explanation of social and economic linkages and political interaction and interdependence (Rosenau, 1969). Recent works by O'Sullivan (1982) and O'Sullivan and Millar (1983) give a lead to geographers in the study of physical proximity and conflict and the relationship between economic and cognitive distance and the diffusion of conflict.

Global geopolitical studies must be allied to less expansive work on the physical and natural environments of states and the resource characteristics of state territory. The traditional inventorial approach provides no ready-made models of environment-state-conflict relations yet the search for resources and the urge to control resource-rich territories is a strong component of states' policies. Such a vast field of study, if approached with the aim of complete coverage by political geographers, would again lead back to comprehensive empiricism. However two related aspects of resource studies stand out as particularly important in the geographical study of inter-state conflict.

The first aspect concerns the geopolitics of strategic minerals. The size of known domestic supplies of minerals such as oil and uranium, the rates of their use, the location and size of foreign resources and the problems of access to and use of these resources are vital to state security and military strategy. The political geography of oil will increase in importance as the rate of use outstrips the rate of discovery of new sources. The dependence on foreign supplies of the industrial countries of North-West Europe and North America, as well as Japan, allied to the factors of specific resource location mean that oil can be used as a potent weapon of international blackmail. The nature of the component states of the Organisation of Petroleum Exporting Countries (OPEC) has a considerable influence upon the politico-economic objectives of the Organisation which in turn have exerted an increasing influence upon the political behaviour of the foreign oil-dependent states. Japan (90 per cent dependent on OPEC oil) and Western Europe (over 80 per cent dependent) carefully guard their statements on the conflict in the Middle East and are particularly aware of potential Arab reactions to their relations with Israel. Analysis of resource location and its effect upon political and conflict-seeking or conflict-avoiding behaviour however is but one element of geographic study. Such analysis can lead on to the field of military and strategic forward planning. What contingency plans might Japan or states in Western Europe for example evolve concerning maintenance of supply of oil in the event of war, brief or protracted, in the Middle East? Few political geographers have carried resource studies to such logical and politically involved, sensitive end points — in Britain the work of Anderson and Blake (1981, 1982, 1983) is the exception — yet with the growing desire for greater involvement in contemporary issues and the removal of the myth of the geographer's geographical objectivity, such studies are a pointer to the future. At least political geographers could concentrate more on understanding the philosophy and geopolitical perception of existing strategic plans. A useful lead in this direction has been given by O'Sullivan and Millar (1983) who have traced the evolution of United States' military and strategic response planning in the context of invasion of the oil states of the Middle-East by the Soviet Union.

The second conflict-laden aspect of the geography of resources concerns the international transport and supply of scarce raw materials. The study of logistics, that is, the science of movement and supply of raw materials and commodities usually in time of war, has received little attention from political geographers yet the transportation problem is fundamentally geographic. As a first exercise the mapping of scarce and strategic resource flows over politically bounded and controlled lands and seas would immediately establish patterns of dependence and interdependence and highlight specific 'choke points' where limited military activity and game conflict could rapidly reduce the international economic system to chaos and result in widespread violent conflict (Anderson, 1982; Anderson and Blake, 1982). 'Choke points' such as the Mozambique Channel, the Cape route of South Africa and the Atlantic approaches to western Europe having been established, the analysis of types and volumes of commodity flows through these points could lead to an assessment of their conflict potential in a world of increasing interdependence in which, between 1965 and 1975, the world's gross registered tonnage of shipping increased by 130 per cent and the number of fighting ships grew from 4,857 to 5,363 (Borgese and Ginsberg, 1978). Very important, because of their specific physical and locational characteristics, are the narrow strategic straits and waterways of the world.

The Bab-el-Mandeb (18 miles wide) at the Red Sea entrance, the Hormuz Strait (24 miles wide) at the entrance to the Persian Gulf and the Gibraltar Strait (9 miles wide) at the Mediterranean entrance are examples of such physically congested 'choke points' where the extension of territorial waters creates tension between competing riparian states and the states requiring transit rights for their ships (Blake, 1982). With two-thirds of the world's international waterways controlled by developing countries whose share of world shipping in 1975 was only 6.3 per cent, and with future conflict between states increasingly likely to result from the need to maintain and defend supply routes, the study of international logistics in the maritime environment will become vital.

This discussion of the notable areas for geographic study in the physical environment of conflict establishes two general prerequisites of analysis. The first is the requirement that political geographers become familiar with the developing field of transport and military technology. Successful geopolitical analysis at whatever scale depends upon clear recognition of the spatial relationships involved and spatial relationships have meaning only in the context of contemporary technology. The second requirement is that political geographers become familiar with national and international law and its role in conditioning conflict behaviour. Future study of the geopolitics of oceans, seas and straits for example, will be impossible without constant recourse to the emerging Law of the Sea, UNCLOS III (United Nations, 1983).

Finally it is noteworthy that the physical environment and the human environment of conflict (considered in the next section) are not discrete. As Kirk (1951) and Harold and Margaret Sprout (1956) established long ago, there is for every decision-maker a variable and varying relationship between the world as perceived — the behavioural or psychological environment and the real material world — the phenomenal environment. The greater the gap between the perceived and the real, the more difficult it is to formulate effective policies and successfully achieve objectives. Study of the perceptions of national groups and especially of political elites who make or influence state policy has obvious importance for the study of conflict. Thus when President Nixon in 1970 stated 'Now I know there are those that say, well the domino theory is obsolete! They haven't talked to the dominoes,' he was, in the words of the Indonesian government spokesman, arguing 'a gross oversimplification of the historical (and spatial) processes that go on in the area (i.e. South-East Asia). It obscures and distorts rather than illuminates our understanding and offers no guidelines for realistic policy!' (cited in O'Sullivan, 1982, p. 59). An individual's mental map of the world with all its simplifying distortions stubbornly persists despite the constant flow of new information, yet a simplified map or image of geopolitical relations leads to misunderstanding, policy failure and increased danger of conflict. Human perceptions of the physical environment and their political and conflict consequences must be an important theme in political geographic study if progress is to be made in the understanding of conflict between states.

The Human Environment of Conflict

As all human conflict begins in the minds of men so conflict between states finds its origin in variations in human group values, perceptions and attitudes which give rise to divergent national interests and contradictory state goals. Intuitively aware of this, political geographers throughout the twentieth century have studied the population of the state and placed particular emphasis upon the nature and distribution of cultural attributes. Until the last decade homogeneity in language, religion and ethnic type was taken as the prime reflector of group and national solidarity while differences in type and the uneven spread of such attributes were taken to represent diversity and political separation. These studies relied almost totally upon a cartographic method — distributions of cultural attributes were plotted and compared with degrees of spatial correlation of the attributes taken to reflect degrees of cultural integration and division and thus levels of political co-operation and conflict. Such geographical analyses were carried out most frequently in boundary zones where the extent of homogeneity in cultural attributes represented the spatial extent of the nation while the political boundary represented the extent of the state. A non-correlation of state and national extent pointed strongly to the presence of minority problems and boundary disputes; set in a historical context, such findings explained contemporary goal contradictions and highlighted the causes of conflict behaviour.

While studies such as those of House (1959) and Burghardt (1962) provided many valuable insights and considerable empirical clarity, the logical underpinnings of the relationship between cultural homogeneity/heterogeneity and political co-operation/conflict were never strongly established by political geographers. It was Dahl (1956), a political scientist, who clarified the way in which fragmenting and reinforcing attribute cleavages affect human behaviour. As Dahl states in a later work:

> . . . if all cleavages occur along the same attribute lines, if the same people hold opposing positions in one dispute after another, then the severity of conflict is likely to increase. The man on the other side is not just an opponent, he soon becomes an enemy. But . . . if cleavages occur along different attribute lines, if the same persons are sometimes opponents and sometimes allies, then conflicts are likely to be less severe. If you know that some of your present opponents were allies in the past and may be needed again as allies in the future, you have some reason to search for a solution to the dispute at hand that will satisfy both sides' (Dahl, 1976, p. 313).

With the growth of statistical methods in geography, measures such as the Index of Fragmentation (Rae and Taylor, 1970) and the Index of Differentiation (Muir, 1975) were developed and used to quantify the extent of attribute cleavages. Despite certain limitations in logic which reduce their value, the measures have been used by geographers to some effect but largely at an intra-state level (Douglas, 1983). At the inter-state level, attribute analysis has been carried much further by political scientists such as Russett (1975) who used a wide range of attribute variables to delimit international regions of cultural homogeneity, and Rummel (1971) who established that dyadic conflict is most frequent when differences in attributes and status are greatest. Attribute analysis however displays a fundamental weakness when it assumes a direct and universal relationship between attribute diversity and goal contradiction.

Culturally diverse yet relatively peaceful states and peaceful relations between culturally diverse states show that conflict is a consequence of more than differences in cultural attributes.

The deeper insights required were introduced into political geography with the description of the behavioural process and the recognition of its significance (Kasperson and Minghi, 1969). The process describes the set of mental 'black box' activities which predates and conditions human decisions. The mental components on which the process builds are: values, that is, fundamental beliefs and central preferences; perception, that is, the mechanism which controls recognition and selection of environmental stimuli — the experienced world of the individual at any time is called the perceptual field; and attitudes, that is, readiness to be motivated in certain directions. Although separated for the purposes of research the behavioural components and process are complex, interrelated and not easily time ordered as they operate in an environment which constantly changes as a result of information bombardment. The end product of the process is the decision; it represents a choice from among a number of alternative courses of action, the aim being to achieve the desired future state which accords best with the decision-maker's values. Recognition of the importance of pre-decision mental processes and their controls added a vital dimension to political geography and to the study of conflict. Thus the understanding of conflict behaviour, i.e. fight, game or debate strategies or indeed the avoidance of conflict through flight or surrender, could be advanced by the analysis of values, perceptions and attitudes. Such analysis asks the question 'why' in relation to behaviour and adds a functional aspect to the more static constituent approach found in the study of cultural attributes.

Geographical study of the behavioural process has concentrated largely upon the analysis of perception of environment (noted earlier) and of space, both these aspects leading to a concern for mental maps. Also, although to a lesser degree, geographers have studied intra and inter-group perceptions and images. The widespread significance of such group perceptions (and the resultant supportive or derogatory images) for decision-making and for conflict is seen in the works of Lowenthal (1958) on the West Indies, Ginsberg (1968) on China and Boal (1969) on Belfast. As well as pointing toward conflict, group image analysis can help explain lack of conflict or lack of increasing intensity of conflict in situations of civil stress and unrest. The absence of widespread civil war in

Northern Ireland despite terrorist agitation and an active propaganda war owes much, as O'Donnell (1977) has shown, to Protestant and Catholic intergroup images which recognise certain basic similarities and sympathies between the 'ordinary people' in each group. Political scientists have developed further the study of interstate/international perceptions and images. Political geographers in their study of conflict between states could well begin by reading Buchanan and Cantril's (1953) *How Nations See Each Other*, before progressing to the study and application of Boulding's (1959) interstate image matrices to show hostility/friendliness, strength/weakness and dominance/submission perceptions. The work of Goldmann (1973, 1974) which develops theoretical settings and empirical techniques to trace the levels of East-West tension in the perceptions of European elites provides a more recent area for study. Tension, which serves as the central focus of the work, is composed of both conflictual and co-operative components. The relative balance of these components controls the level of tension and the potential for conflict behaviour.

Geographers with their abilities to recognise and represent mental maps could with profit develop further the concept of cognitive distance and investigate how such distance between groups acts and interacts with geographical distance, actual and perceived, to influence group relations. Such work will lead to a better understanding of why, despite close physical proximity, some groups maintain sharply subjective stereotyped images and develop few co-operative contacts. These matters lie at the heart of conflict within and between states with plural societies whether in Ireland (Boal and Douglas, 1983), Cyprus (Patrick, 1976), Israel (Harris, 1980) or elsewhere. Investigation along these lines might also lead to a classification of conflict — particularly armed conflict — based upon perceived triggers. Holy wars, revolutionary wars, wars of liberation, strategic wars, resource wars and wars of national survival overlap in terms of the values, beliefs, ideologies and perceptions on which they are based, causing difficulties for useful classification, yet the development of categories could lead to a better understanding of the intensity of conflict and the possibilities for its resolution.

Apart from the context of voting behaviour the study of attitudes has received little attention from political geographers, yet attitude analysis has considerable potential in the explanation of conflict between states. Attitudes are particularly amenable to study as they are adopted toward individuals or groups as well as toward situations or events. Survey and clarification of attitudes therefore can help establish prime conflict motivators, provide measured assessment of potential conflict and its intensity and, in relation to specific issues, establish the location of groups with particularly intense feelings and the existence of territorial conflict 'hot spots'. Harold and Margaret Sprout (1966) recognised the value of attitude studies in international politics and argued that such studies should have three main elements. These were:

(1) the analysis of attitudes toward national and state communities, that is, attitudes toward loyalty, obedience and acceptance of the political legitimacy of the state;
(2) the study of attitudes toward fellow members of the state which would clarify intra-state social and cultural cleavages and establish group antagonisms;
(3) the survey of attitudes towards other states and members and groups thereof; these attitudes would reflect inter-state antagonisms, selective group associations and potential for co-operation or conflict.

As attitudes can be ranked by intensity and their distributions plotted, such studies encourage the investigation of the spatial/geographical component of conflict. Despite important technical difficulties in data collection and measurement of attitudes and problems concerned with the validity of results over time (Douglas, 1983) — attitudes, unlike values and perception, can change rapidly with new information flows — attitude studies should provide a central focus in the geographical study of conflict between states (Muir and Paddison, 1981).

Unlike attitude studies the value of Transaction Flow Analysis, developed by Deutsch (1966) and based upon his Theory of Social Communication, has been shown to be limited as a measure of political integration and division. The underlying hypothesis that the density of social communication and transactions linking groups or states reflects the level of integration between them provided the starting point for a number of works which skillfully measured socio-economic linkages and so provided an assessment of political association. Of these works, that of Soja (1968) on telephone communication in East Africa, Brams (1966) on world trade and diplomatic linkages and Wittkopf (1974) on foreign aid transactions are deservedly best known. However it is now clear that social communication between groups at any scale can be integrative or disintegrative, the control being the milieu in which the communication and transactions take place. Transaction Flow Analysis is probably most valuable not as a measure of integration and division but as a method of establishing and clarifying economic interdependence between states. Thus Transaction Flow Analysis will be particularly useful in the study of the flows and the logistics of scarce and strategically important materials and natural resources (see the section on the physical environment of conflict).

Reference to the role of milieu in the study of social communication points to the importance of environmental context in the operation and study of the behavioural process. The cumulative cultural experiences of history — former conflict, aggression, atrocity, territorial usurpation — tied to myth and legend usually provide the key to contemporary images and attitude intensity. The importance of context is recognised by Thrift and Forbes (1983) in their recent plea for political geography to become more concerned with people in conflict in place. Political geographers must recognise the interrelationships of the human and physical environments of conflict and the considerable role of the historical context.

Finally in this section the importance of the economic factor in conflict between states must be noted. Diverse levels of economic development over the face of the earth result in inter-state patterns of relative deprivation. Relative deprivation, which can refer to the gap between Developed and Lesser Developed Countries and, perhaps more significantly, to the gap between expected economic achievement and life chances and the actual standards reached within states (Runciman, 1966), has fundamental conflict significance. When allied to rigid social class structures relative deprivation is an active generator of violent conflict: it can provoke terrorist activity and revolution. Such conflict behaviour usually leads to counter-violence which frequently becomes built into the structure of the state; civil war evolves and the vicious circle of violence is closed (Galtung, 1964). Violent conflict, however, seldom remains self-contained within the state. Aid and refuge become international and war has a tendency to diffuse across boundaries (McColl, 1969). With the flagrant failure of efforts to achieve greater global equality of economic development since World World II, the spectre encroaches of inter-state conflict among the Lesser Developed Countries and between the Developed and Lesser Developed states (Galtung, 1981). The causes of continued gaps between developed and lesser developed, north and south, centre and periphery and the reasons why rich states get richer while poor states get poorer, relatively and absolutely, are considered in the final section, i.e. the institutional environment of conflict.

The Institutional Environment of Conflict

One of the most dramatic developments in geography during the past decade has been the growth in policy studies. The trend followed the recognition of the spatial and environmental significance of policy decisions emanating from institutions and organisations at all levels. From the urban manager controlling the housing market, to the regional administrator distributing economic benefits, to the executives of multi-national organisations moving finances and factories from country to country, the dynamic and creative effects of implemented policies are considerable.

In the institutional environment national and local government policies have provided the major focus for political geographers. The activities of these arms of government have been studied largely in the context of the state as the authoritative allocator of scarce resources; through policies which supply and redistribute public goods and arbitrate on competing demands the state decides who gets what, where and when (Dear and Clark, 1978). In this model of the role of the state a direct link exists between institutions and conflict. The social and political geographies of the city, the region, the state and the international group are all the outcome of dynamic competition between non-governmental organised groups and between these organisations and the arms of governments. As the public sector in states grows, authoritative decisions more and more mould the environment; such decisions, however, constantly create gainers and losers among individuals and organised groups at varied scales as the environmental impacts of policies emerge. Access to power, access to the decision makers and ability to influence policy so as to gain advantage or, at least, to avoid disadvantage are persistent aims of all interest-consumer groups. The competing and conflicting goals involved inevitably create conflict. Environmental change is thus the outcome of resolved conflict — in which state governments acting as arbiters will also to some degree be acting as social engineers — and the cause of further conflict (Burton, 1966). The importance of the institutional environment is clear; the essence of politics is struggle and the causes and outcomes of such struggles are seen in the economic and social patterns and distribution of life chances which make up the human environment (Cox and Johnston, 1982; Kirby, 1982).

With the emphasis upon the study of inter-state policies the role of the state as authoritative allocator and generator of geographical change is now widely recognised. Transfer of study to the international level brings more than a straightforward change in scale; the international institutional environment has very different characteristics. The vital difference results from the relative weakness of, or indeed in many cases the total lack of, authoritative allocators. Whether at continental or world scale the inability of overarching institutions such as the EEC, the United Nations and the International Court of Justice to decisively and authoritatively arbitrate on inter-state relations results in more volatile and unpredictable competition which, less restrained by rules and structures, can easily escalate into intense conflict. The power of threat and economic and political blackmail — no less real for being disguised — becomes the basis for solving differences.

In this environment three types of institution are worthy of study. First, the state demands attention with particular emphasis upon international policies designed to protect and defend. Many policies, unilateral or multilateral, fulfil such goals, perhaps most important in conflict terms being those concerned with nuclear defence and the maintenance of strategic or economic bases. The state as a producer and seller of arms is also worthy of study. It is noteworthy that the states of the Developed World are the major providers of arms and the Lesser Developed states form the major market. Between 1973 and 1977 the USA supplied nearly 38 per cent and the USSR almost 33 per cent of all imported arms throughout the world (Kidron and Segal, 1981). International governmental organisations form the second institutional group. As noted earlier such organisations do not remove conflict between states; they do however create a much wider institutional setting within which rules have been developed for the resolution of conflict between member states. Conflict *between* international groupings and the stockpiling of the means of war by each group, e.g. NATO and the Warsaw Pact, provide a sombre but necessary topic of study in the institutional environment (Kidron and Smith, 1983). The third type of institution is the multi-national organisation; the paramount importance of multi-nationals as the *de facto* international allocators of resources and finished goods makes them a potent force for conflict. With great financial strength and bases in many states, multi-national organisations use the greater flexibility of non-discrete economic space and move finance, factories and personnel from political space to political space in the search for maximum profits. The role of multi-national organisations in the development process and in the replication of relative deprivation within and between states demonstrates the importance of institutions as moulders of the human environment and generators of conflict (Galtung, 1981).

In considering such international institutions political geographers must begin to develop general hypotheses about the causes of different levels of conflict intensity and about strategies of conflict behaviour. As noted earlier, McColl's (1983) work on the perceived importance of territory provides a lead-in to the study of conflict intensity. In the examination of strategies of conflict behaviour the many works on group behaviour at local and intra-national levels might be applied to international institutions. As an example the study of Dear and Long (1978) on community strategies in location conflict suggests a number of interesting questions. In what situations can, and under what conditions do, international institutions employ the *exit* strategy and remove themselves from the field of conflict? When will institutions use the *voice* strategy and compete in the conflict through debate and game behaviour? What conditions give rise to the *illegal action* strategy with resulting fight behaviour? Are there situations or conditions in which the *resignation* strategy will be adopted with avoidance of conflict but also with loss of goals, which can generate frustration and increased potential for future agression? (Kriesberg, 1973).

Thus far the institutional environment and conflict have been considered in the context of a pluralist paradigm of world society. Human group divisions are based upon divergent cultural characteristics and the resulting national and political cleavages create conflict. This culturally generated conflict is then viewed within a competitive market economic system in which demand and supply imperfections exacerbate the conflict. Progress in the understanding of conflict can be achieved by considering the role of institutions in alternative paradigms of world society; most significant is the class structured paradigm based on Marxism. In this context the state acts as the ally of capital so helping to maintain the grand cleavage between the custodians of capital and the labouring or working class. Such a view creates different insights into why the state acts as it does, why outcomes of state policies are as they are and why conflict on an economic class basis is so prevalent (Johnston, 1982). The role of the multi-national organisation also takes on new meaning as the international agent of capital which, through its policies, inevitably creates mounting antagonism between the modernised and modernising bourgeoisie and the underclasses within and across state boundaries. In the class structured paradigm the capitalist economic system not only causes inevitable and incurable conflict, it contains the seeds of its own destruction. The economic role of the multi-national organisations is seen in the creation of a world economy in which the skewed distribution of rewards maintains economic cores, peripheries and semi-peripheries. Accepting the view of Wallerstein (1975) that the world economy is the key unit of analysis leads to study and understanding of inter-state conflict in terms of the economically based relationships of core, periphery and semi-periphery. The developing relationships between the states of the core, periphery and semi-periphery as the world economy advances in cycles of depression and prosperity will determine the nature and scale of conflict in the future.

Those who reject the economic determinism of the class structured paradigm in which conflict is a consequence of contradictory material interests and economic processes should not forget that study of the institutional environment of conflict requires an approach flexible enough to cope with the bewildering range of motivations and goals which generate institutional activity.

Conclusion

As a fundamental component of world society, so common as to seem synonymous with life itself, conflict cannot be treated as a peripheral element in politico-geographic study. While the geography of conflict is likely to attract more attention at the intra-state level (the scale of experience), the study of conflict between states (the scale of reality) will ask more significant questions and lead to deeper insights into the causes and conditions which most vitally influence the future of the world. In the analysis of international conflict progress will come with the development of hypotheses about conflict generation and intensity, with the construction of models of conflict behaviour, and from careful scholarship on the physical, human and institutional environments of conflict which will permit the testing of hypotheses and refinement of models.

References

Agnew, J.A. (1983) 'An Excess of "National Exceptionalism": Towards a New Political Geography of American Foreign Policy', *Political Geography Quarterly*, 2, 151–66

Alexander, L.M. (1957) *World Political Patterns*, John Murray, London

Anderson, E.W. (1982) 'The Strategic Significance of the Cape Sea Route', *Paper presented to the International Seminar on Contemporary Problems in Political Geography*. University of Haifa, Israel, January, 1982

—— and Blake, G.H. (1982) *The Transport of Oil and Strategic Minerals: The Cape Route and Key Choke Points*, Ministry of Defence, London

—— (1983) *The Republic of South Africa: a stable supplier?*, Ministry of Defence, London

Ardrey, R. (1967) *The Territoral Imperative*, Collins, London

Aristotle (384–322 B.C.) *The Ideal State*, reprinted in Kasperson, R.E. and Minghi J.V. (1969) *The Structure of Political Geography*, University of London Press, London

Ashworth, G. (1977) *World Minorities, Volume 1*, Quartermaine House, Sunbury, Middlesex

—— (1978) *World Minorities, Volume 2*, Quartermaine House, Sunbury, Middlesex

—— (1980) *World Minorities in the Eighties*, Quartermaine House, Sunbury, Middlesex

Auburn, F.M. (1982) *Antarctic Law and Politics*, Hurst, London

Bergman, E.F. (1975) *Modern Political Geography*, Wm. C. Brown Company, Dubuque, Iowa

Blainey, G. (1973) *The Causes of War*, Macmillan, London

Blake, G.H. (1982) 'Maritime Boundaries and Political Geography in the 1980s', *Political Geography Quarterly*, *1*, 171–4

Boal, F.W. (1969) 'Territoriality on the Shankill-Falls Divide, Belfast', *Irish Geography*, *6*, 30–50

—— and Douglas, J.N.H. (1982) *Integration and Division. Geographical Perspectives on the Northern Ireland Problem*, Academic Press, London

Borgese, E.M. and Ginsberg, N. (eds.) (1978) *Ocean Yearbook, 1*, App. F, 821–33, University of Chicago Press, Chicago

Boulding, K.E. (1959) 'National Images and International Systems', *Journal of Conflict Resolution*, *3*, 411–21

—— (1962) *Conflict and Defense: A General Theory*, Harper and Row, New York

Bowman, I. (1922) *The New World: Problems in Political Geography*, World Book Co., New York

Brandt, Commission (1980) *North-South: A Programme for Survival*, Pan Books, London

Brams, S.J. (1966), 'Transaction Flows in the International System', *The American Political Science Review*, *60*, 880–98

Buchanan, W. and Cantril, H. (1953) *How Nations See Each Other*, University of Illinois Press, Urbana, Illinois

Burghardt, A.F. (1962) *Borderland: A Historical and Geographical Study of Burgenland, Austria*, University of Wisconsin Press, Madison, Wisconsin

—— (1973) 'The Bases of Territorial Claims', *Geographical Review*, *63*, 225–45

Burton, J. (1966) 'Conflict as a Function of Change', in A. de Reuck and J. Knight (eds.), *Conflict in Society*, J. and A. Churchill, London

Cohen, S.B. (1973) *Geography and Politics in a World Divided*, Oxford University Press, London

Coser, L.S. (1967) *Continuities in the Study of Social Conflict*, Collier Macmillan, London

Cox, K.R. (1979) *Location and Public Problems*, Blackwell, Oxford

108   *Conflict Between States*

—— and Johnston, R.J. (eds.) (1982) *Conflict, Politics and the Urban Scene*, Longman, Harlow, Essex
Dahl, R.A. (1956) *A Preface to Democratic Theory*, University of Chicago Press, Chicago
—— (1976) *Pluralist Democracy in the United States*, Rand McNally, Chicago
—— (1982) *Dilemmas of Pluralist Democracy*, Yale University Press, New Haven, Connecticut
Dear, M. and Clark, G. (1978) 'The State and Geographic Process: a critical review', *Environment and Planning A*, *10*, 173–83
—— and Long, J. (1978) 'Community Strategies in Locational Conflict' in Cox, K.R. (ed.) *Urbanisation and Conflict in Market Societies*, Methuen, London
Deutsch, K.W. (1966) *Nationalism and Social Communication*, MIT Press, Cambridge, Massachusetts
Dickinson, R.E. (1943) *The German Lebensraum*, Penguin Books, Harmondsworth, Middlesex
Douglas, J.N.H. (1983) 'Political Integration and Division in Plural Societies — problems of recognition, measurement and salience' in N. Kliot and S. Waterman *Pluralism and Political Geography. People, Territory and State*, Croom Helm, London
East, W.G. and Moodie, A.C. (1956) *The Changing World*, Harrap and Co., London
Elliot, R.S.P. and Hickie, J. (1971) *Ulster. A Case Study in Conflict Theory*, Longman, London
Galtung, J. (1964) 'A Structural Theory of Aggression', *Journal of Peace Research*, *2*, 81–117
Galtung, J. (1981) 'Global Processes and the World in the 1980s' in W.L. Hollist and J.N. Rosenau *World System Structures. Continuity and Change*, Sage Publications, Beverley Hills
Ginsberg, N. (1968) 'On the Chinese Perception of World Order' in Tang Tsou (ed.), *China's Policies in Asia and America's Alternatives*, vol. 2, University of Chicago Press, Chicago
Glassner, M.I. and De Blij, H.J. (1980) *Systematic Political Geography*, John Wiley, Chichester
Goldmann, K. (1973) 'East-West Tension in Europe: 1946–1970: a Conceptual Analysis and a Quantitative Description', *World Politics*, *26*, 106–25
—— (1974) *Tension and Détente in Bipolar Europe*, Scandinavian University Books, Stockholm
Harris, W.W. (1980) *Taking Root. Israeli Settlement in the West Bank, Golan and Gaza-Sinai, 1967–1980*, Research Studies Press, Chichester
House, J.W. (1959) 'The Franco-Italian Boundary in the Alpes-Maritimes', *Transactions, Institute of British Geographers*, *26*, 107–31
—— (1983) 'Political Geography of Contemporary Events: Unfinished Business in the South Atlantic', *Political Geography Quarterly*, *2*, 233–46
Jackson, W.A.D. (1958) 'Whither Political Geography', *Annals, Association of American Geographers*, *48*, 178–83
Johnston, R.J. (1981) 'British Political Geography since Mackinder: a Critical Review', in A.D. Burnett and P.J. Taylor (eds.), *Political Studies from Spatial Perspectives*, John Wiley, Chichester
—— (1982) *Geography and the State. An Essay in Political Geography*, Macmillan, London
Jonsson, H. (1982) *Friends in Conflict: The Anglo-Icelandic Cod War and the Law of the Sea*, Hurst, London
Kamenka, E. (ed.) (1976) *Nationalism. The Nature and Evolution of an Idea*, Arnold, London

Kasperson, R.E. and Minghi, J.V. (ed.) (1969) *The Structure of Political Geography*, University of London Press, London
Kende, I. (1978) 'Wars of Ten Years, 1967–1976', *Journal of Peace Research, 8,* 227–42
Kidron, M. and Segal, R. (1981) *The State of the World Atlas*, Heinemann, London
—— and Smith, D. (1983) *The War Atlas*, Heinemann, London
Kirby, A. (1982) *The Politics of Location*, Methuen, London
Kirk, W. (1951) 'Historical Geography and the Concept of the Behavioural Environment', *Indian Geographical Journal, Silver Jubilee Volume,* 152–160
Kjellen, R. (1917) *Der Staat als Lebensform*, Vowinckel, Berlin
Kriesberg, L. (1973) *The Sociology of Social Conflicts*, Prentice-Hall, Englewood Cliffs, New Jersey
Lee Yong Leng (1983) 'Economic Aspects of Supranationalism: The Case of ASEAN', *Political Geography Quarterly, 2,* 21–30
Lowenthal, D. (1958) 'The West Indies Chooses a Capital', *Geographical Review, 48,* 336–64
—— and Bowden, M.J. (1976) *Geographies of the Mind*, Oxford University Press, London
MacAonghusa, P. and O Réagan, L. (eds.) (1967) *The Best of Connolly*, Mercier Press, Cork
Mackinder, H.J. (1904) 'The Geographical Pivot of History', *Geographical Journal, 33,* 241–4
—— (1919) *Democratic Ideals and Reality*, Holt, New York
—— (1943) 'The Round World and the Winning of the Peace', *Foreign Affairs, 21,* 595–606
McColl, R.W. (1969) 'The Insurgent State: Territoral Bases of Revolution', *Annals, Association of American Geographers, 59,* 613–31
—— (1983) 'A Geopolitical Model for International Behaviour' in N. Kliot and S. Waterman (eds.) *Pluralism and Political Geography. People, Territory and State*, Croom Helm, London
Minghi, J.V. (1963) 'Boundary Studies in Political Geography', *Annals, Association of American Geographers, 53,* 407–28
Muir, R. (1975) *Modern Political Geography*, Macmillan, London
—— and Paddison, R. (1981) *Politics, Geography and Behaviour*, Methuen, London
Nairn, I. (1977) *The Break-up of Britain*, New Left Books, London
O'Donnell, E.E. (1977) *Northern Irish Stereotypes*, College of Industrial Relations, Dublin
O'Sullivan, P. (1982) 'Antidomino', *Political Geography Quarterly, 1,* 57–64
—— and Millar, J.W. (1983) *The Geography of Warfare*, Croom Helm, London
Patrick, R.A. (1976) *Political Geography and the Cyprus Conflict: 1963–71*, Department of Geography, University of Waterloo, Publication Series, No. 4, Waterloo
Pounds, N.J.G. (1972) *Political Geography*, McGraw-Hill, New York
Rabushka, A. and Shepsle, K.A. (1972) *Politics in Plural Societies: A Theory of Democratic Instability*, Merrill, Columbus, Ohio
Rae, D.W. and Taylor, M. (1970) *The Analysis of Political Cleavages*, Yale University Press, New Haven, Connecticut
Rao, P.S. (1975) *The Public Order of Ocean Resources. A Critique of the Contemporary Law of the Sea*, MIT Press, Cambridge, Massachusetts
Rapaport, A. (1960) *Fights, Games and Debates*, University of Michigan Press, Ann Arbor
Rosenau. J.N. (ed.) (1969) *Linkage Politics*, Free Press, New York
Ratzel, F. (1896) 'Laws of the Spatial Growth of States', reprinted in R.E. Kasperson and J.V. Minghi (eds.) (1969) *The Structure of Political Geography*, University of London Press, London
Reitsma, H.J.A. (1983) 'Boundaries as Barriers — The Predicament of Land-locked

Countries', in N. Kliot and S. Waterman (eds.) *Pluralism and Political Geography. People, Territory and State*, Croom Helm, London

Rummel, R.J. (1971) 'A Status Field Theory of International Relations', *Dimensionality of Nations Project, Research Report 55*, University of Hawaii, Hawaii

Runciman, W.G. (1966) *Relative Deprivation and Social Justice*, University of California Press, Berkeley

Russett, B.M. (1975) *International Regions and the International System*, Greenwood Press, Westport, Connecticut

Sack, R.D. (1981) 'Territorial Bases of Power', in A.D. Burnett and P.J. Tayor (eds.) *Political Studies from Spatial Perspectives*, John Wiley, Chichester

Schell, J. (1982) *The Fate of the Earth*, Pan Books, London

Short, J. (1982) *An Introduction to Political Geography*, Routledge and Kegan Paul, London

Siddayao, C.M. (ed.) (1978) *ASEAN and the Multinational Corporations*, Institute of South-East Asian Studies, Singapore

Smith, D.M. (1977) *Human Geography: A Welfare Approach*, Arnold, London

Soja, E.W. (1968) Communications and Territorial Integration in East Africa. An Introduction to Transaction Flow Analysis', *East Lakes Geographer*, *4*, 39–57

Sprout, H. and Sprout, M. (1956) *Man-Milieu Relationship Hypotheses in the Content of International Politics*, Centre for International Studies, Princeton, New Jersey

—— (1966) *Foundations of International Politics*, Van Nostrand Co., New York

Spykman, N.J. (1944) *The Geography of the Peace*, Harcourt, Brace and Co., New York

Starr, H. and Most, B.A. (1976) 'The Substance and Study of Borders in International Relations Research', *International Studies Quarterly*, *20*, 581–620

Statesman's Year Book, 119th Edition (1982) Macmillan, London

Taylor, M. and Thrift, N. (1982) *The Geography of Multinationals*, Croom Helm, London

Taylor, P.J. (1979) 'Political Geography', *Progress in Human Geography*, *3*, 139–42

—— (1981) 'Political Geography and the World Economy', in A.D. Burnett and P.J. Taylor (eds.) *Political Studies from Spatial Perspectives*, John Wiley, Chichester

—— (1982) 'A Materialist Framework for Political Geography', *Transactions, Institute of British Geographers*, New Series, *7*, 15–34

Thrift, N. and Forbes, D. (1983) 'A Landscape With Figures: Political Geography with Human Conflict', *Political Geography Quarterly*, *2*, 247–64

United Nations Organisation (1983) *The Law of the Sea: United Nations Convention on the Law of the Sea*, United Nations, New York

Van Meerhaege, A. (1980) *A Handbook of International Economic Institutions*, Martinus Nijhoff, The Hague

Wallerstein, I. (1975) *Old Problems and New Syntheses: The Relation of Revolutionary Ideas and Practice*, University of Saskatchewan, Saskatchewan

Weber, H. (1968) *Economy and Society*, Free Press, New York

Whittlesey, D. (1944) *The Earth and the State*, Holt and Co., New York

Wittkopf, E.R. (1974) 'The Concentration and Concordance of Foreign Aid Allocations: A Transaction Flow Analysis' in K.R. Cox, D.R. Reynolds and S. Rokkan (eds.) *Locational Approaches to Power and Conflict*, Halsted Press, New York

4 MINORITY GROUPS IN THE MODERN STATE

C. H. WILLIAMS

Introduction

In common with other aspects of political geography, research into the racial, ethnic and cultural characteristics of citizens and unincorporated peoples of multi-ethnic states has flourished of late. The conception of 'the state' and its relationship to constituent social groups has changed markedly in the past three decades. Events in the real world have cast doubts on the adequacy of several key concepts and theories, especially the traditional core themes of political behaviour, such as 'social mobilisation, economic development, political integration and the desirability and successful impact of redistributive welfare policies' (Rokkan and Urwin, 1982, p. 2).

The previous generation's comparative neglect of minority groups has been more than compensated for by today's flood of research on the geography of ethnic and minority relations. This chapter seeks to review the following selected themes suggested by this recent research: core-periphery interaction and state-formation, uneven development and nationalism, territoriality and perception studies, border regions and identity, and finally ethno-regional inequalities.

Ethnicity and the State

Consensus theory has a tendency to treat ethnic behaviour as a patterned response to the disruption of tradition. It suggests that ethnic resurgence in the contemporary industrial state speaks of a wider social tension within the existing order. At a time when class politics should dominate a reversion to the primordialism of ethnic identification smacks of the search for communitarian security, and thus a return to 'pre-modern' forms of political expression. In contrast, the liberated citizenry of the modern state express their interests in terms of political alliances between individuals of similar market position and thus, more generally, social class. Individual achievement determines one's role in society and the state becomes the facilitating agency which encourages upward social mobility through its enfranchisment and education of the populus. In consensus terms the state's principal role is that of reform in the great structural transition from tradition to modernity. In multi-ethnic states mass participation is usually encouraged along lines firmly established by the dominant host group which controls most avenues of socialisation and directs the path of state development.

When minority groups seem to overcome the structural discrimination imposed upon them by the host group and emphasise the ethnic diacritica of their group separateness they are accused of being disruptive, traditional and misguided, for ethnicity is conceived as an ideological blinker which obscures the development of class consciousness. Clearly, we need to discuss both ethnicity and social class within the same organisational framework, if only, as Williams (1980) suggests, to root the problem in social terms rather than to express it in terms of a residual category of culture. He argues that the existence of social class groupings is established by considering the relationship of actors to economic resources, regarding the social formations as somehow 'natural'. By contrast, ethnic groups are established by a consideration of their unique, usually cultural attributes, and the groups are then located in the economic order. As a consequence, 'either the ethnic group is treated as socially uniform, or the problem of ethnicity is reduced to a problem of class. . . . If we accept that groups exist because of an institutionalised discrimination which is manifested in terms of access to economic resources and with the diacritica of ethnicity being the basis for the legitimisation of that discrimination, then ethnic stratification becomes the natural order in the same sense that class is often referred to.' (Williams, 1980, p. 367).

The state is central to the analysis, since in tandem with monopoly capitalism, its interventionist role has grown enormously in the modern period. In order to understand its influence as an 'ethnic-defining' instrument, we will trace the development of state formation, initially in Western Europe, through the central concept of core-periphery interaction.

Core-Periphery Perspectives

Long recognised as a key concept in economic geography and

regional planning, core-periphery interaction has lately provided the basis for a resurgence of interest in state formation, national development and superordinate-subordinate relations within the modern state. Intuitively attractive because of its simplicity, flexibility and inherent spatial connotations, the core-periphery theme is rich in suggestive hypotheses concerning political behaviour at a variety of scales: global, continental, state and regional.

Of the many variants on this theme, perhaps the most comprehensive and stimulating is Rokkan's 'Conceptual map of Europe' (Rokkan and Urwin, 1982; Allardt, 1981). In his attempt to develop a model explaining the processes of state-formation and nation-building in Europe, Rokkan adapts a Parsonian scheme incorporating four functional prerequisites — economy, political power, law and culture. These elements, elaborated upon by Allardt (1981, p. 259) separate from each other in time, but also provide institutional domains within which separate and competitive élites vie for influence at various junctures in the process. The originality of Rokkan's work is that he tied these functional attributes to the constant tension of core and periphery in European development, producing central coordinates for his conceptual map. Broad in design and catholic in execution, Rokkan's four interactive requisites of economy and culture, core and periphery, structure the development of the modern European state system and help locate the ethnic identity of Europe's people within a social and spatial order (Figure 4.1).

A fundamental division reflecting the economy-culture tension, is the North-South axis (cultural) and the East-West axis (economy). Both of these axes can be described by four dominating structural and institutional factors, reported by Allardt as follows:

(1) Network of trading cities
(2) The religious organisations, with a particular emphasis on the unity and strength of the churches and religious bodies.
(3) The linguistic, ethnic and national solidarities and the social formations based on them, and
(4) The patterns of ownership of agricultural lands with a special emphasis on both the relative importance of agriculture and the size of farms and estates (Allardt, 1981, p. 262).

On Rokkan's conceptual map the East-West axis differentiates the economic bases of the state-building centres. They owe their primacy as core locations to their ability to accumulate surpluses from a 'highly monetised economy in the West', and from 'agricultural labour in the East'. In contrast to the key commercial centres of the seaward powers, France and England, the cities of Eastern Europe were much less effective partners in state formation, for they could not 'offer the essential resource base for the building of the military machineries of the new centres at the periphery of the old empire' (Rokkan, 1980, p. 179). The only alternative partners here were the land owners, but their resources of food and manpower were less suitable for the creation of territorial centres of commerce and power. However, Rokkan goes beyond the economic distinctions suggested by Moore's (1966) analysis of political consolidation and highlights the cultural significance of post-Reformation Europe being divided north and south. In the south the Catholic Church dominated the culture, but portrayed it as a universal set of values, thus preserving its hegemony. In the north the state and the dissenting churches of Protestantism became major agencies for producing national aspirations by standardising languages and socialising the masses into unique, national cultures. Thus he concludes that whereas the 'West-East axis differentiates the conditions of *state*-building, the South-North axis (differentiates) the conditions of *nation*-building' (Rokkan, 1980, p. 179) (cf Figure 4.1).

It was in North West Europe that the prime conditions for the development of virulent nation-states were met. Here both state-building and nation-building tended to proceed simultaneously, though admittedly exhibiting tensions at the fringes of authority, between the forces of territorial incorporation and those of irredentism and separatism. Peripheral groups sought to resist their emasculation by core host groups throughout the north: English versus Celts, Danes versus Norwegians and Icelanders, Swedes versus Finns (Rokkan, 1980, p. 182). For Rokkan, trade-belt Europe continued to express its diversity at the cultural interface of Central Europe. In these territories national identity came first, rooted in the inherited language systems of medieval empires, Italian in the south, German in the north. Political unification followed as a very late secondary process. In the 'Lotharingian-Burgundian' zone linguistic borders were hardly ever recognised as territorial frontiers, and a complex set of developments ensued. Switzerland evolved into a plural society, Alsace-Lorraine though decidedly German in dialect, identified mostly with France, Luxembourg oscillated between Germany and France, Belgium

Figure 4.1: Rokkan's Conceptual Map of Western Europe: Principal Features

	WEAK	STRONG	WEAK	STRONG	WEAK
CENTRE FORMATION:					
CITY NETWORK:	WEAK	STRONG	STRONG	WEAK	WEAK
WEST TO EAST	SEAWARD PERIPHERIES	SEAWARD EMPIRE-NATIONS	CITY BELT	LANDWARD EMPIRE-NATIONS	LANDWARD BUFFER TERRITORIES
NORTH TO SOUTH					
ARCTIC PERIPHERIES	Iceland Faeroes Finnmark			Norrbotn	Lappland
PROTESTANT TERR.	Norway Scotland Wales	DENMARK ENGLAND	Hanse Germany	SWEDEN PRUSSIA	FINLAND Baltic Terr.
MIXED/ NATIONAL CATHOLIC TERR.	Scots Highl. Ireland Brittany	FRANCE	NETHERLANDS Belgium RHINELAND GERM. SWITZERLAND		Lithuania Poland
COUNTER REFORMATION	Galicia Navarre Basque	SPAIN PORTUGAL	Rousillon Catalonia	AUSTRIA	Hungary Croatia
MEDITERRANEAN PERIPHERIES	Andalucia Estremadura		Balearic Islands Southern Italy		Dalmatia Albania

Note: Territories sovereign before 1789 are in capital letters.

Source: F.H. Aarebrot, 'On the Structural Basis of Regional Mobilization in Europe' in B. de Marchi and A.M. Boileau (eds.), *Boundaries and Minorities in Western Europe* (Franco Angeli Editore, Milan, 1982).

became a buffer zone between the two great faiths, languages and ideologies of this region.

In the rest of Catholic Europe Rokkan's conceptual map comprises dominant languages at the territorial centres with strong movements of cultural resistance in the peripheries. France, though ruthless in its pursuit of national unification and standardisation, still could not subdue alternative conceptions of 'national identity' in the periphery, in Brittany and Occitania. Spain never succeeded in overcoming the resistance of Basque and Catalonian challenges to the Castilian national ideal, whilst Austria struggled for centuries to make German the dominant language of southeast Europe. Interestingly, Rokkan points to the contrast between Germany and Austria to illustrate the truth of his cultural classification influencing political development. Austria pushed its state apparatus far beyond the borders of the German speech community and founded a multi-lingual empire. Prussia also had ambitions for landward expansion to the east, but in the end turned westward toward the core area of the German nation.

> The Catholic power stuck to the supraterritorial idea; the Protestant power endeavoured to acquire territorial control over the one linguistic community. The struggle between kleindeutsche and grossdeutsche strategies was a struggle over conceptions of the state and nation, a struggle between a political and a cultural conception of territorial community (Rokkan, 1980, p. 183).

The great merit of Rokkan's nation-building models is that they portray the broad brush strokes of European history. His classificatory scheme is both bold and innovative.

Generalised social process can be related to the changing spatial order. Dynamism is inbuilt into the model by his insistence on analysing transactions across territorial boundaries (Allardt, 1981, p. 263). In these economic, cultural and political transactions one can identify various sets of boundary-opening and -transcending as well as boundary-strengthening and -maintaining mechanisms (Allardt, 1981).

However, Rokkan's work has been criticised for dealing mainly with those groups that have survived and were subsequently able to build nation states. It has also been challenged for being too eclectic and 'too willing to always consider new groups and categories' (Allardt, 1981, p. 264). Far from this being a failure I see this as a major source of strength, for too few scholars in this field set out their typologies, let alone embrace new scholarship from other disciplines. In one of his last published papers (Rokkan and Urwin, 1982), Rokkan identifies the main stages, in the development of a typology of territorial structures which should be of lasting relevance for students of state formation and nationalism (Figure 4.2).

The first stage in developing a typology combines information on the unification strategies distinctive of the state-building élites (Rokkan and Urwin, 1982, p. 4). A second stage requires the specification of two spatial contexts within which strain and unification operate. One is conceived as territorial space, the other as membership space. A territorial definition of political identification relates to state-formation. This is generally a process whereby the centre will seek to extend its rule throughout the territory by ensuring 'its political and economic dominance through an efficacious system of administrative control, and to create unity out of diversity through a constant and conscious policy of cultural standardisation' (Rokkan and Urwin, 1982, p. 8). In attempting to make state and nation coterminous this policy seeks to form a new 'national' identity throughout the territorial space of the state through its socialising agencies of education and the law constructing linguistic uniformity, and thereby establishing cultural norms and standards of behaviour.

In contrast, membership space structures an alternative identity. It is largely a defensive reaction against state incursion, and asserts the primacy of group identification over any other source of loyalty. It is rooted in historic tradition and the preservation of territorially varying rights and customs. Whilst territorial space thus implies monocephality, membership space suggest polycephality (Rokkan and Urwin, 1982, p. 9). Territorial space processes suggest the establishment of a unitary nation-state, whilst membership space processes suggest the establishment of a federal, plural state. The utility of these general, ideal-type constructs may be seen by consulting Figure 4.2 where the constructs have been combined with the previously discussed historical sources of strain and unification strategies to produce a most suggestive typology. By including regions as well as states in their typology, they draw attention to a possible range of solutions that might satisfy respective peripheral demands. Thus whilst unitary states, such as Norway and France, have historically militated against the development of regionalism, federal covenant states, such as Switzerland, have incorporated territorial based political activity into their constitutional framework. If this French-Swiss diagonal may be taken as an ideal fit between state and nation-building histories, then Rokkan and Urwin suggest that 'placement in cells away from this diagonal indicates the degree to which there is incongruity between these two processes, and therefore also the potential for varying kinds of territorial politics' (Rokkan and Urwin, 1982, p. 13) (cf Figure 4.2).

A related attempt to explain one aspect of the general problem discussed by Rokkan and his team is provided in Aarebrot's work on ethnoregionalism. Of particular interest is his typology of regionalist goals,(Figure 4.3). Aarebrot frames integration and independence as twin poles of a political continuum within which one may either compare regionalist movements in Europe or alternatively trace the development of a single regionalist movement from one position on the continuum to another. The central column of Figure 4.3 represents the primary stages in the mobilisation of ethnic/national demands, whilst the pyramid structure deftly conveys the image that the more radical and 'profound the planned changes the smaller the popular base' (Aarebrot, 1982, p. 80). The right hand column suggests the political incorporation of these aims in the form of a nationalist movement. Some limited application of this typology is presented in Aarebrot (1982), and is under way in conjunction with the Economy, Territory and Identity Project. It remains one of the most useful ways of structuring the field of ethnoregionalism. It is perhaps symptomatic that, by and large, Scandinavian scholars are those most involved in elaborating structural typologies for comparative ethnic/regional research.

I have attempted to summarise the tensions and processes inherent in the state-building histories of Europe in Figure 4.4. This composite map, derived from the work of Rokkan, Parker (1983), Williams (1980) and others, illustrates the central strategic role of the 'Lotharingian Axis', the principal European axis of trade and communication. Control of this vital corridor of power and commerce has been a persistent feature of modern European history, and a strategic target in most continental warfare since the Thirty Years' War. The map brings into sharp relief the dynamic pressure exerted by expansionist states such as France and England in the west and Germany in central Europe. It also illustrates the marginalised position of peripheral minority groups, such as the Celts, Basques and Catalonians on the fringes of empires and developing states. However, as we shall see, this apparently simple core-

Figure 4.2: A Simple Typology of State-building and Nation-building Processes in Western Europe

Strategies of unification	Territory — Anti-centre		Space/identity characteristics		Membership — Covenant/ toleration
	Anti-centre		*Peripheral protest*	*Regional tension*	*Covenant/ toleration*
Unitary state (Centralizing)	France Denmark Norway Italy (Brittany) (Alsace) (Occitania) (Corsica) (Carinthia) (Sardinia)	Iceland Sweden Portugal Austria	Finland (Swedish Finns)	Belgium	(Berne)
Union state			Netherlands United Kingdom (Friesland) (Cornwall)	Spain (Galicia) (Andalusia)	
Mechanical federalism	(Alto-Adige) (Val d'Aosta)		(Scotland) (Wales)	Germany (Flanders) (Wallonia)	
Organic federalism (Accommodating)	(Faeroes)		(Northern Ireland)	(Bavaria) (Basques) (Catalonia)	Switzerland (Jura)

Source: Reproduced with permission from S. Rokkan and D. Urwin (eds.) (1982) *The Politics of Territorial Identity*, p. 12. Copyright: Sage Publications.

Figure 4.3: The Pyramid of Regionalist Aims: Outcomes Ranked According to Degree of Independence

Type of nationalist/ regionalist ideologies: defined in terms of desired final territorial solution	Stages in an escalation from full integration in a state to independence from a state		Examples of effective political movement particularly relevant to each state
Full independence			
Separatism/irredentism	Full independence	Transfer to neighbouring state	War of independence or state level negotiations
Confederalism	Regional autonomy with a central authority only to regulate inter-regional problems		Threats to secede
Federalism	Shared autonomous powers between a central government and all provinces		Devolution
Regional autonomism	Autonomous status for one particular peripheral region over the rest		Regional party with heavy regional vote
Regionalism	Preservation of cultural characteristics in a peripheral population		Stable regional party running at least in local elections
Peripheral protest	Putting regional demands on the agenda for the central political system		Nation-wide party with a high degree of regional electoral support
Peripheral identity building	Arguing for the unique character of a given territory and its population		Cultural defence associations
Full integration	A province of a state with no separate culture identity		

Source: F. Aarebrot, 'On the Structural Basis of Regional Mobilization in Europe' in B. de Marchi and A.M. Boileau (eds.), *Boundaries and Minorities in Western Europe*. (Franco Angeli Editore, Milan, 1982, p. 81).

periphery tension at the European scale does not necessarily imply a permanent dependency situation for such groups in the European economy or state system. Euskadi, Catalonia and Scotland in particular have good grounds for being classified as well integrated territories within the expansion of modern capitalism.

An alternative, if complementary, approach to the analysis of autonomist nationalism in Europe is outlined by Orridge and Williams (1982). They attempted to separate structural preconditions from triggering factors in the development of nationalist movements. Rather than treat single cases in detail, they sought to locate the origins of autonomist nationalism within certain regular and identifiable sociopolitical milieux. Their structural preconditions include a core territory, some distinctive bases of community (usually language or religion) and an identifiable sub-group that more often than not is superior in political and economic terms to the host group. These structural preconditions locate those areas vulnerable to autonomist nationalism, the places where it is a possibility, and where states so found may be susceptible to the nationalist challenge.

Two key factors affected the development of the preconditions of autonomist nationalism, namely linguistic geography and a key frontier position. By relating these key features to such variables as the European state system and economy, sources of war finance, international cataclysms, and dynastic changes Orridge and Williams demonstrate the utility of adopting a macro-approach to their subject matter. The variation between states is as important as what they share, and generalisations about the development of the preconditions of autonomist nationalism are better obtained at this level than at the level of general models of the individual state. This is because established theories are applied generally to every state and fail to take into account the variations produced by the place in the state system that a country occupies. The place of a country in this system helps produce variations in the preconditions of nationalism; at a later date it also affects the capacity of the state to manage autonomist nationalism and hence the extent to which it is subject to these various factors. Unlike Rokkan and Urwin, Orridge and Williams do not start with a broad canvas of a conceptual map of Europe, but rather search for the underlying generalities, which in the main help to explain the incidence of autonomist nationalism wherever it happens to surface in Europe. In that respect their work is not as ambitious as Rokkan's, but neither does it need as many

Figure 4.4: State-building in Europe: Tensions and Processes

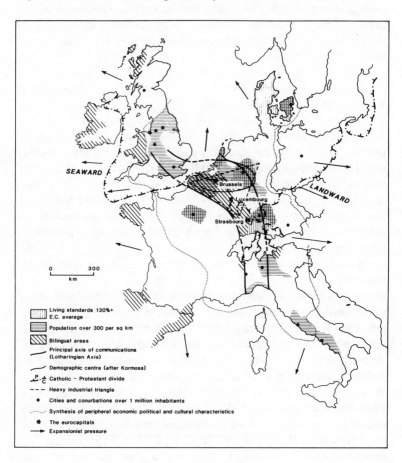

Source: Base map and selected features redrawn with permission of author and publisher from G. Parker, *A Political Geography of Community Europe* (Butterworths, London, 1983, p. 65).

qualifications in its application to historical examples. A fusing of both approaches would prove very fruitful, especially as they both seek to integrate material from history, geography and the social sciences *per se* in their analysis of European state development and autonomist nationalism.

Uneven Development and Nationalism

Whilst Rokkan's core-periphery theorising was a welcome return to the historical and specific analysis of inter-group and inter-national relationships, it could not provide an overall global context, within which developments in Europe could be related to those elsewhere. The development of a materialistic framework promised to provide just such a global context. Its holism, complexity and versatility offered the possibility of replacing the fragmented structures of social science with a unified framework within which 'all political activities may be viewed' (Taylor, 1981, p. 166). The world-economy approach provided 'an opportunity for political geographers to return to the global scale of analysis without paying homage to Mackinder' (ibid.). Wallerstein, Braudel and Nairn were to be our new heroes. Taylor sketches an outline of a materialist framework for political geography and deftly summarises Wallerstein's (1974) argument that the post-1648 European state system was concomitant with the growth of capitalism as a world-economy. This process produced two legitimising ideologies, statism and nationalism (Taylor, 1982, p. 27). Whilst statism, the 'claim for increased power in the hands of the state machinery' (Wallerstein, 1974, p. 102) did not necessarily relate political development to the fortunes of the masses, nationalism certainly sought, as its prime rationale, to re-interpret reality in such a way that populist destinies were seen as central to the whole process of group political development. This guaranteed its role as the articulator of structural change in post-revolutionary Europe, stirred from its absolutist slumbers by the uneven penetration of advanced capitalism. But why nationalism?

For Nairn, capitalism's uneven development is necessarily 'nationalism-producing' (Smith, 1981, p. 37) because development always comes to the less advanced peoples within the 'fetters of the more advanced nations' (France and England). In order to avoid or reduce their dependency situation the intelligentsia of the

underdeveloped regions have to espouse nationalist ideology. Traditional institutions and the state apparatus being barred to them, the
bourgeois intellectuals retreat to mobilise the one resource they have
access to: the people (Smith, 1981, p. 38). Thus a new historicism of
the intelligentsia, imbued with its own imminent self-realisation and
pledged to develop the 'national culture' of the masses, becomes a
driving force in European and ultimately world-history. Cultural
differences, of language, religion, myth and shared oppression
became the ammunition for a new attack on statism, in the name of
the people. Nationalism thus becomes 'a crucial, fairly central feature of the modern capitalist development of world history' (Nairn,
quoted in Taylor, 1982, p. 28).

In this framework, the only logical scale for understanding the
recent growth of nationalism is global. Core, semi-peripheral and
thence peripheral relations structure the spread of capitalism from
its origins in the sixteenth-century onwards producing an emergent
system of sovereign states. Thus

> the world-economy became basically structured as an increas-
> ingly interrelated system of strong 'core' and weak 'peripheral'
> states, in which inter-state relations — and hence patterns of
> state formation and, in that setting, the formulations of nation-
> ally-organised 'societies' — are continually shaped and in turn
> continually shape the deepening and expanding world-scale divi-
> sion and integration of production. These basic trends are funda-
> mentally antipathetic and what the states try to unify, the world-
> economy tears asunder (Wallerstein, 1977, p. 2, quoted in
> Pettman, 1979, p. 166).

That capitalist development and nationalism are related is not a
new conclusion. What is new in this framework is the insistence that
the only adequate frame of reference for analysing the interplay
between them is world history, As Nairn notes

> Most approaches to the question are vitiated from the start by a
> country-by-country attitude. Of course it is the ideology of world
> nationalism itself which induces also this road by suggesting that
> human society consists essentially of several hundred different
> and discrete 'nations', each of which has (or ought to have) its
> own postage stamps, and national soul. The secret of the forest is
> the trees, so to speak (Nairn, 1977, p. 332 quoted in Taylor, 1982,
> p. 28).

Inherent in this process are two sets of contradictory forces, the tension between universal capitalism and a particularistic nationalism, and that between an integrative statism and a fragmenting world-economy. In essence, is not this the substance of much 'traditional' political geography? What is novel in this account is the global context and the stratification of participants according to their predetermined role in the world system, reflecting the operation of global division of labour.

Such a dynamic comparative and historical approach has proved very influential of late, but is not without its weaknesses. Of the many critiques I want to concentrate on Smith's work (1981) for he is especially concerned with explaining the role of ethnicity in the modern world-system. Smith argues that Nairn is surely correct when he suggests a close relationship between nationalism and foreign domination. Quite often nationalism is stimulated by war, and the role of warfare in nationality-formation is an underdeveloped area of study (Smith, 1983). Further, capitalist development is recognised as being much more than a process of economic imperialism. It involves psychological and cultural conflicts, value and identity conflicts, ultimately producing group antagonisms and often bitter hatred between the oppressor and the oppressed.

Of greater import is Nairn's emphasis on the state as the mediator of capitalist development. The state is central to our understanding of both capitalism and nationalism. What is lacking in this account, though, is an explanation for the anti-imperialist response. For, if the state is no more than a vehicle of capitalist development, asks Smith, 'how do we arrive at the ethnic content, the nationalist aspiration? Why should the unevenness of capitalist advance correspond to cultural division'? (Smith, 1981, p. 40). The answer, in part, rests with the tremendous ability of the state to direct and reproduce culture in a particular form. We are beginning to specify the manner in which state structures operate to favour some groups over others, but the ethnic content of such formulations has often been relegated to a residual category as many analysts preferred a primarily class-specific framework. An additional failure was the inability to relate structural features over time to key developments in the relationship between dominant and subordinate groups within the state. This is seen in using geographic regions as surrogates for groups in conflict. This has led to some gross exaggerations and historically inaccurate portrayals of regional consciousness and popular will acting as if they were independent

causal forces influencing national development and state formation. It was recognised in the late 1960s that fresh theoretical concepts were needed; concepts which would allow for spatial aspects to
be included as part of the analysis without either leading to spatial
determinism or spatial fetishism. This concern, despite a decade of
lively research, is still a major feature of the geography of ethnic and
minority relations, as it is, of course, within political geography writ
large.

The origins of this concern lie in recent developments within
political sociology and political economy, especially in relation to
the concept of internal colonialism. This thesis suggests that
expanding nation-states incorporated not only overseas colonies but
also internal colonies, that is, ethnic enclaves within their own
boundaries. The result of continued economic exploitation of the
ethnic periphery produced a clearcut cultural division of labour, 'a
system of stratification where objective distinctions are super-
imposed upon class lines!' (Hechter, 1975, p. 30). For Nairn (1981)
this thesis holds promise for sustaining a general theory of nationalism, and for Hechter (1975) it offers the basis for a general theory
of the development and maintenance of ethnic boundaries in
advanced industrial states.

In the United Kingdom, for example, economic progress was
instrumental in delaying the development of the periphery and thus
facilitated the maintenance of a distinct ethnic identity there until
well into the late twentieth century. By encouraging core-periphery
interaction, industrialisation further reinforced the dependence of
the periphery, creating lower levels of prosperity, forming exposed
and dependent economies tied to the primary sector, and producing
a consequent cultural stratification, a cultural division of labour.
Industrialisation, by strengthening economic and cultural contact,
has accentuated the persistence of cultural inequalities, or 'peripheral sectionalism'. Ethnic nationalism in the Celtic regions of the
United Kingdom thus becomes a reaction to an exploitative indus-
trialism and its associated hierarchical cultural division of labour.
Because the bureacratic state is responsible for this failure of
regional development and this hierarchy, 'the most recent crystal-
lization of Celtic nationalism may ultimately be understood as a
trenchant critique of bureaucratic centralism' (Hechter, 1975,
p. 310, quoted in Smith, 1981, p. 32).

Though intuitively attractive, especially with its recent modifications (Hechter and Levi, 1979), this thesis has been criticised

on a variety of grounds. The most telling criticism is the historical relevancy of the term 'internal colonialism' in describing the relationship between Wales, Scotland, Ireland and England. Whilst some authors recognise that the thesis 'illuminates the many ways in which political domination has utilised economic policy to perpetuate the subordination and sometimes impoverishment of peripheral populations' (Smith, 1981, p. 32), others claim that it 'mishandles the central reality of uneven development and it therefore often reads consequences as causes' (Williams, 1982, p. 192). Williams (1982, p. 197) reminds us that a colonial core-periphery interpretation for the economic development of Wales is ideologically blinkered. For the use 'of the term internal colonialism to describe the historical conjuncture precisely reverses the reality; it is the contradictions of an imperial capitalism we are dealing with, not those of one of its satellites.' Any other interpretation of South Wales's history would presuppose a nationalist view of an incipient satellite being exploited by an ever-voracious imperial core, centred on London.

A second difficulty relates to Hechter's national framework. The thesis suggests, too neatly, that capitalist development and exploitation must reinforce ethnic cleavage, thereby minimising the degree of socio-economic and structural similarity which exists between the deprived regions of the core national area, and the subject periphery, e.g. between the industrial history of Lancashire or Tyneside and South Wales. If the cultural division of labour is paramount, then an alternative explanation must be found for cases of high development accompanied by great deprivation within the national community. Uneven development theorists assume the existence of multiple ethnic identities and envisage uneven development as working on them to transform them into a dominant national community coincident with the boundaries of the state. But, as Orridge (1979) has pointed out, this raises fundamental questions about the nation-defining capacities of economic differences.

A third difficulty is the problem of timing (Smith, 1981, p. 33; Williams, 1982, p. 190). Why did Welsh and Scottish nationalism gain wide political support in the 1960s and not at an earlier date? Smith comments that Hechter has recently identified state policies as the basic determinant of the timing of separatism, thus introducing political factors rather than economic forces as the prime determinant of ethnic reaction. But this modification does not do justice to the specific emergence of an ethnic movement in the periphery. Smith's critique is especially good on the problem of the relationship between economic factors and ethnic change.

> For, if economic factors operate independently of ethnic ones, and ethnic protest can emerge independently of economic changes, then the central failures of the 'internal colonialism' model to explain why social discontent is focussed upon ethnic identities becomes apparent. . . . The plausibility of Hechter's model derives from the fact that many ethnic groups populate a single, readily identifiable territory, and hence suffer the disadvantages (or enjoy the benefits) of that terrain, with its soil and climate, distance from trade routes, possession of valuable minerals, strategic importance, communication networks and the like (Smith, 1981, p. 35).

But we know that ethnic groups are not necessarily coextensive with an economically defined region. Neither are they undifferentiated social wholes. Ethnic groups manifest internal social variations, which by definition the internal colonial thesis must subsume to the core-periphery social differentiation, maximising dissimilarity rather than those cross-cutting social bonds between exclave and enclave social formations.

Equally, within the periphery *per se*, there are often clear cases of core-periphery duality, replicating at that lower level the precise relationships that are deemed to predominate at the state level, viz. the Cardiff-Swansea axis versus the west and north of Wales, the Glasgow-Edinburgh axis versus the north of Scotland, each operating their own internal division of labour. Finally the thesis shifts attention away from the autonomous cultural and social reproduction of the peripheral minority group. Many commentators suggest that nationalism is both a necessary and specific response to the uneven economic development of the periphery. Economic considerations are paramount in their taxonomy of the structural preconditions for ethnic mobilisation. Far from there being an overriding necessity for nationalist reaction, the history of the United Kingdom has demonstrated that accommodation, incorporation, even assimilation have been embraced by large numbers in the 'periphery'. And this not just because they have been 'bought off' by English patronage, or have subsumed their ethnic loyalty to a larger (spurious) British loyalty. Rather it is often the result of a calculation that in order to change the material basis of their social/economic existence, access to central power and decision-making is paramount. But even if one were to concentrate only on the early development of nationalism in Scotland and Wales, one would readily recognise that issues of religion, education and language conservation dominated their discussions. It is only rather recently that any real heed has been paid to the necessity of sound economic arguments for nationalist mobilisation and representation.

Despite these several problems, Hechter's contribution to core-periphery theorising and ethnic relations has been profound. He has combined theoretical innovation with time-series data measurement in a most sophisticated manner, and his work serves as a model attempt to challenge the orthodox interpretation of English-Celtic relationships in the formation of the British state. In particular, one may summarise four principal contributions of Hechter's 'Internal Colonialism'.

(1) His work illumines key economic relationships in the past.

(2) By emphasising the spatial consequences of uneven economic development he reinforces the geographic element in political sociological research.

(3) His work has stimulated political geographers and others both to test the accuracy of his explanation for British national development, and to apply the principles of internal colonial theory in a wide range of case studies (Stone, 1979; Drakakis-Smith and Williams, 1983).

(4) Political activists within nationalist movements have often embraced the logic of Hechter's work and have commissioned research reports on some of its implications. Incidentally, some have also embraced the language of internal colonial theory for it serves to legitimise their grievances in an historical context and provides a conspiracy theory of the state (unintended by the author) which justifies their complaint of being exploited by the current economic and political system.

From a narrower, disciplinary perspective, Hechter's work is one of the landmarks of the 1970s. It has stimulated very fruitful exchanges between geographers and other social scientists and has served to provide a common theme for cross-cultural comparative research in which both theory and application are given due weight.

In a recent revision of his theory Hechter paid greater attention to the emergence of a segmental cultural division of labour in addition to hierarchical ones. He argued that, once a region had achieved a degree of institutional autonomy, ethnic specialisation would ensue where incumbents recognised that they owed their positions within the bourgeoisie to the existence of cultural distinctiveness in the region.

> In this way Scotland's institutional autonomy is responsible for producing a substantial material incentive for the reproduction of Scottish culture through history. It also serves to anchor the social base of Scottish ethnicity firmly within the bourgeoisie. The existence of these institutions insures that nearly all strata in the population come into regular contact with the peripheral culture and thus are likely to identify with it (Hechter, 1983, p. 36).

He recognises that more attention should be paid to the material interests that bind individuals into solidary groups and the normative sanctions that a group is able to impose on 'free-riders' in order to integrate them into the group's collective interest and mobilise their support for political action. Hechter's revised position is that his theory was not so much incorrect as incomplete because it took 'too narrow a view of the conditions that promote common materials interests among culturally distinct populations' (Hechter, 1983, p. 40). We await the empirical validation of his revised theory with great interest.

Territory and Group Identity

In recent years geographers have increasingly sought to measure the subjective relationship between people and place, whether that relationship be expressed through literature (Pocock, 1979), art, politics or the built environment. Following from an initial lead in perception studies given by Swedish geographers such as Hagerstrand and Lundén, a number of investigations have sought to specify political identification and loyalty in territorial terms.

Human territoriality is a vast and fascinating field of study. We now appreciate that for many peoples territory is not just an objectively defined 'given' portion of space, but is also capable of being constructed to fit an ideal. Williams and Smith (1983) have demostrated how since the age of nationalism it has served the cultural needs and social interests of nationalist élites and followers to shift the emphasis away from the objective interpretation of reality, that is, the 'givens' of space, and towards the subjective malleable aspects of 'the land'. A measure of their success in this enterprise has been their ability to enforce a new definition of space and reconstruct their environment as a political territory. The net result of this shift has been to

> deliver exceptional political power and cultural control into the hands of zealous nationalist élites and their parties, a power and a control that they have utilized to effect perhaps the most radical transformation in society's relationship with its environment since the Neolithic revolution' (Williams and Smith, 1983, p. 514).

Truly, a 'national' construction of social space has been effected, in which we see a filling in of power vacuums and the utilisation of all areas for social benefit and communal power. This structural transformation has reified the nation, and exalted it as the ultimate locus of political loyalty. It has also generated new sources of tension for the 'universalism of the prenationalism era has given way to a nationalist vision of the globe which is simultaneously involved both with the unique, the nation, and the general, the relationship between constituent nations in an international system' (Williams and Smith, 1983, p. 514).

At one level of analysis the new international 'nationalist' order has freed many peoples from the fetters of colonialism and explicit domination. But, for the 'subject nationalities' which remain, the new order poses severe impediments for group development. This is especially so when marginal minorities inhabit territories which, though meaningful in terms of their own internal values system, are not recognised in the legal-administrative apparatus of the host state. Traditionally, geographers have focused on the constitutional implications of granting or denying the moral imperative of self-determination and have addressed the consequent problems of boundary delimitation and adjustment when that principle of independence has been endorsed. More recently attention has been paid to analysing several cases where an ethnic group inhabits an informal homeland, in order to explain the relationship between a group's identity and its territorial context.

In a study set in the Canadian Maritimes Williams (1977) constructed 'mental maps' to reveal the perceived limits of ethnic territory amongst Francophones and Anglophones in New Brunswick. The findings show that, despite official attempts to dissipate any sense of regional-cum-national identity amongst the Acadians since 1755, local inhabitants continue to recognise Acadia as a national homeland, but that such perceptions are different for Francophones and Anglophones. This type of research is important, in my view, in an applied sense, because as part of its Maritime Union programme the Canadian government incorporated discussion on 'Acadia' as a regional unit in a proposed new political structure for the Maritimes. Such government thinking assumes what has to be demonstrated, namely the regional boundaries of this historically cherished but poorly defined homeland.

A comparative study was undertaken in Wales using the same methodology and sample selection process of senior high school students socialised in different milieux separated by language, religion and region into distinct socio-cultural backgrounds. The study (Williams, 1981) identified a perceived core area of 'y Fro Gymraeg' (The Welsh Heartland) centred on Gwynedd, though the extent of the area subsumed depended upon the sample's location and linguistic affiliation. The salience of social communication flows is acknowledged in this type of research, especially that of the filtering processes of cultural reproduction, involved in the socialisation of different language groups, who share a common territory, but who are separated by perceived cultural distance. In the Welsh and Acadian cases (representative of many bicultural communities) we would need to examine what effect an attenuated culture region has on the predisposition of non-Welsh or non-French speakers to learn the language given that the range of speech situations (in geographic terms) is diminishing. We would also need to investigate the powerful emotional attachment of minority culture groups to their territorial homeland and examine to what extent this concern over loss of territorial dominance becomes translated into political activism in its myriad forms. Finally we would need to be able to anticipate the likely reaction of the constituent language communities were the 'unofficial' homeland of the minority to be declared an official region of state, with possible implications for the establishment of unilingual régimes and consequent disputation over language planning and group rights (Williams, 1982).

The spatial context is paramount in this regard, for traditionally a homeland produced a complex range of speech domains within which the minority language was spoken as a matter of course. In situations where the territorial frame is being attenuated, the pattern of language domain dominance is undermined and a constant tension ensues between traditional and intrusive speech forms. In functionally bilingual societies, such as Wales and Acadia, the minority group can only survive if it establishes alternative speech domains, not dependent on territory, for that is eroding, but rather dependent upon the institutionalisation of the language as the medium for social communication. Thus bilingual education, public administration, the legal system and the media all become targets for group penetration, couched in the form of language equality so as to produce a system of legitimate domains, tied now to the legal apparatus of the state, not to the territorial frame of group settlement. Of course, this transformation implies a new source of dependency on the legal-rational largesse of the state and is not without its long term problems.

In analysing such changes, some geographers have been prone to treat cultural minorities *as if* they were primarily spatial entities, rather than material social groups who occupy specific territorial contexts. In emphasising spatially delimited concepts, such as culture areas or speech communities, emphasis can be shifted away from the power relations inherent in conflicting language groups or religious parties. This switch in attention is often accompanied by a consensus view of social change and leads the analyst to a statist position where the failure of the minority to integrate is seen in negative terms as the failure of upwardly mobile individuals to grasp the opportunities afforded by the liberalism of the benign host society. The ideological implications of this approach should be evident. If, for example, language minorities persist in demanding bilingual education within their territory, this is attacked from a consensus perspective as perpetuating the dependency and backwardness of the minority, for they characterise such language and educational rights as a reversion to primordialism or tradition, and a barrier to full integration. They fail to appreciate that not only do the minority often wish to maintain their separateness, but also wish to appropriate for themselves the ideological power inherent in the socialisation process of mass education. Of course, in the long run, such cultural autonomy is severely limited by the power of the state and the international economic system, but its control is often perceived as being vital for group survival, and hence education and language become inherently political battlegrounds within which the power relations between majority and minority become mediated.

Cultural Integration and Division

In its broadest sense culture embraces politics. The motivations for political activity are often inculcated in us by our respective cultural experiences, whether drawn from childhood or specific junctures in our adult life. But the link between a predisposing cultural system and our resultant political orientations is often difficult to specify because of the diversity of political issues one is asked to address in any conscious speculative effort. For members of beleaguered groups speculation is often concentrated in one or two key dimensions, namely survival and representation. All other nuances of political life are relegated to a secondary, dependent status, and flow from changes in the primary struggle. Nowhere is this evidenced more strongly than in Northern Ireland, a troubled territory which receives more than its fair share of attention as an example of almost every conceivable theory of religious, class, ethnic and material conflict. That there exist considerable grounds for harmony and social integration is often, understandably perhaps, overlooked by many in their accounts of 'the Troubles'. In addition many applied studies provide a partial account of the situation, focusing on constitutional or socio-economic issues, but hardly ever both in tandem. Others hinge their analysis on a truncated view of history and a conscious neglect of periods of cultural harmony if not actual cultural integration.

Given these failings it is heartening that a group of geographers from Northern Ireland have produced what I consider to be the most comprehensive overview of any 'conflict situation' in the past decade. Certainly it is the most lucid and wide-ranging of the many contending 'explanations' for the Ulster situation yet produced. Boal and Douglas (1982) provide a detailed outline of the main dimensions of the situation by reviewing the various territorial, demographic, socio-economic, political and behavioural attributes. They then relate these attributes to the process of integration and division, recognising the complexity of their task, but providing a sufficiently strong structure within which the other contributions may be discussed. Their structure (Figure 4.5) is derived from the

Figure 4.5: Integration and Division: Attributes and Processes

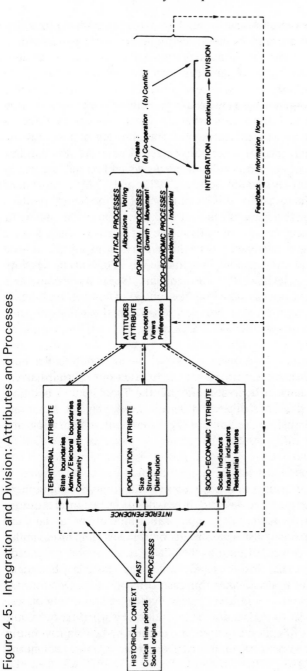

Source: Reproduced with permission from F.W. Boal and J.N. Douglas (eds.) (1982), *Integration and Division: Geographical Perspectives on the Northern Ireland Problem*, Figure 1.1 p. 3. Copyright: Academic Press Inc. (London) Ltd.

plural society model and is used with such sensitivity that the dynamism of integration and division as processes is highlighted.

The editors describe both integration and division as continuous processes, deriving from significant decison-making which is related to considerations of the balance of power in the territory. The complexity and dynamism of integration is reflected in their definition which states 'that integration (that is, the act of integrating) results from a process whereby members of a culture group develop an escalating sequence of social linkages and contacts which create cohesion and establish behaviour norms which become legitimised through time' (Boal and Douglas, 1982, p. 10.) (The process of division is the reverse of this.) Complementing the central political dimension of their analysis is a careful reasoning of the impact of locational decisions on group advantage and disadvantage, a feature examined in the detailed work of Osborne on locating a second University in Ulster, and in Singleton's analysis of housing development in the Poleglass (Boal and Douglas, 1982). What many outsiders fail to realise is that within the context of competitive defence of limited vested interest *any* decision which threatens change is treated with distrust, what Edwards calls a

'conspiracy consciousness', in which most resource allocation decisions are seen as favouring one or other of the groups and in which Catholic-Protestant differentials are frequently interpreted in terms of deliberate discrimination, no matter how complex the actual explanation for the differentials may be (Boal and Douglas, 1982, p. 342).

In response to this pervasive situation of strong competition over scarce economic and political resources the volume suggests that groups in the province develop three types of behavioural strategy: defensive territoriality, dominance-subordination behaviour and social closure. Whilst the first two are well known adaptive strategies in conflict situations the latter needs elaboration. Parkin suggests that social closure includes not only exclusionary behaviour (which relates to dominance) but also behaviour derived from the excluded themselves (which relates to avoidance of dominance) as a direct reaction to their status as outsiders. Usurpationary closure strategies, as might be expected, are deemed to be common in this context of 'competitive communal coexistence' (quoted in Boal and Douglas 1982, p. 347).

Whilst the research represented in this book points to a more comprehensive understanding of the many-layered tensions inherent in Northern Ireland, the solutions to reduce such tensions are by no means obvious. The editors reject the pessimistic claim that there is no solution, for in characteristic manner they suggest that the 'desired solutions tend to define the problem' (p. 353). Three solutions are discussed. The first is dominance, a situation likely to engender further conflict, which is passed over quickly in favour of a consideration of territoriality and partition. This would necessitate a redrawing of the international boundary and population transfer, but still leave an unpalatable situation. The third possibility is the most humane, and initially least likely to be adopted in view of current problems with power sharing. It is the mutuality solution, fundamental to which is a recognition of the territory's dual identity, British and Irish. Under joint protection of the two sovereign powers, both communities would have the right to vote separately on key constitutional issues and structures, thereby minimising the threat of a 'sell out' by one party. The withdrawal of absolute sovereignty as a precondition of mutuality would stop short of independence for Northern Ireland but would allow a considerable degree of autonomy within the 'supportive framework of Great Britain and the republic of Ireland' (p. 353).

Border Regions

Related work on territorial identification, particularly in border regions continues to produce extraordinary insights about both the manipulation of regional/spatial orientation and the formation of social networks. Scandinavian geographers and historians have been in the forefront of boundary contact studies. Sven Tägil (1977) and his co-researchers at Lund have developed a general theory for explaining boundary conflicts which deserves much wider attention within geographic circles. They identify key values which, when threatened, predispose groups to mobilise their resources and engage in forms of conflict, particularly boundary conflict. Central to their analysis is a view of human nature as essentially responsive to environmental pressures. But this does not predispose them to a determinism, so often seen in early geographic treatises. Rather they conceive of *man as an active being*, who, guided by his values, is able to create his environment at the same time that he is influenced by his environment. According to this premise, man is free and is able to create his own history. He can and *should* abolish the conditions which make him unfree' (Tägil, 1977, p. 36).

Such an epistemological premise not only affects the researcher's position, but also, claim Tägil *et al.*, the perception of the actor's relationship to reality. In consequence appropriate research objects consist of *actions* rather than events. This identifies them in the subjectivist camp in the current controversy in conflict research between 'subjectivist' and 'objectivist' conflicts. Their empirical examples of boundary contact behaviour are replete with new insights and a sensibility of the many layers of explanation one may identify therein. Of particular merit is their discussion on an old controversy in social science writ large, namely to what extent is it possible to draw conclusions about the intentions of individual members from studying group behaviour, and, vice versa, to draw conclusions about the group from the individual level? Reductionism and imputing motivation to key decision makers are critical problems in boundary conflict analysis (as in many other problem areas), particularly when contending explanations for the historical processes of resolving boundary disputes abound in any single case. The merit of their work is that it integrates much macro-sociological and geographic theory (core-periphery perspectives again) and modifies such theory in the light of detailed examination of specific European boundary problems during the interwar period, 1918–1939.

Thomas Lundén (1973), in contrast, concentrates his attention on one 'open' boundary, the southern portion of the Swedish-Norwegian border. His research focuses on two interrelated processes: (a) the integrative process of state activities, and (b) the behaviour of local residents on either side of the international boundary in adjusting to their specific geographic position as border zone dwellers. In developing his schema for relating these two processes Lundén (1982) distinguishes between three levels of social organisation: (a) the state as a system and a territory; (b) a more diffuse level of voluntary associations and regions; and (c) the individual level which forms the basis of social organisation. Each level of analysis implies its own related set of behaviours forming a complex whole. Actions and reactions in the border area have to be seen as part — not only of the constituent state system, but also in terms of the wider geopolitical milieu. Thus

> a boundary is a secondary phenomenon in relation to the binding power and the bounded objects. To understand the meaning and impact of boundaries we therefore have to look at those systems which end and meet at the boundary and those which overlap or are translated at the boundary. (Lundén 1982, p. 151).

In an impressive empirical exercise Lundén measures the state integrative forces of education, mass communications, and political directives which so powerfully bind people into 'national communities'. He also measures the incidence of trans-border cooperation and contact via telephone calls, postal services, journey-to-work patterns and accessibility to retail and service provision centres in the border region. Despite relative accessibility, and the occasional social overlapping, e.g. marriage patterns and social club membership, communities on either side of the boundary are increasingly socialised to relate to their co-nationals elsewhere in the state, rather than to their physical neighbours across the open border. This trend is accelerated by locational decision-making, the siting of high schools, state supported churches, health clinics and the like. In the highly organised societies of Norway and Sweden policy proposals continually seek to reduce inequality between individuals and regions. Paradoxically, this equalisation often results in growing inequality at the border area, for example, in accessibility and place utility (Lundén, 1973, p. 198). It also influences individual spatial perception and behaviour in a border area whilst predisposing whole communities to re-orientate their activities to cues and promptings which emanate from deep within their respective state system.

Clearly one could cite opposing examples of trans-frontier cooperation and of the weakening of national integration consequent upon increased boundary transformations as in the Friuli-Venetia Julian interaction with Carinthia and Slovenia, or the Alto-Adige case outlined in Strassoldo and Delli Zotti (1982), or in many newly integrated societies in the Third World where irredentist claims are still virulent, as in the Ogaden dispute between Ethiopia and Somalia or in the Kurdish problem. However, the significance of Lundén's pioneering work is that he has both measured and mapped the operation of such processes, rather than merely discussed them in theoretical terms, and has reconstructed the effects

of living in an open border zone on the lifestyle and habitual preferences of such communities. In an increasingly technological
society this emphasis on social responses to space-diminishing processes seems eminently suited to political geographic inquiry concerned with the political effectivness of state integrative forces.

Ethno-regional Inequalities

Information derived from behavioural studies of national integration, such as the perceptions and attitudes of the inhabitants
towards the state, assists in measuring the degree of ethno-regional
support for statehood and state policies. However, alternative
structuralist approaches, based upon aggregate socio-economic
data can highlight regional inequalities and suggest areas of possible
anti-régime resistance, if diffusion hypotheses of political mobilisation are to be believed. Disaffection and opposition, particularly in
Third World states, are held to be aggravated by a combination of
factors, such as regional inequality, mobilised political parties and
a sense of alienation from state directives and actions. Clearly
questions of land tenure, the direction, pace and rewards of development, the desire to be free from the fetters of neo-colonialism are
central in the formation of a revolutionary ideology which seeks to
challenge the ideological and materialist basis of social existence
under capitalism. Evidence of such stirrings abounds, particularly
in Southeast Asia and has been analysed by geographers primarily
through positivistic frameworks. In an informed discussion of the
relationship between economic underdevelopment and political
resistance Lee Yong Leng (1979) cites the examples on Mindanao,
Sabah, Sumatra and the Huk-balahap rebellion in the Philippines
during the 1950s and mid 1960s as reactions to the imbalance of
wealth and regional economic development. Attempts by governments to reduce poverty and economic imbalance may give rise to
frustration and resentment on two grounds. The first is economic:
as patterns of land tenure are modified (albeit too slowly for the
majority) acute frustration is accentuated by the close relationship
between the political élite and the landowning class. In the Philippines Lee Yong Leng suggests that often appropriate land reform
schemes are emasculated by the time they pass through Congress.
The highly skewed pattern of land ownership maintains the rural
peasantry in a permanent dependency situation, consigned by the

system to a precarious status of share-tenancy or a landless existence as occasional workers.

Alternatively government policy aimed at reducing ethno-regional inequality may attack the socio-structural persistance of discrimination. This is particularly apposite in situations where an intrusive ethnic group has benefited from colonialism and modernisation to the disadvantage of the indigenous population. In Malaysia it was the Chinese and Indians who achieved initial advantages during the colonial period. On independence in 1957 it was recognised that long-established patterns of urbanisation, education and employment had created an urban-rural dichotomy along ethnic lines with the Malays in a subordinate position. Various crude attempts at positive discrimination in favour of rural development to equalise opportunities for Malays and to reverse their low socio-economic position have threatened the basis of Malaysian political stability, as Chinese and Indians perceive their position within the new state as increasingly untenable. Watson (1980) demonstrates the impact of positive discrimination in favour of Malays in education and training, particularly at the tertiary level where three new universities were created. Judged by the evidence of the Majid Report (1971), and measured by the increase in the numbers of Malays enrolled in all courses (Tables 4.1 and 4.2) and particularly in science, engineering and medical courses, it can be seen that the pro-Malay policy of Tun Abdul Razak achieved startling results in a short time (Watson, 1980, p. 169).

However successive governments have recognised that positive discrimination bred ethnic resentment which threatened the internal security of the state. Thus the Third Malaysia Plan (1976−80) promoted a national policy of economic reconstruction, regardless of ethnic considerations. Watson reports that through education and economic development some observers see a new Malaysian value system emerging, as the ruling élite become increasingly Malay-educated and Malay-speaking. Though, he cautions, that ethnic harmony itself will depend in great measure on whether or not

the gap between privately educated Chinese and publicly educated Malays grows: whether the socio-economic gap between the bumiputras in the rural areas and those Malaysians living in urban areas can be bridged; and how far Malays will be prepared to recognise Malay-educated, Malay-speaking non-Malays as partners in citizenship (Watson, 1980, p. 171).

Table 4.1: University Student Enrolments by Faculty (1966/76) at University of Malaya (percentages)

Year	Ethnic group	Arts	Science	Engineering	Agriculture	Education	Medicine	Economics and Public Administration
1966/7	Malays	42.5	7.5	1.6	30.3	28.3	15.9	36.8
	Chinese	39.7	81.5	90.0	61.6	46.6	73.6	54.2
	Others	17.8	11.0	8.4	8.1	25.1	10.5	9.0
1970/1	Malays	61.1	11.5	1.3	28.1	53.4	20.3	37.5
	Chinese	26.6	82.0	93.1	64.2	33.3	66.1	48.8
	Others	12.3	6.5	5.6	7.7	13.3	13.6	13.7
1976/7	Malays	71.1	21.9	13.4	86.7	37.2	33.6	68.4
	Chinese	18.6	67.9	81.3	13.3	52.1	56.1	22.2
	Others	10.3	10.2	5.3	—	10.7	10.3	9.4

Source: Majid Report. Reproduced by permission of K. Watson, 'Cultural Pluralism, Nation-Building and Educational Policies in Peninsular Malaysia', *Journal of Multilingual and Multicultural Development, 1* (1980), p. 168.

Table 4.2: Enrolments in Malaysian Tertiary Education by Race
(1970/5)

	Malay	Chinese	Indian	Other	Total
1970					
Diploma and	2865	537	36	19	3457
Certificate courses	(82.9)	(15.5)	(1.8)	(0.6)	
Degree courses	3237	4009	595	307	8148
	(39.7)	(49.2)	(7.3)	(3.8)	
Pre-University courses	520	1141	47	11	1719
	(30.3)	(66.4)	(2.7)	(0.6)	
Totals	6622	5687	678	337	13324
	(49.7)	(42.7)	(5.1)	(2.5)	(100)
1975					
Diploma and	11579	1810	138	20	13547
Certificate courses	(85.4)	(13.4)	(1.0)	(0.2)	
Degree courses	8153	5217	743	141	14254
	(57.2)	(36.6)	(5.2)	(1.0)	
Pre-University courses	815	2751	157	5	3728
	(21.9)	(73.8)	(4.2)	(0.1)	
Totals	20547	9778	1038	166	31529
	(65.1)	(31.1)	(3.3)	(0.5)	(100)

Note: Figures in parentheses are percentages. Reproduced by permission of K.
Watson, 1980, p. 170.

An additional complicating factor is the internal orientation of
those non-Malays who were prepared to make concessions for the
peace of society. Watson speculates on the possibility of increased
enrolments in private Chinese-medium schools leading to divisions
in the Chinese ranks — between the privately Chinese-educated and
the publicly Malay-educated. Lee Yong Leng (1979, p. 347) adds
ironically that in attempting to defuse an economic time bomb,
Malay education and economic policies may be building up another
political time bomb, as the Chinese come to recognise and resent
their periodic exclusion from the opportunities afforded by the new
social structure.

Few sociologists or geographers have sought to trace the spatial
patterns of national integration using multivariate analysis (for
exceptions see Hechter, 1975; Allardt, 1981; and Williams, 1982).
However, Drake (1981) demonstrated the utility of adopting factor
analytical techniques in explaining the spatial pattern of economic
development and national cohesion in Indonesia. Her study sought
to examine the relevance of the core-periphery model to understanding the process of national integration. But instead of validating

the dichotomous core-periphery relationship, her analysis of *per capita* characteristics of the three composite dimensions of integration (socio-cultural, interaction and economic), demonstrated that Java did not exhibit many of the features expected of a national core. Only its principal city, Jakarta, fulfilled anticipated core functions. In many respects the shift in productive capacity away from sugar as a prime export crop (grown on Java) towards petroleum, timber, rubber and tin exploitation on the Outer Islands has changed Indonesia's internal political and economic relationships. Drake's analysis points to the need for state integrative social and economic measures to be promoted in peripheral and marginal regions, particularly West and East Nusatenggara and South-east Sulawesi if fissiparous tendencies are to be discouraged.

Whilst commending the empirical basis and methodological diligence of this type of research we need to consciously assess the primacy given to state stability in national-integration studies. Granted, studies of this type address the question of regional diversity, and demonstrate the nature of pluralism in Third World societies. But too often geographers espouse a statism in their work, derived from a consensus view of political legitimacy and social change. This can lead to an interpretation of ethnic promotion being dysfunctional in the contemporary state. It is but a short step from this to equating limited group self-determination with a threat to state stability in order to preserve the *status quo*. This is especially pressing as political leaders themselves face the same sort of dilemma in promoting territorial unity. Smith has framed the dilemma thus:

> to preserve the fragile state and its artificially-created territorial domain, the leaders must centralise the means of administration and coercion, and place a heavy emphasis upon the inviolability of the territorial *status quo* and the need for political order. On the other side . . . to inspire people to make sacrifices for the ideals of development and national dignity, to get them to raise productivity, man institutions effectively and improve a weak infrastructure, the masses need to be mobilised and educated and politicised. But mobilisation and politicisation may well rekindle the fires of ethnic conflict. . . . Therefore to tap the sources of popular zeal and commitment can jeopardise the stability and integrity of recently formed states, which have no real basis in popular assent (Smith, 1983, p. 128).

If this is a major problem for the emergent states which espouse citizen equality, it is even more fundamental for political control in states which have institutionalised discrimination within their constitutional and economic framework. A particularly good example of the institutionalisation of group inequality under the law is South Africa.

The paradox and tragedy of 'separate development' continue to occupy the attention of the international academic community, let alone reluctant participants in the apartheid process. In the main, geographers have concentrated on methodologies and empirical analyses of several universal socio-economic processes, seeking to explain how such processes are modified in a Southern Africa context. Detailed studies are available on urbanisation in Southern Africa (Kay, 1970; Davis, 1972) modernisation and industrial development (Bell, 1973), together with comprehensive geographic texts on the region (Christopher, 1982). Other studies covering the African continent have substantial southern African contributions (Knight and Newman, 1976).

In describing and explaining apartheid's influence on the internal structure of the state and of the relationship between its constituent groups, geographers have concentrated on four main issues. First they have sought to outline the problems involved in homeland consolidation and securing appropriate capitals for the homelands (Best and Young, 1972a, 1972b). Secondly, they have attempted to measure rates of change in internal migration and urbanisation patterns both within the homelands and between the homelands and the rest of South Africa. For example, Smit, Olivier and Booysen (1982) demonstrate the dependent nature of homeland settlement. Most of the new towns lack an economic base and function as dormitory towns for white urban areas. Such towns have little functional connection with their hinterland and are typified as 'islands in a sea of underdevelopment'. The artificiality of their settlement structure is also clearly indicated in several chapters in Smith, D.M. (1982). Migrant labour, both the keystone and Achilles's heel of apartheid, has received due attention, most notably by Lemon (1980) who argues that the need for a skilled Black labour force to underpin a dynamic economy creates problems for the satisfaction of apartheid's ideological commitment to racial segregation at both macro- and micro-levels. Tension between the ideological and economic forces within the state can be mediated in a number of ways. One is to guarantee urban Blacks their Section 10 (1) (b) rights to residence under the Riekert Report's recommendations allowing domicile rights to those who had worked for one employer for an unbroken period of ten years (Lemon, 1982, p. 87), thus creating the possibility of a permanent Black middle class and widening the gap between the 'haves' and 'have-nots' with respect to Section 10 rights. A second thrust is to transfer the social costs of labour repro- duction (identified by Lemon, 1982, p. 89 as education of workers' children, social services, housing of squatters, welfare benefits, etc.) from 'white' South Africa to the 'independent' states. This would guarantee the availability of migrant labour for the industrial needs of South Africa but displace costs and problems on to the shoulders of township governments within the homelands. The concept of frontier community, developed by Lemon (1982), is one of the most instructive developments in the field for it articu- lates the 'inequity of locating labour supplies in distinct geo- graphical areas, at considerable inconvenience and cost to the people concerned, and then shedding responsibility for those areas by decreeing them to be part of independent states' (Lemon, 1982, p. 87).

Thirdly, geographers have demonstrated the persistence and functional necessity to apartheid of urban racial segregation. At a general level Smith (1982) analysed the role of urbanisation in changing both the racial composition and class construction of the relationship between whites, coloureds and Blacks in South Africa. Of particular import is his treatment of race and class in tandem, as simultaneous processes, for the development of a coloured bour- geoisie and a Black urban home-owning class threatens the privilege of whites. Inevitably the system's creation of a skilled African labour force has threatened to undermine the status of the white working class as a labour aristocracy. Spatially, industrial employ- ment demands on the Black labour force have produced sponta- neous settlements, e.g. Crossroads, in locations deemed to be 'white' territory. Economic factors continue to cut across the ideal of apartheid's separate development plan. As Smith argues 'apart- heid may remain functional to capitalism for some time to come, but the state is likely to find it increasingly difficult to handle the tensions generated by the interplay between the traditional inter- racial antagonisms and the emerging trans-racial class alignments' (Smith, 1982, p. 45).

The link between structural patterns and individual experience is also becoming evident in geographic research on South Africa.

Preston-Whyte (1982) focuses on the functions of racial separation in maintaining white supremacy. Her analysis of the racial ecology of Durban stresses the economic importance of service personnel in white areas. Despite being shunned as 'social beings' she claims that Blacks have adapted to working and living in white areas without succumbing to their employers' paternalism. An analysis of township life indicates that non-resident domestic servants can create an atmosphere of mutual collective support and a relative autonomy denied to resident domestic servants. It is quite another question of course to ask to what extent they perceive themselves able to change aspects of their present existence so that their mutual support could become anything other than the desolate comforting the desolate.

Fourthly, some geographers have sought to demonstrate within the context of South Africa that space is more than a 'given'; it is a resource also, capable of being used for political and ideological ends. Western's (1982) treatment of Cape Coloureds in Capetown tackles this question of spatial manipulation head on. He takes issue with the conventional critique of spatial relations as deriving from social positions rather than vice versa i.e. that space is merely the mirror of society. His claim is that the ruling racial oligarchy maintains its hegemony by as many means as possible, including spatial means, and cites the use of the Group Areas Act to examine this contention. Clearly the Cape Coloureds' position over the past thirty years has been eroded by laws passed by whites. 'Not coincidentally, at the same time coloureds were being distanced in social relations, their place in spatial relations was changing also: from limited overlap with white residential areas to the passive reflection of social change or that *human social relations are also space forming*' (Western, 1981, p. 7). Another reflection of such spatial changes occurs in territorial bonding. When Non-whites are resettled, the white government, claims Western, has achieved its aim, because a 'cowed and atomised mass of Non-whites has been placed at a "safe" distance' (Western, 1981, p. 7). But as Soweto demonstrated, Non-whites may defend their 'ghettoised space' as a reaction to the distancing forced upon them. This produces a government counter-reaction which sets in train a policy of continued removal to forbid place-specific identification. 'Otherwise, the hand that endeavoured to manipulate space may find it has used an uncontrollable tool. A contradiction can arise in time: Society's rulers create an apartheid space, and space is used for domination; yet, subsequently the dominated may begin to find in space an ally in challenging the domination' (Western, 1981, p. 7). His work is replete with insights and explanations which not only improve the outsider's understanding of apartheid in operation, but also impart a feeling of the remarkably bleak daily round of most Capetownians. Tension, fear and repression call from each situation and make the volume indispensable reading for political geographers. Whilst undoubtedly economic issues will continue to dominate geographic research within Southern Africa (Beavon and Rogerson, 1981) there are signs that some geographers recognise the need to go beyond the 'economic basis of discrimination' and enlarge upon Western's concern with political conflict. Wellings and McCarthy's (1983) critique calls for greater attention to, and involvement in, such issues as 'transport boycotts, rent struggles, patterns of resistance to "resettlement" and conflict in general with the state over that component of the "social wage" that receives expression in urban infrastructure and amenities' (p. 341). They warn that unless positivist researchers recognise the fundamental political and exploitative nature of the processes that they study they are 'likely to remain imprisoned within the most restrictive of "iron cages" to understanding' (p. 342). In consequence of these realisations some have called for the 'decolonisation of the existing colonial geographies and attitudes concerning Southern Africa' (Crush *et al.*, 1982, p. 197) and for a shift away from modernisation theory because the 'rejection of diffusionism and its attendant modes of spatial fetishism is. . .a crucial facet of geography's "decolonisation" ' (Wellings and McCarthy, 1983, p. 340). This is a major programme of action critical to the development of a more autonomous scholarly position within Southern Africa.

Conclusion

This review has highlighted the need for greater research on the role of the state in its interaction with minority communities, for it is this struggle that forms the basis of ethnic politics. Whilst great potential is seen in a materialist theory of the state which stresses ideology and conflict, over and above consensus theory and liberalism, care should be taken not to dismiss the actions of ethnic minority members as merely reactive urges to the dictates of the modern state, or to reduce the origins of ethnic activism to a social class formulation. Given the current interest and talent evident in recent geographic

writings on ethnicity and the state we may conclude with the promise
of more interesting work in the future.

References

Aarebrot, F.H. (1982) 'On the Structural Basis of Regional Mobilization in Europe'
in B. de Marchi and A.M. Boileau (eds.), *Boundaries and Minorities in Western
Europe*, Franco Angeli Editore, Milan, pp. 32–91
Agnew, J.A. (1981) 'Structural and Dialectical Theories of Political Regionalism' in
A.D. Burnett and Taylor, P.J. (eds.), *Political Studies from Spatial Perspectives*,
John Wiley, London, pp. 275–90
Allardt, E. (1979) 'Implications of the Ethnic Revival in Modern, Industrial Society',
Commentationes Scientarium Socialium, 12
—— (1981) 'Ethnic Mobilization and Minority Resource', *Zeitschrift für Soziologie*,
10, 427–37
—— (1981) 'Reflections on Stein Rokkan's Conceptual Map of Europe', *Scandina-
vian Political Studies*, 4, 257–71
Beavon, K.S.O. and Rogerson, C.M. (1981) 'Trekking On: Recent Trends in the
Human Geography of Southern Africa', *Progress in Human Geography*, *5*,
159–89
Bell, T. (1973) *Industrial Decentralisation in South Africa*, Oxford University Press,
Cape Town
Best, A.C.G. and Young, B.S. (1972) 'Capitals for the Homelands', *Journal for
Geography*, *3*, 1043–55
—— (1972b) 'Homeland Consolidation: the case of KwaZulu', *South African
Geographer*, *4*, 63–74
Boal, F.W. and Douglas, J.N. (eds.) (1982) *Integration and Division: Geographical
Perspectives on the Northern Ireland Problem*, Academic Press, London
Braudel, F. (1977) *Afterthoughts on Material Civilization and Capitalism*, Johns
Hopkins University Press, Baltimore
Breuilly, J. (1982) *Nationalism and the State*, Manchester University Press,
Manchester
Burnett, A.D. and Taylor, P.J. (eds.) (1981) *Political Studies from Spatial Perspec-
tives*, John Wiley, London
Carter, G. and O'Meara, P. (eds.) *Southern Africa: The Continuing Crisis*,
Macmillan, London
Christopher, A.J. (1982) *South Africa*, Longman, London
Crush, J., Reitsma, H. and Rogerson, C. (eds.) 'Decolonizing the Human Geog-
raphy of South Africa', *Tijdschrift voor Economische en Sociale Geografie*, *73*,
whole issue
Davies, R.J. (1972) *The Urban Geography of South Africa*, Institute of Social
Research, Durban
Day, A. (ed.) (1982) *Border and Territorial Disputes*, Longman, London
de Marchi, B. and Boileau, A.M. (eds.) (1982) *Boundaries and Minorities in Western
Europe*, Franco Angeli Editore, Milan
Drakakis-Smith, D. and Williams, S.W. (eds.) (1983) *Internal Colonialism: Essays
Around a Theme*, Developing Areas Study Group Publication, Salford
Drake, C. (1981) The Spatial Pattern of National Integration in Indonesia, *Transac-
tions, Institute of British Geographers*, *6*, 471–90
Fouere, Y. (1980) *Towards a Federal Europe*, Christopher Davies, Swansea
Gottmann, J. (ed.) (1980) *Centre and Periphery: Spatial Variations in Politics*, Sage,
London

150   Minority Groups in the Modern State

Haugen, E. *et al.* (eds.) (1981) *Minority Languages Today*, Edinburgh University Press, Edinburgh

Hechter, M. (1975) *Internal Colonialism: The Celtic Fringe in British National Development*, Routledge and Kegan Paul, London

—— (1983) 'Internal Colonialism Revisited' in D. Drakakis-Smith and S.W. Williams (eds.), *Internal Colonialism: Essays Around a Theme*, Developing Areas Study Group Publication, Salford

—— and Levi, M. (1979) 'The Comparative Analysis of Ethnoregional Movements', *Ethnic and Racial Studies*, *2*, 260–74

Kay, G. (1970) *Rhodesia: A Human Geography*, Africana Publishing, New York

Knight, G.C. and Newman, J.L. (eds.) (1976) *Contemporary Africa*, Prentice-Hall, London

Krejci, J. and Velimsky, V. (1981) *Ethnic and Political Nations in Europe*, Croom Helm, London

Lee Yong Leng (1979) 'Southeast Asia: The Political Geography of Economic Imbalance', *Tijdschrift voor Economische en Sociale Geografie*, *70*, 339–49

Lemon, A. (1980) 'Migrant Labour in Western Europe and South Africa' in A. Lemon and N.C. Pollock (eds.), *Studies in Overseas Settlement and Population*, Longman, London

—— (1982) 'Migrant Labour and Frontier Commuters: Reorganizing South Africa's Black Labour Supply' in D.M. Smith (ed.), *Living Under Apartheid*, George Allen and Unwin, London

Lincoln, D. (1982) 'State, Capital and the Reserve Consolidation Issue in South Africa', *Tijdschrift voor Economische en Sociale Geografie*, *73*, 229–36

Lundén, T. (1973) *Individens Rumsliga Beteende i eft Gränsomrade*, Kulturgeografiska Institutionen, Stockholm

—— (1980) 'Language, Geography and Social Development in Norden', *Discussion Papers in Geolinguistics*, *3*

—— (1982) 'Linguistic Minorities in Boundary Areas: The Case of Northern Europe', in B. de Marchi and A.M. Boileau (eds.), *Boundaries and Minorities in Western Europe*, Franco Angeli Editore, Milan, pp. 149–63

Meinig, D.W. (1983) 'Geography as an Art', *Transactions, Institute of British Geographers*, *8*, 314–29

McCann, L.D. (ed.) (1982) *Heartland and Hinterland*, Prentice-Hall, Scarborough, Canada

Mabogunje, A.L. (1980) 'The Dynamics of Centre-Periphery Relations: The Need for a New Geography of Resource Development', *Transactions, Institute of British Geographers*, *5*, 277–96

Moore, B. (1966) *Social Origins of Dictatorship and Democracy*, Beacon, Boston, Massachusetts

Nairn, T. (1981) *The Break-Up of Britain*, Verso, London

O'Keefe, P. (ed.) (1983) 'South Africa in the Global Division of Labour', *Antipode*, *15*, whole issue

Orridge, A.W. (1979) *Structural Preconditions and Triggering Factors in the Development of European Sub-State Nationalism*, P.S.A. conference paper, Sheffield

—— (1981) 'Uneven Development and Nationalism', *Political Studies*, *29*, 1–15, 181–90

—— and Williams, C.H. (1982) 'Autonomist Nationalism: A Theoretical Framework for Spatial Variations in its Genesis and Development', *Political Geography Quarterly*, *1*, 19–39

Pearson, R. (1983) *National Minorities in Eastern Europe, 1848–1945*, Macmillan, London

Pettman, R. (1979) *State and Class*, Croom Helm, London

Pirie, G.H., Rogerson, C.M. and Beavon, K.S.O. (1980) 'Covert Power in South Africa: The Geography of the Afrikaner Broederband', *Area*, *12*, 97–104

Pocock, D.C.D. (1979) 'The Novelist's Image of the North', *Transactions, Institute of British Geographers, 4*, 62–77

Poggi, G. (1978) *The Development of the Modern State*, Hutchinson, London

Preston-Whyte, E. (1982) 'Segregation and Interpersonal Relationships: A Case Study of Domestic Service in Durban' in D.M. Smith (ed.), *Living Under Apartheid*, George Allen and Unwin, London

Pryce, W.T.R. (1982) 'The Idea of Culture in Human Geography' in E. Grant and P. Newby (eds.), *Landscape and Industry*, Middlesex Polytechnic, London

Rogerson, C.M. and Beavon, K.S.O. (1982) 'Getting By in the "Informal Sector" of Soweto', *Tijdschrift voor Economische en Sociale Geografie, 73*, 250–65

Rokkan, S. (1980) 'Territories, Centres and Peripheries' in J. Gottman (ed.), *Centre and Periphery*, Sage, London, pp. 163–204

—— and Urwin, D.W. (eds.) (1982) *The Politics of Territorial Identity*, Sage, London

Smith, A.D. (1981) *The Ethnic Revival*, Cambridge University Press, Cambridge

—— (1982) 'Nationalism, Ethnic Separatism and the Intelligentsia' in C.H. Williams (ed.), *National Separatism*, University of Wales Press, Cardiff, pp. 17–42

—— (1983) *State and Nation in the Third World*, Wheatsheaf Books, Brighton

Smith, D.M. (1978) Involuntary Population Movement in South Africa, *Area, 10*, 87–8

—— (ed.) (1982) *Living Under Apartheid*, George Allen and Unwin, London

Stone, J. (1979) Special Issue on Internal Colonialism. *Ethnic and Racial Studies, 2*, 3

Strassoldo, R. and Delli Zotti, G. (eds.) (1982) *Cooperation and Conflict in Border Areas*, Franco Angeli Editore, Milan

Tägil, S. ed., (1977) 'Studying Boundary Conflicts', *Lund Studies in International History*, Lund University, Sweden

Taylor, P.J. (1981) 'Political Geography and the World Economy' in A.D. Burnett and P.J. Taylor (eds.), *Political Studies from Spatial Perspectives*, John Wiley, London, pp. 157–72

—— (1982) 'A Materialist Framework for Political Geography', *Transactions, Institute of British Geographers, 7*, 15–34

Wallerstein, I. (1977) 'Patterns of Development of the Modern World System', *Review, 1*

Watson, J.K.P. (1980) 'Cultural Pluralism, Nation-Building and Educational Policies in Pennisular Malaysia', *Journal of Multilingual and Multicultural Development, 1*, 155–75

Wellings, P.A. and McCarthy, J.J. (1983) 'Whither Southern African Human Geography', *Area, 15*, 337–45

Western, J. (1981) *Outcast Cape Town*, George Allen and Unwin, London

Williams, C.H. (1977) 'Ethnic Perceptions of Acadia', *Cahiers de Geographie de Québec, 21*, 243–68

—— (1980) 'Ethnic Separatism in Western Europe', *Tijdchrift voor Economische er Sociale Geografie, 71*, 142–58

—— (1981) 'On Culture Space: Perceptual Culture Regions in Wales', *Études Celtiques, 18*, 273—96

—— (ed.) (1982) *National Separatism*, University of Wales Press, Cardiff

—— and Smith, A.D. (1983) 'The National Construction of Social Space', *Progress in Human Geography, 7*, no. 42

William, G. (1980) 'Review of E. Allardt's Implications of the Ethnic Revival in Modern, Industrial Society', *Journal of Multilingual and Multicultural Development, 1*, 363–70

—— and Roberts, C. (1981) 'Language and Social Structure in Welsh Education' in J. Megarry (ed.), *World Yearbook of Education: Education Minorities*, Kogan Page, London, pp. 147–63

Williams, G.A. (1982) *The Welsh in their History*, Croom Helm, London

5   LOCAL GOVERNMENT AND THE STATE

R.J. Johnston

A system of local governments is characteristic of most states. Each local government provides services for the population of a defined territory, raises at least some of its revenue from the residents and/or land users within that territory, and is accountable to others — to the central government that provides the legislative framework within which local governments operate and, in many cases, to the electorate within its territory. Because of the accountability, within any system there are both common elements and differences; local governments exist to perform certain functions, but interpret their roles differently because of variations in the constituency served.

There is no substantial tradition of work on local government by geographers — in part because of the relatively low level of interest in political geography and the focus of the few political geographers on the larger-scale spatial phenomenon of the nation-state. There has been some interest in the definition of local government boundaries — stretching back to Fawcett's (1919) work and continued by Freeman (1968) — and a major function of local government in many countries, land use planning, has been a topic of investigation (not least because of its role as a potential employer of geographers). In recent years, the growing realisation among geographers that the state is a central element in the production of spatial structures, and the consequent rejuvenation of political geography (Taylor, 1977), has focused attention on local government.

In developing work on local government, mainly during the 1970s, geographers have drawn on studies in other disciplines, especially those which displayed the same philosophy of social science that characterised the 'new' geography of the time. The emphasis was on work that sought generalisations, that identified — usually statistically — cause-effect relationships. Geographers promoted a particular perspective — that of the role of space as an influence; they sought to explain variations in local government activity and to improve efficiency in state operations (Johnston, 1981). More recently, geographers have become aware of the relative poverty of understanding that results from their sophisticated descriptions of what is done where, and with what it is correlated. Arguments that understanding requires a theoretical appreciation of the nature of local government have led to explorations of theories of the state and of the role of local government within the state apparatus.

This chapter reflects the two strands of work identified in the previous paragraph, and it reviews the current situation regarding geographical analyses of local government. ('Geographical' is not used to confine the discussion to work by 'professed' geographers. The review covers all work within the context that geographers currently adopt.) Thus after a brief discussion of definitions, the chapter deals first with work analysing spatial variations in local government activity. The argument is then introduced that such work treats local governments, and those who operate them, as independent actors. Two brief case studies are used to indicate the constraints — both economic and political — upon independent action; these lead into discussions of the functions of the state in modern society and of the roles allocated to local government. The aim, therefore, is to illustrate both the diversity of geographical work on this topic in recent years and the major differences in approach that follow from the adoption of separate perspectives.

Some Definitional Preliminaries

Before proceeding further, it is necessary to establish clear definitions of the major terms being used in this chapter. *The state* is defined here as a sovereign body, whose existence, territorial limits, and (accepted) power over its citizens are widely, if not universally, recognised, both within and without. Virtually all states contain some dissidents who question the use of sovereign powers (and most states take a spatial solution; they confine the dissidents). Many states are in some dispute with others, too — over the extent of their sovereign territories, for example. But in general, a state is a fixed territory, within which, and on behalf of whose population, power is wielded by a recognised government, that rules with the (apparent) consent of the population and whose right to rule is respected by the governments of other states. *A local government* is also a bounded territorial unit, administered by an accepted authority (which may be elected). It differs from the state in one crucial respect — it lacks any sovereign status and therefore any independence of existence; it is there because the central government allows it to be. It has been created, and can be modified, even removed, by the central government. (There are usually constitutional and legal controls on central-local government relationships, but since only the former, as the sovereign body, has the power to alter those controls it alone is the repository of ultimate power. The situation is slightly different in federal states.)

The relationship between central and local governments is that between a dominant and a series of subordinate bodies, therefore. This does not mean that local government is merely an administrative arm of the state (though it could be, if the central government so decrees). The concept of local government implies some local freedom in deciding who shall rule, and how that rule will be exercised. But because of its sovereign status, the central government has the power to interfere in and with that local freedom.

Recently, a third term has been introduced to the literature — the *local state*. This term was apparently coined by Cockburn (1977), who identified local government as being one part of a unitary body, the state: 'our local councils don't spring from some ancient right of self-government but are, and under capitalism have always been, an aspect of national government which in turn is a part of the state (p. 2)'. This is little more than a strong statement of the dependent relationship between local and central government. The term local state implies an equivalence on the crucial element of sovereignty, however, and its use is widely criticised (even when it is defined as 'any non-sovereign body concerned with the government of a constituent area of a sovereign state': Johnston, 1982a, p. 183). There has been a considerable debate on this terminology (see Dear, 1981; Dear and Clark, 1981; Paris, 1983). Saunders (1982) concludes from it that 'to talk of a "local state" . . . is simply misleading' (p. 65). This is the position taken here: local government refers to the operation of local administration, set within the context defined by the central government, the recognised administration of the sovereign body, the state.

Local Government in Action

Local government operates those aspects of state policy that the central government considers should be administered within subareas of the national territory. In addition, it undertakes activities which the local residents (via the local administrators) consider desirable, and which are not denied to it by central legislation. (There are differences between countries in control of the latter function. In some, local governments can only do that which is allocated to them in law — anything else is *ultra vires* — whereas in others they can undertake any tasks that are not proscribed in law.)

The diversity of functions undertaken by local governments is great (as illustrated in the list of those undertaken in England since 1974; Richards, 1973). In general terms, these relate to: the maintenance of law and order; the provision of various social services (health, education, welfare etc.); and the control of nuisances and the planning of an orderly pattern of land use.

Geographical concerns with the local government cover a variety of topics, such as the spatial conformity between local government boundaries and the extent of a built-up area/urban region. Recently, much attention has focused on two topics: inter-government variations in activity — which services are provided, and to what extent; and intra-government spatial variations in service provision. Both of these areas are heavily populated; neither has produced clear conclusions.

Inter-government Variations

It is a commonplace observation in most countries that some local governments spend more on certain services than do others. This in itself provides material to be mapped and analysed, with the analyses increasingly focusing on general models of the determinants of spending (some of which are reviewed in Johnston, 1979, 1983a). The independent variables in such models almost invariably include indices of:

(1) *Need*: the greater the local demand/need for a service, the more likely it is to be provided and the greater the level of spending on that service.
(2) *Resources*: the greater the volume of resources available to a local government, the better able it is to meet the demands made of it.
(3) *Political inclinations*: the more favourably inclined those in political power are towards both a particular service and those who benefit from it, the more likely that the service will be provided and the greater the spending on it.

This model has much to commend it in general terms. (For general reviews of its use see, *inter alia*, Fried, 1975; Kirby and Pinch, 1983; Knox, 1982a.) Its first two variables suggest the operation of general demand/supply considerations (hence the economic models presented and tested by Nicholson and Topham, 1971), whereas the third introduces the role of local political actors as interpreters of what is needed and should/can be supplied. (Although the usual format in which the models are tested implies that similar people will always react in similar ways.) But the model is extremely difficult to operationalise, for two sets of reasons.

First, there are problems of *measurement*. How, for example, are needs to be measured? What are the 'needs' for a police service, or a library service, or various paramedical services? In general terms, it could be argued that, for example, the need for a police service reflects the crime rate, but there is an element of circular reasoning here (as well as problems of defining crime). Most studies represent the needs for a service by a surrogate measure, such as the size of the target group. For some services this is sensible — the age group 5–16 represents the 'demand' for a compulsory education service in Britain, for example, although there are problems with regard to the proportions of children who are educated outside the public sector and of those who need special provision. For others, it is less so; the age group 65 and over may contain all those eligible for certain services, but their needs for those services can vary substantially — according to age, health, wealth etc.

With resources, the problems of measurement are in general less than they are with needs. Most local governments have a given resource base, reflecting the taxation and other powers allowed to them by the central state. Thus for local governments that raise their revenue from a property tax, the value of local real estate indicates their resource base, whereas for those that rely on a local income tax it is the incomes of their residents that provide the relevant source. For both, the size of the resource base is also a foundation on which they might borrow. (For general treatments of this subject, see Bennett, 1980, 1982.)

Finally, there are measurement problems with regard to political inclinations. For example, it is generally assumed in Britain that local governments with the Labour Party in political control favour high levels of spending, whereas those with the Conservative Party in control do not. This, however, conceals considerable variations within each party (a paternalistic Labour district council in the south of England is very different from an aggressively socialist one in

South Yorkshire) and fails to take into account other contextual variables. Local governments in large cities have greater demands placed upon them because of the high-order central place functions that they have to perform, relative to those in smaller towns, for example. And high spending might be required of certain Conservative-dominated local councils by their constituents, because this provides a necessary base for local business — as in tourist resorts, for example (see Newton, 1982). There is also the issue of the electoral mandate. Does a party with a small majority on a local council introduce its partisan policies regardless of possible future electoral defeat; does a party only act in particular ways when it has a secure electoral (or other?) majority; or does a party only act on certain issues when it seems as if the probable beneficiaries could swing the election result (Johnston, 1979)?

The second set of problems refers to *model specification*. In particular, there are problems of collinearity among the three sets of independent variables. Districts with high levels of demand for certain services, particularly those social and other services from which the relatively poor benefit most, tend also to be those: (a) with relatively poor resource bases on which to draw to provide those services; and (b) strong political inclinations to provide the services. Disentangling the relative importance of such closely linked sets of variables in multivariate statistical analyses is far from easy (Johnston, 1983a).

Given all of these problems, it is not surprising that the many studies of inter-government variations are far from unanimous in their conclusions. Indeed, reworkings of the same materials, using slightly different methods, have been undertaken in the hope of confirming one point of view and disproving another (as in Fenton and Chamberlayne, 1969). In very general terms the model provides a reasonable fit, especially with regard to the first two sets of variables. The greater the needs and the greater the resources, the greater the spending; local governments provide more where more is needed, if they can afford it. (Even so, the use of correlations in such work can obscure the detail. A high positive correlation between need for a service and spending on it could nevertheless — if the standardised regression slope is substantially less than 1.0 — mean that, per recipient of the service, spending declines with increasing levels of need.) All of this is perhaps somewhat unsurprising.

What is much more in doubt is the importance of the political set of variables. Many studies find little or no relationship between the nature of party control and levels of spending — holding needs and resources constant. In part, this is because political interpretations of the desirability of meeting needs can vary — as outlined above. In part, also, it reflects the operation of other variables. In the USA, for example, there is considerable debate over whether low levels of welfare spending in the southern States reflect poor resources, the electoral safety of incumbent governments, or the racism of white-dominated power elites in areas where blacks are the main beneficiaries of welfare (see Johnston, 1983a). The level of aggregation of the studies is crucial; analyses of particular services suggest that local governments dominated by left-wing politicians are more favourable to high levels of spending in personal services (education, health, social services) whereas those run by right-wing politicians are inclined to favour property-related services (e.g. fire, police). Even so, politicians are not the only influences on the level of spending — the bureaucrats play a crucial role in many places, in their structuring of the political agenda. (See the examples referred to in Johnston, 1982a, pp. 229–31.)

Intra-government Variations

Some of the services provided by a local government are targetted at the entire population; others are aimed at particular client groups only. Whether every member of the potential user-group is equally well served depends upon a variety of factors. Among these, and of particular interest to geographers, are policies with regard to the spatial allocation of services.

Some publicly provided services are equally available to all (a good example is a national defence strategy against potential outside invaders) whereas others are equally available to all providing that they have the wherewithal to benefit from the service (as with a national public broadcasting system). But many — probably most — are 'biased' in their availability, because of where they are provided.

Three types of public goods and services can be identified (Johnston, 1982b):

(1) *Pure public goods*, which are equally available to all. There is no spatial variation in their provision within the territory concerned.

(2) *Impure public goods*, which are provided at fixed locations, and therefore are more beneficial to certain groups — in the vast

majority of cases those who live near to the locations — than to others. Many local government services — parks, libraries, bus routes — occupy fixed locations, from which, given the well-known frictional effect of distance hampering use of a facility, local residents benefit more than those who live further away. People manipulate the property market to benefit from these impure public goods, which involves using land-use controls, that almost invariably also come within the province of local governments (Johnston, 1980a, 1984a).

(3) *Impurely distributed public goods*, which are not provided at fixed locations only but which are distributed unequally. Police services may be unevenly distributed, for example, with certain areas receiving a higher level of policing than others; so might educational services, with the quality of provision varying from place to place.

Attention naturally focuses on the last two categories.

In terms of analysis, there has been much concern with the determinants of the spatial allocation policies operated by local governments (general reviews include Rich, 1979, 1982a, 1982b; Kirby, 1983; Knox, 1983). A modification of the inter-government variations model provides a popular overall framework for such work — although the resources variable is usually irrelevant because local governments do not have spatially varying property or income taxes operating within their territories. Thus it is suggested, as an ideal against which reality can be compared, that the distribution of a service should reflect the spatial pattern of need. Once again, there is the problem of defining and measuring need. Also, it is hypothesised that political variables may influence which areas get what services reflecting, *inter alia*, the impact of local (ward or district) elected representatives on the allocation procedures, the inclination of a party with political control in a local government to favour the areas which return it to power, and the importance politicians attach to wooing votes in marginal areas.

Testing this model is not straightforward, and the plethora of empirical studies set at least partially within that framework is far from unequivocal in its findings. Particular attention has been paid to the political variable, but there is little that can be generalised from the findings. Some claim to show a clear political bias; others say that there is none. Methodological difficulties abound. Many of the services discussed are provided both for residential and non-residential land users (as with fire and police services, for example), so that it is difficult to identify needs, and then to portion those out to see whether political influences have 'distorted' the distribution. Analysts just cannot agree. (A recent example — pro political influence — is Bolotin and Cingranelli, 1983.) Of course, this may be simply because in some situations there have been political influences, whereas in others there have not. (On this topic, more generally, see Johnston, 1980b, and Rundquist, 1982.) There is, however, one area in which political influence has been proven in many cases, beyond any doubt. This is the link between racial residential segregation on the one hand and unequal service provision on the other. South African cities show it at its sharpest, but there is also a long history of it in American cities, as successful court actions have shown (Johnston, 1984a).

In the field of intra-government variations, more so than with inter-government variations, it is possible for client groups to seek influence over the allocation policies. They can, for example, collectively protest against certain decisions and petition that others be made, or they can make individual contacts with the decision-makers — thereby hoping to influence, both positively and negatively, what is put where. (Reviews of the literature regarding protesting and petitioning are provided in Burnett, 1981; Burnett, Cole and Moon, 1983: see also Cox and Johnston, 1982.) Whether they are successful depends on many factors, among them the electoral and political importance of the protesters, their ability to manipulate the local political system (on this, see Saunders, 1980), and the efficacy of the individuals contacted. Again, no invariant relationships have been uncovered in analyses of the efficacy of various types of protest activity.

Rather than seek influence over allocation policies via political activity, individuals can instead adjust their locations to the existing allocations (Orbell and Uno, 1972). Thus people wishing a public park in their locality might choose a home with that in mind. Others may move in order to get the package of public goods that they require (Tiebout, 1956; Clark, 1981); a family may, for example, seek to move into the catchment area of a desirable school. But households vary in their ability to rewrite the social geography of an area in this way. In the private housing market, the competitive bidding process excludes people from certain desirable areas; in the public sector, allocation policies are difficult to counter without certain criteria being met (Taylor, 1979). Thus many have to accept their particular location within the geography of public-service provision.

From Functional Description to Realistic Explanation

The literature just reviewed is typical of the positivist approach to social science, which has a strong (if often implicit) determinist element. Observed events and patterns are examples of general laws and tendencies. The events — and the constellation of events that produce a spatial pattern — may be unique (there is no other quite like any one of them) but they are not singular. There are general processes operating, and these combine in different ways to produce unique events. Thus the latter can be explained, providing that we know the laws. The empirical studies discussed above use sets of events to provide the evidence from which the laws can be derived. Given success, the result will be that history is post-dictable, and the future is predictable.

There are several objections to this philosophy of social science. One is that it — usually implicitly — derogates human decision-making power, and posits a human automaton responding to given stimuli in a pre-programmed manner. (Sometimes the response is not as predicted, which means either that the model is not yet properly specified or that the decision-maker has acted irrationally!) A second objection is that it is essentially a static approach, for it cannot incorporate change. Finally, although the approach may be more than adequate as a description of empirical realities (a useful description, none the less; needs, resources and political inclinations do influence people's perceptions of and decisions about who gets what, where) it offers no valid answers to questions such as: why have local governments?; why have the particular local governments that we have?

Two Case Studies

Examples of the force of these criticisms can be given by recent events in Britain and the USA, in each of which there has developed what has been dubbed by some as a 'local fiscal crisis' (see Sharpe, 1981). The models of inter-government spending discussed above are relative only: they can suggest why some local governments spend more on service x that others, but cannot say why total spending is z rather than zt.

A major influence on why spending is only $z is external to the local government itself. This is illustrated by the fiscal crisis of New York City in the 1970s. There, while the resource base was substantial the provision of services grew, with little political debate over the distribution. Then, from about 1963 on, resource availability began to grow more slowly and there was considerable political controversy over budget allocations — in which two constituencies, the trade unions representing the service providers and the local minority groups representing increasingly active claimants, were particularly involved. Meeting their claims put increased strains on the local resource base, and on the ability to use this base to underwrite loans (Ziegler, 1981). As economic decline set in, and the base was further eroded — in part by fiscal migration of businesses away from New York — so the City became increasingly unable to support such demands from claimants. Indeed, it was close to bankruptcy, and was only saved after 1975 by a 'business takeover' which insisted on what the banks saw as prudent fiscal policies (similar to those imposed by the IMF on impoverished national governments; Johnston, 1982a.) Local political independence was thus transitory, and ultimately subservient to business interests (David and Kantor, 1979).

In Britain, the unwillingness of the central government to give local governments taxing powers on other than property values has long resulted in a situation in which the local governments are unable to raise sufficient revenues to meet increased demands (Newton, 1981, provides a good discussion of the 'fiscal squeeze'). Thus, the central government has found itself obliged to provide much of the needed revenue, in the form of grants (Bennett, 1981, 1982). The formulae used in the grant allocation procedure encouraged spending, so that although the central government only contributed a fixed percentage of the estimated total expenditure there was considerable incentive to local governments to pursue their political inclinations and meet perceived needs.

As problems of economic recession increased during the 1970s, so central governments became more concerned about the size of the grant to local governments and the total volume of local spending. Measures were sought to restrict local autonomy, and the Conservative government (elected in 1979) introduced a new grant procedure (see Bennett, 1982) which: (a) determines what the total expenditure of each local government should be; (b) fixes what proportion of that will be met by a central grant; and (c) penalises (by the withdrawal of grant) those local governments that overshoot the centrally defined target. In this way, the central government — despite an explicitly stated belief in local democracy and autonomy (Duncan and Goodwin, 1980) — promotes its economic policies (based on the assumed equation between reduced public spending, reduced public borrowing, lower interest rates and, therefore, industrial investment) by constraining local governments. Directives to the latter have been issued that not only remove fiscal autonomy but elements of other decision-making autonomy too: local governments were required to offer public housing for sale to sitting tenants, with the Secretary of State for the Environment able to intervene and take over the selling process if the central government was not satisfied with the progress on sales (see Johnston, 1983b).

From the Particular to the General

These two brief case studies are of very different responses to symptoms of the same problem, often termed the 'fiscal crisis of the state' (see O'Connor, 1973). In New York, higher level governments — notably the Federal Government — distanced themselves from the fiscal problems of the local government, in the expectation that sounder policies would eventually be imposed by the dictates of the market. If the City of New York could not raise money, it would have to introduce policies (layoffs of public employees; reductions in social service programmes) that would make it more acceptable to those able, but currently unwilling, to provide financial support. It very soon did, and the City's budgetary procedures were restructured along lines acceptable to finance capital. In Britain, central government insisted on similar disciplines.

In both of these cases, therefore, we see that what a local government can do is circumscribed by external influences. Local governments are not autonomous, because they lack any sovereign status. They exist at the behest of central governments, and they have no autonomy beyond that which central governments are prepared to grant them. (And if and when they challenge that authority, the consequence may well be that autonomy is removed from them, in the field of the challenge; the British health services and public utilities illustrate this, as do the 1983 proposals to abolish the metropolitan counties.) Financially, too, local governments are constrained. They have no fiscal autonomy beyond that allowed by central governments (as cogently argued by Dear and Clark, 1981), as restructuring of the fiscal system by the latter can ensure that local governments remain in a politically inferior position.

To understand the nature of local government — what it is and does, and why — it is necessary to understand why local governments exist. And if, as argued here, the existence and operations of local governments are very much dependent on the central government organisation, then one can only understand local government by understanding the nature of the state, of which both central and local governments are part.

The State and Local Government

The state exists as part of the necessary institutional structure of society; its function is to maintain that structure, facilitate its continuation, and provide the environmental context within which its goals can be achieved. Different forms of society have different goals, and hence make different demands of the state. In feudal societies, for example, the state guarantees property rights and provides the institutional structure within which respect for those rights, and payment of the relevant dues, occurs. In mercantile capitalist societies, the state protects and promotes the trade system. And in socialist societies, it provides an administrative framework that ensures that each contributes according to ability and receives according to need.

The mode of production operating in much of the world at the present time is industrial capitalism, based upon the buying and selling of labour power. The state provides the environment for that mode of production to operate within, including a legal system that governs all sorts of contracts between buyers and sellers, and a system of money that protects investments in productive capacity (Harvey, 1982, p. 281).

The capitalist mode of production is based on the accumulation of surplus value. Capital is invested in labour power, to produce commodities that can be sold and can yield surplus value to the investor — that is, the wage paid to labour is less than the price received for the product. This surplus value must then be reinvested, to stimulate further accumulation. If investment is not forthcoming, labour is unused, commodities are not produced, and the quality of life deteriorates.

The capitalist mode of production does not follow a linear trend of progress. It has inbuilt contradictions within it which produce cyclical sequences of crises and booms, as capital is directed away from increasingly unattractive areas of investment and seeks new centres of potential profitability. (Profit is surplus value expressed as a ratio of production cost.) Those with capital invested wish these cycles — or at least their crisis components — to be at least damped, if not eradicated. This is the role accepted by the state — as a *promoter of accumulation*. It involves many activities including: ensuring 'sound money and credit'; securing a properly trained labour force; promoting means by which surplus value extraction, and hence profit, can be increased — including increased productivity; and providing an infrastructure of fixed capital, such as roads.

The capitalist mode of production is based on exploitation, in particular on alienation from the worker of part (the surplus value) of the product of labour. Accumulation requires that this exploitation be not only sustained, but also advanced — by increasing productivity; if it is not, investment will be withdrawn, with clear consequences. Thus in promoting accumulation, the state is promoting exploitation of most of the people it is supposed to represent (directly, in an electoral democracy, or indirectly in other states via the ideology of the state apparatus). To counter this situation of the state as the promoter of exploitation, it is necessary for the state to adopt a second role — as *the legitimator of the mode of production*. It has to convince the 'exploited' — who are the vast majority of the population — that the system is working for their benefit as well as for those who reap the rewards of accumulation: if there were no investment, there would be no jobs and no profits, no incomes to be taxed to provide needed public goods and services; if workers do not accept innovations aimed at increasing their productivity, their industries will decline in competitiveness and their jobs will be in jeopardy; enterprise must be encouraged, since it buys benefits for all. (Much of this legitimation ideology is nationalistic. There is not one state but a system of many, inherited and modified from the pre-capitalist situations. Each government advances the interests of its own workers, arguing that if the ideology of competition — that is, increasing productivity and accumulation — is not accepted, then investment will be channelled to other states.)

The legitimation role of the state is not solely ideological. It must, at least at the level of appearances, seek to promote the interests of the workers, winning 'concessions' for them — shorter working hours; better safety at work; higher real wages; wage-bargaining powers for trade unions; better public services etc. These may be 'real' concessions, identified by those operating the state as necessary if legitimation is to be maintained. But many of them may be 'disguised' concessions, that bring as many benefits to the exploiters as to the exploited. Cohesion — particularly national cohesion — must be maintained if all are to benefit from the successful operation of the capitalist system. Thus, allied to the state's legitimation role is its function as *the maintainer of law and order*; without regulation, the system will fail.

So Why Local Government?

The rationale for local government usually stresses three related aspects. First, by having decisions made at the local level the state is able to ensure that local needs are appreciated and that local resources (supplemented where possible and necessary from central sources) are brought to bear on them. Secondly, by having local-level decision-making, authority and power are allocated to people at that scale, encouraging participation and countering potential alienation from, and apathy — even hostility — towards, a distant central government. Finally, by involving people locally in control of their own affairs they are protected against an authoritarian central state apparatus.

This rationale promotes the concept of local autonomy. It is part, as Taylor (1981) and others have argued, of the legitimation ideology — it gives the appearance of local freedom when the reality is very different. The capitalist system operates at a world scale. It is experienced at the local scale, whereas the national scale is used as the ideological level countering international movements. But nation-states cannot successfully isolate themselves within capitalism; national governments must work with it, to promote local accumulation and legitimation. The territories of local governments certainly cannot be isolated within capitalism, and if they act contrary to its tendencies they may harm not only local people but also those elsewhere in the state. Thus, as the case study examples earlier in this chapter showed, local governments are ultimately subservient to capitalist forces and their interpretation by central governments.

Why then have local governments? In part because the ideological rationale is correct; it is more efficient and effective to have decisions made, and participated in, locally, so long as the disciplines are such that local power cannot counter central direction. In part, fragmentation serves the legitimation purpose. By setting area against area, in the competition for resources, the central government may not only be defusing potential antagonism to the capitalist system as a whole, but may also be promoting accumulation — in order to attract jobs, local governments may subsidise investment (see Herr, 1982; Fincher, 1981, 1982).

Within limits, many of the areas handled by local governments are local and, in a national context, trivial. It may be irrelevant to national economic and social policy that the elected government of local authority x provides a free family planning service, whereas that in y does not. Policies that run counter to a national government's ideology — selective schooling, say, or subsidies to public transport — may call for the disciplining of the local government. As Saunders (1982) has pointed out, however, local government is generally concerned with three areas of responsibility: the provision of certain public goods and services (usually termed social consumption, and part of the legitimation exercise); the meeting of local needs; and regulation of activities (as in land-use planning and the control of nuisances) in 'the public good'. But in a capitalist society, the provision of public goods and services comes second to the promotion of accumulation, on the argument that without capitalist success in the provision of jobs all else is irrelevant (hence cuts in social services at times of economic crisis); local democratic accountability must take second place to meeting the needs of the corporate bodies that facilitate accumulation; and 'the public good' must be set against individual property rights. Promoting accumulation, treating with corporate bodies, and the protection of property rights, are central government roles: thus local government is subservient, and its policies must be in line with those instituted centrally.

This does not mean central dictatorship. (Even in a highly centralised, socialist state some local freedom of action is allowed — but it is trivial.) Local governments do make decisions, but not in circumstances of their own choosing.

The Mosaic of Local Governments

Given that a system of local governments, suitably constrained by constitutional and other legal devices, can provide a satisfactory means of promoting state policies, especially with regard to legitimation, the question arises whether certain structural arrangements are better than others. Cross-national comparisons (e.g.

Johnston, 1984b) indicate substantial variations in the organisation of local government. These may reflect differences between countries in the goals set for local governments. In addition, they are likely to reflect differences in historical context and in political structure. (Most local government systems have evolved in a piece-meal manner, with very few major reorganisations.) In France, for example, the organisation of local government is strictly controlled from Paris, with the departmental prefects acting as agents of the central government in their supervision of local administration (see Meny, 1980, 1983; in the former publication, Meny describes the powers of local governments as 'essentially powers of manage-ment' — p. 143). In Britain, there are no centrally imposed administrators within local government. Instead, central govern-ment chooses to constrain by regulation and by control of the purse-strings. As Miliband (1982, p. 139) expresses it:

> For all the rhetoric about local democracy, citizen participation, and the like, local government in Britain is a greatly constrained and limited business. . . . No council can ever fail to be mindful of what central government can ultimately do to it if it seeks to resist commands from the centre.

In the United States, on the other hand, a much more anarchic system appears to operate (for descriptions, see Johnston, 1982c, 1984a).

Why such variations? One reason is that within the political con-flict that characterises every state, the local government system has been employed in a variety of ways. Societies comprise many interest groups that are opposed to each other, and individuals also compete for benefits. Thus the local government system may be employed in the ongoing intra-class conflict. It certainly is in the United States, where, as elsewhere, people dislike paying taxes. A package of local government reform measures adopted in most States in the early twentieth-century allowed some groups within society (basically the affluent, plus industrial/commercial opera-tions able and willing to migrate from the inner cities) to translate this dislike into practice. Relatively liberal incorporation laws, combined with limits on taxing and borrowing, have allowed the creation of small, fiscally independent local governments; in the suburban rings of most metropolitan areas this has resulted in a contorted, highly fragmented mosaic of small municipalities. In most States, each of these is responsible (with very little central control) for land-use planning and they are the main local spenders (apart from the school districts, which are separate from the municipalities in most States). Manipulation of the planning system has allowed the creation of residential areas, from which undesirable uses and users (industry, much of commerce, apartment buildings, the poor, blacks etc.) are excluded; this in turn has given the residents of such areas close control over the social environment of local schools (a crucial element of class conflict: Johnston, 1980, 1984a) and has allowed them to escape from making fiscal contributions to the costs of running other parts of the urban area. To some free-market theorists (e.g. Tiebout, 1956; Whiteman, 1983) this fragmentation allows choice, with residents selecting those areas offering the set of services and taxes that they prefer. However, although many might prefer to live in exclusive, low-tax suburbs, free of the negative elements of the inner-city, only the affluent are allowed in. Choice is limited to those who can afford to choose, and the local government system is employed to structure the choices.

Whereas in the United States the central governments have been unwilling to interfere with the manipulation of local government as it has evolved, this is not the case in Great Britain. (Constitutionally, the Federal Government in the USA has no powers over local governments: see Johnston, 1984a, 1984b). British local government has become increasingly 'nationalised', with the national political parties competing for control of local governments. Initially, this 'nationalisation' was largely an urban phenomenon, but it is now general. The parties see local governments as laboratories for experiments with new policies (and politicians, for whom it is a training ground: Newton, 1976); the party in opposition in the national Parliament also sees local governments as arenas for contesting the policies of the party in power. (For this reason, local election results are increasingly used as barometers of the popularity of central governments.)

The political parties in Britain have not been content with 'nationalising' local politics and thereby deflecting local attention at elections from local issues. (These may, of course, dominate the election in a particular local government area if they arouse sufficient interest: Hampton, 1970.) They have also manipulated the geography of local government to their own ends, both in the definition of boundaries and in the allocation of functions to the two tiers of government — county and district. The reorganisations of local government in London (introduced in 1964) and in the rest of England (1974) were both undertaken by Conservative governments at the national level; part of the goal was to create units likely to have a Conservative-dominated council and to allocate functions so that most power rested with Conservative-dominated authorities. (Also promotion of large units with 'professional' managements furthered Conservative interests; Dearlove, 1980; Cockburn, 1977). Policies which favour such authorities then follow. There is little doubt that the allocation of central grants to local governments in the period from 1974 reflected central partiality toward types of authority likely to be governed by the same party (Bennett, 1981, 1982). Further, central government attempts to direct the activities of local governments appear to have contained strong political directions; a recent analysis of the operations of the Local Government (Miscellaneous Provisions) (Scotland) Act 1981 suggests that the central government's choice of local governments for its 'hit list' of over-spenders was political:

> the Government's methodology for identifying excessive and unreasonable expenditure *lacks intellectual credibility*. The case is certainly *not* as watertight as Ministers implied it would have to be under the Act, for authorities have not been clearly isolated as being excessive and unreasonable (Midwinter, Keating and Taylor, 1983, p. 405)

New Tiers and Ad Hoc Authorities

Throughout the chapter so far, the discussion has focused on all-purpose territorial local governments. In most countries these comprise a basic framework of local administration, which exhausts the national territory and within which other all-purpose authorities (most of them serving urban areas, or parts thereof) may be defined. In addition, however, many countries also have special-purpose local governments, operating a single function only.

The reasons for the creation of such special-purpose authorities are several. In some cases, they reflect the irrelevance of the existing structure of all-purpose authorities for a particular function, because of their territorial extent (or lack of it). Many special districts in the USA are of this type, providing library, fire, park, planning and other services more effectively than might be the case with fragmented provision (Barlow, 1980); many of them also have been created because of the limitations on the taxing and borrowing powers of municipalities, and the confused picture that they create leads to resident ignorance about who controls what, leaving power in the hands of the few interested local politicians plus the bureaucrats. Thus the ability to create special districts suits the particular groups using the local government system to advance their own interests (maintenance of separate school districts illustrates this very well), and at the same time fragments conflict over the built environment.

Other *ad hoc* territorial local governments may be centrally created, as a means of bypassing local electoral accountability. The organisation of certain public services and utilities in Britain reflects this — notably in the health and water services, and, according to the 1983 proposals, increasingly in fire and police services too. Although the elected local governments within the relevant areas have some representation on the 'regional' bodies, the latter are not accountable to the electorate, are more likely to be controlled by professional bureaucrats, and are more readily manipulated by central government. (The new boards proposed for metropolitan areas in 1983 will have their budgets centrally determined.) Their creation may in part represent a need for administrative efficiency that is not possible at the local scale, but it is also a reflection of the desire of the central government to avoid conflict with local governments over expensive services.

Central governments are increasingly aware of the benefits of replacing accountable local government by appointed local administrators. In Britain, for example, *ad hoc* authorities have been created to plan and administer redevelopment programmes in depressed inner-city areas (such as the Liverpool and London docklands), whereas other areas have been released from some local controls (e.g. enterprise zones). Such acts involve the central government superseding the powers of local governments.

There are many political moves at present for decentralisation of power from central government, rather than the opposite. Some of these are nationalist in their organisation, although many have an economic foundation and the creation of nationalist enclaves within a state's territory represents past economic policies. Others are anti-centralist, and seek to place more power at the local — usually regional — level. Such decentralisation, it is argued, will aid in the promotion of regional economies, by placing control in local hands. But central governments appear entirely unwilling to give regional authorities the fiscal and monetary powers necessary for economic competition in the international capitalist economy; even if they did, the experience of decolonisation suggests that most regions would benefit little from such additional powers.

Conclusions

Local government is part of the apparatus of the state. It has no independent existence, and the functions it is called upon to perform represent — in both quantity and quality — perceptions of the role of local government held by those who control the central state apparatus.

This conclusion does not imply that local government is a subject unworthy of detailed study. It is, for many people, the only level of government of which they have any direct experience, and its actions and inactions impinge directly and indirectly on most daily lives; as such, it is a valid focus of analysis. Furthermore, how it operates reflects much variability in the interpretation of its roles — both by those who run local government (the elected politicians — plus their non-elected party machines — and the appointed bureaucrats) and by those in control of central government. As illustrated here, this variability provides a rich field for analysis.

Analysis of how local government operates (including its increasingly complex relationships with central government (Ashford, 1980a; Jones, 1980)) and of how those operations are experienced can provide sophisticated descriptions. It cannot, however, do any more than ask the questions that relate to an understanding of local government — of what it is, why it does what it does, and so on. For a fuller appreciation a theoretical understanding is needed, focusing on the social relations that underpin the institutional appearances (Dunleavy, 1980). In capitalist systems, those relations concern the class structure of the society, and include 'the process of capital accumulation by the bourgeoisie from the working class' (p. 177). The state is an integral part of the institutional structure of such a society, promoting the process, and legitimation, of accumulation.

The underlying processes are fundamental to capitalism, as is a class structure. But the system is far from deterministic. It is left to individuals to work out how accumulation should be promoted and legitimated. In general, in the 'developed countries' legitimation includes allowing electoral democracy, whereas in the 'developing countries' such a concession is rare, at least for long periods, because it cannot be afforded in the face of economic difficulties (Johnston, 1984c). In general, too, the 'developed countries' have welfare state systems. Their goals are economic stability, equitable distribution of rewards (while not penalising 'enterprise'), and resource allocation to promote growth (Ashford, 1980b).

There is no agreed 'best' way of achieving those goals (at least in part because people in different countries are viewing them from different starting points, and through different cultural lenses). It is open to individuals to use the state apparatus, including local government, to chart what appears to be a realistic route. Nor must it be assumed that these individuals operate other than with the best of intentions, and sometimes with substantial success — as Miliband (1982) puts it

> In countless different ways, local councillors were able to make some contribution to the improvement of health, housing, educational and other facilities in their area . . . a visible sign that immediate activity for practical reform was not in vain . . . (and that) working men and women were able to achieve direct participation in the making of decisions (p. 137)

But their decision-making has to be within the context of the economic system within which they operate — and if they get it wrong, either by opposing the policies of a more powerful body or by stimulating local economic decline rather than growth, then they and their policies have failed. Individuals are free to interpret their roles as they wish, within a system that is fairly robust. But the system has its limits, and eventually those that transgress are brought back into line.

During the period from the mid 1950s to the mid 1970s, geographers exploring the literature of the other social sciences were attracted much more to the empirical and methodological than to the theoretical and philosophical. They added their spatial perspective, and promoted the study of 'spatial variations in . . .' such an approach characterised work on local government, with a concentration on empirical analyses of the correlates of inter- and intra-authority expenditure patterns. More recently, geographers have turned to the theoretical and philosophical literature, seeking to account for what it is they have become so expert at portraying. The present chapter has drawn on both strands, outlining the findings of the empirical analyses and setting them in the context of a theory of the state. Local government and the state are inseparable — the former is a part of the latter. Realisation of this is aiding the pursuit of 'Progress in Political Geography'.

References

Ashford, D.E. (ed.) (1980a) *Financing Urban Government in the Welfare State*, Croom Helm, London
—— (1980b) 'Central-local Financial Exchange in the Welfare State' in D.E. Ashford (1980a), pp. 204–20
Barlow, I.M. (1980) *Spatial Dimensions of Urban Government*, John Wiley, Chichester
Bennett, R.J. (1980) *The Geography of Public Finance*, Methuen, London.
—— (1981) 'The Rate Support Grant in England and Wales 1967–8 to 1980–1: a Review of Changing Emphases and Objectives', in D.T. Herbert and R.J. Johnston (eds.) *Geography and the Urban Environment, Volume IV*, John Wiley, Chichester, pp. 139–92
—— (1982) *Central Grants to Local Governments*, Cambridge University Press, Cambridge
Bolotin, F.N. and Cingranelli, D.L. (1983) 'Equity and Urban Policy: the Underclass Hypothesis Revisited', *Journal of Politics, 45*, 209–19
Burnett, A.D. (1981) 'The Distribution of Local Outputs and Outcomes in British and American Cities' in A.D. Burnett and P.J. Taylor (eds.), *Political Studies from Spatial Perspectives*, John Wiley, Chichester
Burnett, A.D., Cole, K. and Moon, G. (1983) 'Political Participation and Resource Allocation' in M.A. Busteed (ed.) *Developments in Political Geography*, Academic Press, London, pp. 303–36
Cockburn, C. (1977) *The Local State*, Pluto Press, London
Cox, K.R. and Johnston, R.J. (eds.) (1982) *Conflict, Politics and the Urban Scene*, Longman, London
David, S.M. and Kantor, P. (1979) 'Political Theory and Transformations in Urban Budgetary Arenas: the Case of New York City' in D.R. Marshall (ed.), *Urban Policy Making*, Sage Publications, Beverly Hills, pp. 183–220
Clark, G.L. (1981) 'Democracy and the Capitalist State: Towards a Critique of the Tiebout Hypothesis' in A.D. Burnett and P.J. Taylor (eds.), *Political Studies from Spatial Perspectives*, John Wiley, Chichester, pp. 111–30
Dear, M.J. (1981) 'A Theory of the Local State' in A.D. Burnett and P.J. Taylor, (eds.), *Political Studies from Spatial Perspectives*, John Wiley, Chichester, pp. 183–200
—— and Clark, G.L. (1981) 'Dimensions of Local State Autonomy', *Environment and Planning A, 13*, 1277–94
Dearlove, J. (1980) *The Reorganisation of British Local Government*, Cambridge University Press, Cambridge
Duncan, S.S. and Goodwin, M. (1980) 'The Local State and Restructuring Social Relations: Theory and Practice', Working Paper 24, Urban and Regional Studies, University of Sussex
Dunleavy, P. (1980) 'Social and Political Theory and the Issues in Central-Local Relations' in G.W. Jones (ed.), *New Approaches to the Study of Central-Local Government Relationships*, Gower Press, Farnborough, pp. 116–36
Fawcett, C.B. (1919) *Provinces of England*, Hutchinson, London
Fenton, J.H. and Chamberlayne, D.W. (1969) 'The Literature Dealing with the Relationships between Political Processes, Socioeconomic Conditions and Public

Policies in the American States. a Bibliographical Essay', *Polity*, *1*, 388–404

Fincher, R. (1981) 'Local Implementation Strategies in the Urban Built Environment', *Environment and Planning A*, *13*, 1233–52

—— (1982) 'Urban Redevelopment in Boston: Rhetoric and Reality' in K.R. Cox and R.J. Johnston (eds.) *Conflict Politics and the Urban Scene*, Longman, London, pp. 220–40

Freeman, T.W. (1968) *Geography and Regional Administration*, Hutchinson, London

Hampton, W.A. (1970) *Democracy and Community*, Oxford University Press, Oxford

Harvey, D. (1982) *The Limits to Capital*, Blackwell, Oxford

Herr, J.P. (1982) 'Metropolitan Political Fragmentation and Conflict in the Location of Commercial Facilities' in K.R. Cox and R.J. Johnston (eds.), *Conflict, Politics and the Urban Scene*, Longman, London, pp. 28–44

Johnston, R.J. (1979) *Political, Electoral and Spatial Systems*, Oxford University Press, Oxford

—— (1980a) *City and Society*, Penguin, London

—— (1980b) *The Geography of Federal Spending in the United States*, John Wiley, Chichester

—— (1981) 'Political Geography' in N. Wrigley and R.J. Bennett, (eds.), *Quantitative Geography*, Routledge and Kegan Paul, London, pp. 374–81

—— (1982a) *Geography and the State*, Macmillan, London

—— (1982b) 'The State and the Study of Social Geography' in P. Jackson and S.J. Smith, (eds.), *Social Interaction and Ethnic Segregation*, Academic Press, London, pp. 205–22.

—— (1982c) *The American Urban System*, Longman, London

—— (1983a) 'Politics and the Geography of Social Well-being' in M.A. Busteed, (ed.), *Developments in Political Geography*, Academic Press, London, pp. 189–250

—— (1983b) 'Texts, Actors and Higher Managers: Judges, Bureaucrats and the Political Organisation of Space', *Political Geography Quarterly*, *2*, 3–20

—— (1984a) *Residential Segregation, Constitutional Conflict and the State*, Academic Press, London

—— (1984b) 'Human Geography as a Generalising Social Science: Trans-Atlantic Contrasts in Local Government', *Geographical Journal*, *150*

—— (1984c) 'The Political Geography of Electoral Geography' in P.J. Taylor (ed.), *Agendas in Political Geography*, Croom Helm, London

Jones, G.W. (ed.) (1980) *New Approaches to the Study of Central-Local Government Relationships*, Gower Press, Farnborough

Kirby, A.M. (1983) *The Politics of Location*, Methuen, London

—— and Pinch, S. (1903) 'Territorial Justice and Service Allocation' in M. Pacione (ed.), *Progress in Urban Geography*, Croom Helm, London, pp. 223–50

Knox, P.L. (1982a) *Urban Social Geography*, Longman, London.

—— (1982b) 'Residential Structure, Facility Location and Patterns of Accessibility' in K.R. Cox and R.J. Johnston (eds.), *Conflict, Politics and the Urban Scene*, Longman, London, pp. 62–87

Meny, Y. (1980) 'Financial Transfers and Local Government in France' in Ashford (1980a), pp. 142–57

—— (1983) 'Permanence and Change: the Relations between Central Government and Local Authorities in France', *Environment and Planning C*, *1*, 17–28

Midwinter, A., Keating, M. and Taylor, P. (1983) 'Excessive and Unreasonable: the Politics of the Scottish Hit List', *Political Studies*, *31*, 394–417

Miliband, R. (1982) *Capitalist Democracy in Britain*, Oxford University Press, Oxford

Newton, K. (1976) *Second City Politics*, Oxford University Press, Oxford
—— (1981) *Balancing the Books*, Sage Publications, London.
—— (1982) 'Central Places and Urban Services' in K. Newton (ed.), *Urban Political Economy*, Frances Pinter, London, pp. 117–36
Nicholson, R.J. and Topham, N. (1971) 'The Determinants of Investment in Housing by Local Authorities: an Econometric Approach', *Journal, Royal Statistical Society, A*, *134*, 273–320
O'Connor, J. (1973) *The Fiscal Crisis of the State*, St. Martin's Press, New York
Orbell, J. and Uno, T. (1972) 'A Theory of Neighbourhood Problem-solving: Political Action versus Residential Mobility', *American Political Science Review*, *66*, 471–89.
Paris, C. (1983) 'The Myth of Urban Politics', *Environment and Planning D, Society and Space*, *1*, 89–108
Rich, R.C. (1979) 'Neglected Issues in the Study of Urban Service Distributions: a Research Agenda', *Urban Studies*, *16*, 143–56
—— (ed.) (1982a) *Analyzing Urban-Service Distributions*, Lexington Books, Lexington, Massachusetts
—— (1982b) *The Politics of Urban Public Services*, Lexington Books, Lexington, Massachusetts
Rundquist, B.S. (ed.) (1982) *Political Benefits*, Lexington Books, Lexington, Massachusetts
Richards, P.G. (1973) *The Reformed Local Government System*, Allen and Unwin, London
Saunders, P. (1980) *Urban Politics*, Penguin, London
—— (1982) Why Study Central-local Relations? *Local Government Studies*, 55–66
Sharpe, L.J. (ed.) (1981) *The Local Fiscal Crisis in Western Europe*, Sage Publications, London
Taylor, P.J. (1977) 'Political Geography', *Progress in Human Geography*, *1*, 130–5
—— (1979) ' "Difficult-to-let", "Difficult-to-live-in", and sometimes "Difficult-to-get-out-of": an Essay in the Provision of Council Housing with Special Reference to Killingworth', *Environment and Planning A*, *11*, 1305–20
—— (1981) 'Geographical Scales within the World-economy Approach', *Review*, *5*, 3–11
Tiebout, C.M. (1956) 'A Pure Theory of Local Expenditures', *Journal of Political Economy*, *64*, 416–24
Whiteman, J. (1983) 'Deconstructing the Tiebout Hypothesis', *Environment and Planning D: Society and Space*, *1*, 339–54
Ziegler, D.J. (1981) 'Changing Regional Patterns of Central City Credit Ratings: 1960–1980', *Urban Geography*, *2*, 269–82

6 URBAN POLITICAL PROCESSES AND RESOURCE ALLOCATION

A. Burnett

Urban political geography *per se* has never been recognised as a separate or distinctive sub-discipline. But in recent years many books and articles have been written by geographers and others on spatial aspects of the government and politics of cities. Such topics as locational conflict, political participation (at and between elections), jurisdictional boundaries, and service provision have been investigated. A number of political geographical texts have devoted several chapters to urban issues (Burnett and Taylor, 1981; Short, 1982; Paddison, 1983; Busteed, 1983; and Taylor and House, 1984). In the meantime political scientists and sociologists have also been active in undertaking theoretical and empirical case studies. While much of this work has not been explicitly geographical, that is not to say that political scientists have ignored or neglected spatial and environmental aspects of urban politics (Jones, 1980; Lineberry, 1978; Sharpe and Newton, 1984). Spatial variations in service provision at intra-and inter-city scales have been a major focus for recent research by geographers and social scientists alike (Rich, 1979; Kirby, Knox and Pinch, 1983a). While some studies have examined only who gets what, and where, by way of municipal spending and provision, the majority have also attempted to identify the causal mechanisms underlying unequal/unfair patterns of public resource allocation. Ecological, statistical methodology has generally been employed in accounting for variation in spending between local authorities while intra-urban studies often used a more process-orientated case study approach with the emphasis on decision making.

The focus in this chapter is on the latter, although the scope and content of 'output' studies will be briefly reviewed. The causal link between political process and resource allocation will also be discussed. The roles of key actors involved — the public, elected representatives and officials will be noted. A number of causal models contributing to an explanation of urban policy-making will be mentioned including the pork barrel, incrementalism and bureaucratic decision rules. Finally these concepts will be illustrated with reference to a case study of resource allocation in one British city.

The aim of the chapter is thus to discuss fully the problems and potentialities of studying the geography of local urban allocative and distributional decision making. Selected recent research is cited but the purpose of the chapter is not merely to present a literature review since that task has been attempted elsewhere (Burnett, 1981, 1983). Rather the basic aim is to shine a torch (searchlight?) into the 'black box' of local urban political systems to illuminate (1) who makes decisions; and (2) how and why municipal spending and provision in the form of facilities and services are decided. It is not disputed that much that goes on in city halls and civic offices in Western cities is influenced by the policies of central and higher tiers of government and wider economic forces (Taylor, 1982), nor that environmental factors are, in a sense, determinants or at least constraints of resource allocation by local authorities. Rather, what is being argued, and hopefully demonstrated, is that some patterns of urban provision can be best explained by the workings of urban political systems that are crucial intervening variables between the environment and outputs of local political systems. It is not adequate merely to point to a list of factors which may explain spatial variation in spending between or within local authorities (Pinch, 1980). Rather the dynamic character of the political process which is composed of 'a series of decisions over a period of time, each decision is the result of interaction among individuals, organised groups and various public agencies; involving consultations, smaller decisions, communications and various pressures and manoeuvres by interested parties' (Merkl, 1970, p. 387) must be understood and closely investigated.

Inter-authority Output Studies

One of the most popular forms of analysis of resource allocation is the approach which correlates environmental, socio-economic, and political characteristics of local jurisdictions or neighbourhoods with levels of public expenditure or service provision. The distinction between aggregate-area (output) studies and case studies of individual cities has been clarified by Hoggart (1983).

Case studies characteristically examine the development of policy in a temporal setting focusing on the decision-making processes that produce policy change or maintenance whereas output studies predominantly associate attributes of the socio-economic, political, administrative environment with variation in output levels at one point in time; case studies treat the local environment as given whereas output studies treat the temporal processes leading to a particular pattern of outputs as given.

In recently published research the same author has incorporated a temporal dimension into an analysis of capital investment and spending by English county boroughs. He has shown that 'contextual' factors do constrain budget making over time, that much of resource allocation is decided on an incremental basis, and that fluctuations in central government grants, national legislation and environmental changes are among the principal determinants of output change. He concludes that 'at present local outputs literature is superior over the case study approach' (p. 66).

The output approach has also been subjected to sustained serating and criticism by Newton and Sharpe (1977). Their most recent reflections, on, as well as findings of, research undertaken into the relative significance of party political and geographical influences on spending by English and Welsh authorities are contained in a recently published book seemingly somewhat mistitled *Does politics matter*? (Sharpe and Newton, 1984).

The authors take a critical stance on much of the published output research. They point to the degree of multi-collinearity among groups of independent variables that measure the socio-economic environment of local authorities, which are 'somehow' converted into policies. They believe that the statistical analysis of socio-economic variables derived from the characteristics of the resident population of the jurisdiction represents 'a mode of analysis which has come to something of a dead end' (p. 20). Their preferred approach is to explain the mix of, and level of expenditure on, different services in terms of (1) a city's role as a service centre within the national urban hierarchy, and (2) its location and economic role. Thus, for example, conurbation centre, country town and seaside resort authorities will be characterised by distinctive packages of resource allocation between different services. It is suggested that 'geographical' determinants, which are external to the political process, condition and constrain local councils in their resource allocation — 'city fathers cannot of course make their domain into something fundamentally different from their community's inherent character'. On the other hand it is recognised that 'political choice and judgement determine how opportunities are taken' (p. 215). Using a 'league table' approach (described by the authors as a 'string and sealing wax' method) which involved ranking authorities from highest to lowest spenders on each service, they found that a clear pattern emerged wherein (1) certain service expenditures such as police, highways, parks, libraries and sports facilities were related to a city's position in the urban hierarchy and (2) a city's local economy and location 'was associated with higher or lower expenditure in certain services'. For example coastal cities and towns spent less on sewerage disposal unless they were holiday resorts; conurbation centres, such as Manchester and Leeds, spent more on parks (being far from the open country) than did free-standing country towns. Major provincial centres also invested heavily in highways (to assist commuters get into the Central Business District), museums (in line with their regional role), police (presumably to combat central and inner city crime and control football crowds) and environmental health (to inspect central restaurants).

The authors make a convincing case for their 'unitary' model of local authority spending whereby each unit has its own set of inter-ests and expenditure package the level and mix of which is a factor in part at least of its geographical location and character. However they do introduce some significant caveats to the major thrust of their case. While they argue that 'city fathers cannot . . . make their domain into something fundamentally different from their commu-nity's inherent character' that does not mean that these 'external' factors predetermine the policies that local decision making chooses (p. 215). They dispute the relevance of 'the bargaining model' which assumes that local policies are best understood in terms of competition between local agencies and groups within each authority. Nonetheless the significance of the local bureaucracy and Party control and the role of leadership and incrementalism in fiscal decision making is recognised, as are the constraints imposed by central government.

Despite the substantial evidence produced by Sharpe and Newton that the spending patterns of authorities in England were linked to their geographical situation they are at pains to point out that in the final analysis 'all outputs should be seen as being a product of the political process' (p. 206). While flour, yeast and sugar are vital ingredients of bread it is the *baking process* that transforms them into a loaf! Likewise, an understanding of the operation of political process, is crucial in attempting to explain the package of policies pursued by urban authorities.

While the baking analogy is convincing, less so is their assertion (p. 3) that 'all in all the output approach has a lot to commend it as a method for elucidating the political process'. Their self-confessed 'string and sealing wax method' involving as it did the ranking of authorities from the highest to the lowest spenders on each service and puzzling over the league tables thus produced, would on the face of it appear to tell us little about the political causes of variations in local spending. They would seem to be on stronger ground in pointing to regularised decision making routines/rules adhered to by agencies, local party control, and political traditions as having a decisive impact on the process of decision making and also policy outputs. Likewise the incremental nature of budget making is freely admitted — 'the budgetary process mainly comprises the standard operating procedure of adding a marginal and regularised increase, or decrease (the increment) to the preceding year's allocation' (p. 81).

The value of Sharpe and Newton's text is that it provides a critique of traditional output studies which leapt straight from environment to policy without considering the intervening political process. Thus not only can they be deemed to be theoretically weak, but they also, not surprisingly, failed to explain variations in resource allocation adequately. However, the authors also point to key geographical background factors which apparently explain variation in service spending by local authorities and help to bridge the gap between ecological and more process orientated approaches.

Political Process and Resource Allocation: Key Concepts and Possible Causal Links

There is then no shortage of studies that have used correlation and regression techniques to search for significant relationships between the environmental/social/political characteristics of jurisdictions and expenditure on services. But what alternative theoretical models and research strategies are available to explain the allocation of resources and their spatial distribution? The one that is favoured here is described as a 'systems model of process' which focuses on how political demands from outside the political system are processed by officials and elected representatives and under certain circumstances converted into authoritative policies and decisions. The key points to be examined in this approach are *if, how, when and where* political demand-making by pressure groups and individuals influences the social and spatial distribution of public largesse. In this context, political participation is visualised as a bargaining process and an unequal one at that. The interests of mobilised citizens and official decision makers are likely to be both congruent and conflicting, depending on the issues. And of course political demands can be suppressed, diluted and manipulated by those in power. Key political actors naturally have their own perceptions of need, and they may be unwilling and unable to accede to pressure because their allocations are governed by bureaucratic rules and conventions, existing budgetary commitments, and financial and other constraints. At the end of the day whether or not politicians and officials are willing and able to accede to demands and make concessions is an empirical question. Furthermore it should *not* be assumed that local pressure from outside the political system is indeed a significant factor in determining policies and decisions affecting resource allocation.

As Richardson (1983) states . . . 'the consequences of participation are highly unpredictable . . . one cannot assume particular results on the basis of the intentions of the participants or the structures through which they are involved' (p. 78). Causal relationships between demands and resource allocation are difficult to prove. Schumaker and Getter (1983) summarise the nub of the problem:

> a causal view of power asserts that influence has been exerted when policy makers modify their decisions because of the real or potential application of resources by participants . . . a non-causal view is less concerned about the reasons motivating policy makers than it is concerned about whether or not their decisions are simply consistent with the preferences of participants. For example, a city council may wish to build an expressway through a particular neighbourhood opposing the project. If the council changes its policies because of neighbourhood protests then influence has been exerted. If the council changes its policies because of cost considerations and ignores completely

neighbourhood protests the neighbourhood would of course have no influence but the council would of course have been responsive to its preferences. Demands need not be the causal agents bringing about policies, they need only achieve policies consistent with their preferences.

There are then difficulties about establishing that political demands by interested parties actually influence resource allocation decisions 'beyond reasonable doubt', but the same is true with respect to the influence of any relevant independent variable. However additional hurdles have to be overcome in the task of systematically examining the influence of certain variables on patterns of resource allocation. In discussing the operation of the 'pork barrel' in the local urban context Hoare rightly notes that 'the task of identifying quite what level of resource allocation has been received by what ward over a given time period can be a major research task in its own right (Hoare, 1983, p. 420). In this respect it may be useful to distinguish between allocation and distributional decisions, that is, the former referring to major budgetary allocations for different services and the latter to more specific decisions about individual public facilities and services. No reference is made here to purely 'symbolic' responses to political demands which do not involve tangible resources. On the other hand regulative activities which involve actual resources of the time of staff and money being spent will be investigated. But whichever scale of resource allocation is being considered and whatever form it takes — allocating teachers between different schools, capital expenditure on new classrooms or revenue on books and equipment — the task of actually measuring spatial variation is formidable. That is not to say that there has not been notable recent research which has successfully formulated a methodology to measure financial contributions and spending patterns on services (education, fire protection, library provision and swimming pools) within a single British authority (Whitehead, 1983).

Before examining the links between political demands and resource allocation empirically there are some notable elements of the political process which should be first clarified. Crucially important is the question of the relative role of elected politicians *vis-à-vis* their full-time, and in Britain, appointed officials, in converting demands into policies (or not, as the case may be). In other words who decides whether and when demands from the public should be merely taken into account, or actually acceded to in terms of making tangible concessions? The issues which mobilise citizens to contact their electoral representatives publicly or privately have been illuminated in Western cities (Cox and McCarthy, 1980; Burnett and Hill, 1981; Davidson, 1979) Likewise the legal and formal channels which are used to consult people affected by official proposals and plans are well known, as are the more spontaneous mechanisms of protest such as petitioning, demonstrating and individual contracting (Burnett, Cole and Moon, 1983). But what is not at all clear is who decides what and why in the process of responding to demands — conflicting or otherwise — from interest groups and individuals.

Councillors and Officers

The framework, and in some instances the detailed procedures, by which the public are practically involved have been incorporated in legislation and circulars emanating from central governments. Nonetheless individual urban authorities still have considerable discretion in who is given the opportunity to participate, how, and when. Given that such discretion exists there remains the question as to who it is within each authority and constituent department that devises and implements the form that local arrangements take. How far do senior councillors of the controlling party set the tone in establishing the parameters for public consultation? Do experienced officers in major spending departments which interact with large numbers of ratepayers and consumers decide, or at least recommend, what procedures are adopted? It is likely that individual authorities have developed over the years a distinctive set of procedures and institutions to involve the public. Deputations may be permitted to attend and plead their case before meetings of the full council as well as several of its committees. Some authorities have allowed co-opted tenant representatives to sit on the Housing Committee or its sub-committees, and have given advisory bodies some formal powers. The pattern however is far from static and changes are likely to have occurred during the 1970s and early 1980s.

A related topic is the extent to which officers and councillors are involved in the operation of participatory schemes. It has been suggested, for example, that professional planners have tended to be more involved than councillors in participation in planning whereas councillors have often taken a greater interest than the officers in tenant participation schemes (Richardson, p. 46). Involvement by officers may also depend on seniority, with chief officers and their deputies eschewing such activities because of other more pressing commitments.

Another empirical problem concerns the question of who are the targets for complaints and demands from the public. Pahl (1979) has suggested that major issues will end up upon the desks of senior officials whereas routine, mundane requests will be directed to and dealt with by middle ranking or junior municipal employees. Newton (1976) found that contact with departments and officials was thought to be the most effective choice of interest group leaders while contact with individual councillors came a poor second. Gyford (1976) also noted that groups wishing to affect policy or its implementation would seek out appropriate officials and only when that did not pay off would councillors become targets for lobbying.

Even more important in terms of understanding the process whereby demands are evaluated and dealt with by those in authority is identifying the locus of power between elected members and bureaucrats. Conflicts and tensions of course occur in their relationship both over overall priorities and on individual issues. In the case of the latter there exists in every agency a well established set of decision rules to guide officers in the advice they give to relevant committees (planning principles in relation to planning applications and points allocation systems in relation to applications for Council dwellings). Complaints and demands from the public are commonly also considered in this manner. In contrast, elected representatives with their party affiliations and ward allegiances often respond to demands, and the advice which they receive, more intuitively. Probably in all cases the costs and benefits of acceding to demands are calculated by both sets of political actors in terms of perceived individual and organisational interests and in the light of financial and ecological constraints. Most planners do have clear ideas of their own about the need for differential service provision.

In the last resort power is crucial in analysing the impact of participation in practice. Councillors may have formal power but in the complexities of housing and educational provision and land use and traffic regulation the informed expertise of the professional officer counts for a lot. It is possible that when 'major' issues are highly politicised and involve conflict, that councillors will assert their authority, whereas more routine and less controversial cases will be decided purely on the 'technical' advice of officials.

Benyon (p. 53) has pinpointed the crux of the matter as follows:

> it is sometimes argued that a fundamental tenet of our local government system is that councillors make decisions on the advice of officers which the latter then implement. However a number of studies have produced evidence which shows that representative local democracy does not operate as the popular model suggests it should. An alternative view which has been called the technocratic model emphasises the role of the expert in local government. Within this model the professional officer assumes a position of pre-eminence while councillors serve as channels from their wards, and as a means of legitimising the technocrats' decisions. Councillors' deference to skilled officers giving objective and impartial advice means that they are reluctant to question recommendations which the officers make.

From the perspective of those in authority participation may perform other functions. Dearlove subsumes the argument as follows:

> participation can force or educate the participants to gain an awareness of government problems and policies and this will not only inhibit the public from pressing for solutions to their own problems but will enable the authorities to legitimise their decisions with the stance of public approval' (Dearlove quoted in Richardson, 1983, p. 37).

Fostering participation and permitting demand-making by the public can be interpreted primarily as a management technique. The public as service consumers and residents will provide information about the actual or likely effects of proposed decisions as well as feedback on past ones all of which are not easily obtained by other means. In some cases the sheer number of the public potentially affected by a policy or proposal may make consultation, by one means or another, essential or desirable.

To politicians, participation offers an opportunity to build support amongst ratepayers and voters. Even those representing safe seats want to show their gratitude and reward their supporters by being seen to keep in touch, and take up issues of concern to their constituents. Officers may well perceive such public consultation as good professional practice and anyway 'they need to know what is publicly acceptable in order to advise councillors in a sensitive manner' (Richardson, 1983, p. 109).

Phases in the Process of Allocating Resources

The interaction of the public with elected and appointed decision makers is, as has already been suggested, a complex process often involving a series of events and phases. Political demands are not simply or immmediately either 'converted' into policies or alternatively ignored and rejected. Some would argue that a valid distinction can be drawn between pre-legislative, legislative and post-legislative steps in the process. Merkl (1970) identifies no less than seven such phases — (1) taking official notice of an issue or problem; (2) fact finding and consultation; (3) formulating alternative policies; (4) public deliberation; (5) authoritative decision; (6) implementation and (7) feedback. As far as British local authorities are concerned the actual legislative process is based on recommendations by functional committees being endorsed by full councils at their periodic meetings. Of course, detailed procedures followed will differ as between authorities and individual service departments depending on the institutional structures and their rules and standing orders. In the British context departmental autonomy and hierarchical structures of decision making largely dominate the process whereby budgetary allocations are resolved and decisions on what should be spent where and when are subsequently made and implemented.

It is rare for citizens to actually take authoritative decisions affecting the location of new facilities, the closure of existing ones or the allocation of grants or public sector dwellings. But still political participation can result in potential involvement in any of several stages. Thus the public may be permitted or encouraged to (1) place items on the agendas of official committees and advisory bodies; (2) provide information as to the consequences of alternative courses of action; (3) have their preferences and priorities placed alongside other criteria and considerations and (4) monitor, and if they wish attempt to modify, the implementation of decisions once taken. Regrettably all too often the public are misled into believing they are actually being asked to take a decision when in fact they are merely being consulted. At local public enquiries on planning issues the quasi-judicial atmosphere leads some to believe that an inspector's word is law, when it may be and not infrequently is, overturned by government ministers and their advisers.

The Role of the Public Agencies and Bureaucratic Rules

While powerful individuals who make allocational decisions do so partly on the basis of their own beliefs and preferences, they do not operate in a vacuum. In cities 'raw' political demands are aggregated and articulated in the form of policy proposals by neighbourhood associations and (more ephemeral) protest groups, by employees' organisations and trade unions and a host of other local pressure groups. It is not necessary to be entirely persuaded by the pluralist model of political systems to recognise that organisations that represent the interests of their members and supporters play a part in local politics. These groups vary greatly in their interests and characteristics, the degree to which they, and their demands, are recognised as acceptable and legitimate, and their ability to prevail in zero-sum struggles such as in the case of locational and land use conflicts.

Success or failure in attempting to gain a favourable allocation of resources (and avoid outputs with negative impacts or financial penalties) depends on a number of considerations. As already noted, these include the cost of acceding to a demand and whether what is being demanded coincides with the commitments, and conventions, of the agency adjudicating and allocating resources. Undoubtedly all organisations, including public agencies, will attempt to enhance their domains by maximising their autonomy and own resources. Thus councillors will adhere to pre-agenda party group decisions and officers will, depending on their seniority, role and amount of discretion they are allowed, conform to the established conventions and rules of their individual bureaucracies. The pork-barrel principle of allocating resources to reward supporters, and influence voters in marginal electoral areas has been shown to operate, albeit more explicitly in the American political system, especially in national politics (Hoare, 1983). Senior councillors of the political party in power in a City Council may also be willing and able to channel funds into their own wards. However it is senior officials who are likely to have a dominant say over budget making and the resulting level of resources devoted to different departments and how, when and where funds are actually spent during the subsequent financial year.

Clearly, organisational decision rules are important, indeed Hoggart (1983) has suggested that 'decision routines set up and followed by officers and councillors alike can override the effects of changes in party control or administrative personnel' (p. 66).

Bureaucratic decision rules are the formal and informal guidelines that direct service personnel in making the myriad choices with which they are confronted about resource allocations both on a daily basis and more episodically. Such rules are generally justified in terms of professional standards aimed at ensuring efficiency, openness and effectiveness in service delivery. They may also deflect public criticism by providing a rationale for decisions.

Thus they are conventions and procedures which determine, for example, who will be allocated a given service — including eligibility rules based on age, income and residential location. They are norms accepted by professional officers which govern how a service is produced and delivered within broad policy and financial constraints, and how various categories of citizens and consumers are treated. They are more likely to be based on 'technical-rational' definitions of need rather than overtly 'political' criteria.

Such rules exist basically to ensure equity or equality, fairness and consistency in the allocation and provision of public services. While individual cases may be treated on their merits, especially if discretion is given to officers, a framework of decision rules is said to reduce costs and minimise conflict by, for example, determining need, entitlement and eligibility. Thus individual decisions do not have to be made in isolation. Such rules may be invoked by officials when politicians and/or the public question and challenge their decisions.

While some rules are based on national legislation and others emanate from professional organisations, many are decided by municipal departments at the local level. In most cases the details will be formulated by senior officials and then formally agreed by councillors. The actual operation of such rules will be left to 'street level bureaucrats' — inspectors, operatives, receptionists, junior officials (those who deal with the public directly on an everyday basis). However, senior officials may also monitor their overall operation and adjudicate when disputes arise.

Depending on the type of service concerned and the circumstances, rules may be (1) very specific and strictly enforced, that is, they prescribe detailed courses of action; (2) more general norms, guidelines, or benchmarks which may be interpreted by officials using their own discretion, local knowledge and judgement. Under some circumstances, e.g. where agencies have centralised control systems, where scarce resources are at stake, and individual members of the public are involved directly, such rules are likely to be more explicit and officials will be at pains to abide by them and be seen to be doing so.

Although bureaucratic rules are 'neutral' their effects are significant determinants of who (what areas) gets what level of resources from local authorities. They represent *one* sort of criteria governing the distribution of expenditure on such items as: inspections; repairs; facilities being opened or closed; staff additions or reductions; grants; permissions and prosecutions; street cleaning; lighting and patching; the location of bus stops, clinics, centres, schools, taxi ranks, etc. In other words, what is spent, located and provided where within a given city or borough. The amenities of different areas and the wellbeing of ratepayers, tenants consumers and visitors may thus be affected.

Some examples of bureaucratic decision rules include the following:

(1) New library books will be allocated to branch libraries on the basis of borrowing/circulation rates; opening hours will be the same in all branch libraries.

(2) Domestic refuse will be emptied once a week; new dustbins will be provided and special collections will be made on request.

(3) Trees in public places will be trimmed and grass mowed on a 'systematic geographical rotation' basis.

(4) In wintry conditions snow will be cleared and gritting undertaken in the first instance on bus routes and major roads linking emergency service facilities (hospitals, ambulance and fire stations).

(5) Road maintenance will be done on the basis of the state of repair of the surface, volume of traffic, the plans of public utility companies, and complaints by the public.

(6) Identical teacher-pupil ratios between schools of similar status will be achieved by adjusting for changes in school rolls. Children travelling to schools located more than a certain distance from their homes will receive free bus passes. Allocation to schools will be primarily on the basis of living in designated catchment areas.

(7) Police response times will depend on the 'seriousness' of a reported crime, e.g. crimes of violence will take precedence over parking offences.

(8) Places of residence and income will govern, eligibility for council housing, a 'points' or 'date order' system will operate in allocating dwellings of varying size, age, type and location to those on the waiting list or seeking transfers.

(9) Planning applications will be refused or allowed on the basis of constraints imposed by structure and local plans, the scale of objections, and the precise nature of the application.

The relative merits of rules versus discretion in resource allocation are beyond the scope of this chapter but are debated at length in a text edited by Adler and Asquith (1981). Suffice to say at this juncture that to understand how and why public agencies allocate resources a knowledge of the internal procedures and rules is essential.

Key Concepts and a Case Study

Thus far it has been argued that whatever the merits of alternative approaches to explaining patterns of resource allocation by urban public authorities a process-orientated perspective that focuses on the interaction between individuals and organisations constitutes a searchlight with a powerful beam to illuminate the causes of patterns of resource allocation. Output studies have their place although it is difficult to see the justification for the conclusion by Sharpe and Newton (1984, p. 3) that 'all in all the output approach has a lot to commend it as a method for elucidating the political process'. Certainly variations in expenditure on different services on the part of authorities has been shown to be influenced by the character of their jurisdictions. Yet even if constraints and opportunities impinge upon the autonomy of local politicians and officials it is they who make fiscal and service decisions.

The roles of councillors, officers and the public have been discussed and will be examined in relation to the question of who decides what and why over the making of traffic regulation orders in one British city. It has been stressed that patterns of financial or other resources which can be observed on the ground are generally the result of a lengthy and complex process in which the relation of power and pressure exerted by participants is crucial. Organisational interest and decision rules are also important as are the electoral consequences to local politicians of action taken and money spent.

A large number of studies of intra-city distribution of service expenditure have been undertaken in recent years, mostly by political scientists in American cities (Boyle and Jacobs, 1983; Levy *et al.*, 1974; Linebery, 1977; Mladenka and Hill, 1977). (Geographers have tended to focus primarily on the distribution of public facilities.)

One of the distinctive features of these studies is that they are basically concerned with analysing the equalities in the distribution of service provision whether measured by expenditure or differential accessibility to facilities, i.e. do different socio-economic/racial groups in different neighbourhoods get a better or worse deal? Only then are a number of explanatory variables investigated using bivariate correlation techniques. These studies, including those conducted in Britain and elsewhere (Adrian, 1983; Goschel *et al*; Webster *et al.*, 1982) have shown that resources in the form of services are often distributed on the basis of 'unpatterned irregularity'. Thus although there are substantial disparities in the results of empirical studies none of these investigations found conclusive evidence that confirmed the underclass hypothesis that is, that the poor consistently had the least money spent on them or inferior services provided. Although such studies concentrate on outputs rather than processes they have revealed there are whole sets of determinants of the inter-neighbourhood allocation of expenditure. These include past decisions, population movements, demands and protests, ecological constraints (e.g. the lack of sites available) and above all allegiance to professional standards and reliance on technical-rational criteria on the part of bureaucrats. Mladenka (1980) for example concludes that organisational rules provide a better explanation of who gets what than any combination of distinctly political and electoral variables.

The case study presented here consists of a detailed analysis of the decision-making process involved in formulating and making traffic regulation orders, over a two-year period in the City of Portsmouth, England. In a sense such orders, which are designed to control the movement of traffic and parking in the interests of good safety, improvement in amenity and accessibility are essentially regulative. But they are also allocative in the sense that considerable money is spent, and staff time and effort expended, in their introduction. Also since the orders involving one-way systems and parking restrictions are location-specific, they have a significant spatial dimension.

Traffic Regulation Orders

Traffic regulation orders are made by the Portsmouth City Council acting as agent for Hampshire County Council under Section 1–9 of the Road Traffic Regulation Act, 1967 as amended by the Highway Act, 1980. (Only the Department of Transport can make orders relating to motorways and trunk roads and District Council's direct powers cover only the making of bye-laws e.g. concerning hackney carriage ranks and dogs fouling footways.) Such orders are made to avoid danger to persons or damage to vehicles, to prevent the use of a road by traffic for which it is deemed unsuitable, to preserve and enhance the amenity of the area through which a road runs, and to control the speed of vehicles and prevent congestion and obstruction of the highway. Orders once made are permanent and can be revoked or changed only by a further order (under Section 9 orders can be experimental for 6 months). Examples of different types of order include: no waiting; limited waiting; prohibition of through traffic; no entry; temporary closure; one-way traffic; weight restrictions or prohibition of HGVs; bus lanes and clearways; and speed limits. It is not uncommon for exemptions to be made in the provisions of such orders, e.g. for disabled persons' vehicles and for picking up and setting down passengers.

The statutory procedure governing the making of such orders is laid down by the Local Authorities Traffic Orders (England and Wales) Procedure Regulations, 1969 (see Table 6.1) and the time scale is shown in Figure 6.1. Every traffic or speed limit order must comply with this statutory procedure and failure to carry out any of the steps laid down will lay an order open to challenge in the courts. In addition in two specific circumstances (1) a proposed ban on loading and unloading where there are objections, and (2) a proposed one-way traffic or no entry order where objections by a bus operator are not withdrawn, the holding of a public enquiry is obligatory. (Such inquiries are held by an Inspector selected by the authority from a list supplied by the Secretary of State.) Further, local councils are advised to arrange inquiries when a major and complex traffic management scheme is proposed.

Figure 6.1: Time Scale for Traffic Regulation Orders

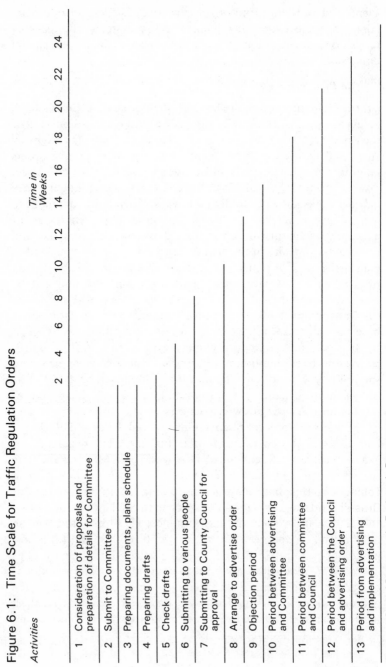

Activities

Time in Weeks

1 Consideration of proposals and preparation of details for Committee

2 Submit to Committee

3 Preparing documents, plans schedule

4 Preparing drafts

5 Check drafts

6 Submitting to various people

7 Submitting to County Council for approval

8 Arrange to advertise order

9 Objection period

10 Period between advertising and Committee

11 Period between committee and Council

12 Period between the Council and advertising order

13 Period from advertising and implementation

Source: City of Portsmouth, Engineer's Department

Public Consultation over Traffic Regulation Orders

Under the Road Traffic Regulation Act (1967) Section 1 as amended by the Highways Act 1980, the City Council acting as agent for Hampshire County Council are required to consult the public before making a traffic regulation order. These govern the movement of vehicular traffic in the miles of carriageways in the city. During the latter part of the 1970s the City Council passed a substantial number of orders in the interests of road safety, access, and the free flow of traffic. The total annual number of orders was as follows: 1976–36, 1977–47, 1978–52, 1979–47, 1980–45. The Council have a statutory obligation to inform those members of the affected public about the aims, scope and likely effect of draft orders and take into account objections. They also consult widely with interested bodies as a matter of course. The detailed processes of making an order and procedures for involving the public are outlined in Table 6.2.

Table 6.1: Statutory Procedure Governing Traffic Regulation Orders

(1) Consult police.
(2) Publish notice of intention to make the order in at least one local paper and the London Gazette and consult other bodies as necessary e.g. AA, RAC. Notice must also be posted in the road concerned.
(3) Allow a minimum period of 3 weeks from date of publication to allow objections. During this time the notice, draft order, plan and statement of reasons for making the order must be available for public inspection.
(4) All objections must be considered by the (Transportation) Committee which may approve, modify or abandon proposals in the light of objections.
(5) Objectors advised of Committee decision.
(6) If approved or modified so as to be less restrictive — signs erected, order sealed, advertised and brought into operation. If modifications are more restrictive, proposal has to be re-advertised and procedure restarted.

Table 6.2: Decision Making and Consultation in Making an Order in Portsmouth

1 *DEMAND FOR ACTION* by groups of residents, councillors, businesses, traders GIA residents' committees, the police or emergency services (some initiatives also arise from within the City Engineer's Department).
2 *INVESTIGATION* of the issues by engineers in the Traffic Management Section of City Engineer's Department.
3 *PRELIMINARY CONSULTATIONS* with County Surveyor and the police.
4 *EXPLORATORY TALKS* with groups of local residents, e.g. GIA committees in road concerned (if requested to do so by ward councillors or a major scheme proposed).
5 PREPARATION OF DRAFT ORDER and report setting out the background, aims and need for the proposed action for the Transportation Committee

(Passenger Transport and Traffic Management).

6 *PRE-AGENDA MEETING* between senior officials of section and Chairman and Vice Chairman of Transportation Committee.

7 *RECOMMENDATION BY TRANSPORTATION COMMITTEE* that a draft order be made.

8 *CONSULTATION* with statutory and other interested bodies (AA, RAC, RHA, Chamber of Commerce, Trades Council, British Telecom, Public Utilities and emergency services).

9 *NOTICE OF THE DRAFT ORDER PUBLISHED IN THE 'NEWS'* with details of the measure, the address and times, the names of roads affected, the addresses and times (in the Civic Offices) at which the order together with plans and statement of reasons for the proposal may be inspected and deadline for written objections to be submitted.

10 *DISPLAY OF SITE NOTICES* at the end of, and at intermediate points in, each of the roads to which the traffic measures apply. The notices contain an outline of the scope of the proposal and details of how and where to object. They are stuck to hardboard squares attached to lamposts and covered to ensure legibility.

11 *PERIOD IN WHICH OBJECTIONS ARE RECEIVED* (if any) (3 weeks). Informal discussions and explanations are held with those inspecting the plans in the offices of the Secretariat and/or City Engineer's Department (both in the Civic Offices). Written objections including grounds for objection are received including those submitted marginally beyond the deadline. Some objections are withdrawn after clarification by officials. An informal local hearing may be heard at the discretion of the Council. (The Director of Engineering has delegated powers to implement an order where no objections are forthcoming, without going through Council and Transportation Committee for a second time.)

12 *PREPARATION OF A REPORT ON THE DRAFT ORDER FOR TRANSPORTATION COMMITTEE* setting out the objectives of the proposal; the number and substance of objections and by whom they have been made; comments on the merits and demerits of the objections and a recommendation to confirm the order as advertised in whole, or parts thereof, or as amended.

13 *MEETING OF TRANSPORTATION COMMITTEE* to recommend that the order be made. Prior to this meeting details of objections including copies of actual letters and petitions and summary of grounds for objections and comments by City Engineers are sent to each member of the Committee (and since 1983 to all ward councillors). These meetings are open to the public and deputations of objectors are permitted to speak (for 10 minutes) at the discretion — invariably exercised — of the Chairman.

14 The City Council must hold a LOCAL PUBLIC INQUIRY if they wish to proceed with an order where objections have been made and not withdrawn against a proposed ban on loading and unloading or where a bus operator objects to a one-way system or road closures.

15 *CITY COUNCIL CONFIRMATION OF THE ORDER* (Details of the draft order and objections to it and comments are included in an appendix to the Council agenda).

16 *OBJECTORS ARE NOTIFIED IN WRITING* of the Council's decision.

17 *CONFIRMATION* of the order by Hampshire County Council (see standard form of consultation).

18 Notice of the order placed in the News.

19 Objectors may challenge the order in the High Court within a specified period.

20 *ORDER IMPLEMENTED* in whole or part.

The latter section of this chapter examines the scope and impact of involvement by the public in objecting to and occasionally supporting draft orders and decisions made by officers and councillors. It examines whether or not public initiative and acceptance of traffic regulations are an important factor in influencing decisions by the Transportation Committee and Council. What weight is attached to the advice of other agencies such as the police? What professional technical criteria govern the framing of orders and their spatial allocation? What part do councillors play in the process? Finally, what proportion of orders are implemented and why?

Traffic Regulation Orders during 1977 and 1978. A two-year period was chosen to analyse the extent of public consultation in the making of traffic regulation orders. During this 24-month period a total of 78 orders were made (orders initiated in 1977 but completed in 1978 were excluded but all 1978 orders even if they were not implemented until after December 1978 are included). 26 orders were for a prohibition of waiting only (105 roads); 7 orders incorporated both prohibition and restriction of waiting (29 roads); there were 8 temporary orders (8 roads); 14 orders comprised multiple regulations (49 roads); finally there were 24 orders regulating the flow of traffic (one-way order, prohibition of driving, no entry, etc.) (69 roads).

Study of the pattern of streets covered by these orders show that they are concentrated in the inner city, especially in and around the main shopping centres and along the main shopping streets where pedestrians, buses and private cars compete for space on the city's often narrow and congested Victorian roads. The other main foci for orders are the areas which were declared as General Improvement Areas during the mid-1970s. In these areas improvement schemes given incorporating traffic management schemes, are worked out by traffic engineers in conjunction with local residents' committees.

The Public as Instigators of Traffic Regulation Orders. It is apparent that the public plays an important role in demanding traffic orders. No less than 17 orders are known to have been started when groups of residents complained to the Council about traffic problems which were presumably adversely affecting them. Of course in many other cases it was Council Officers (responsible for passenger transport and refuse collection, for example) who intervened to get the process started. In some cases such as the relocation of the Isle of Wight Ferry Port in Old Portsmouth and the pedestrian precinct in Southsea, draft orders are necessitated by major council plans and actions. Nonetheless it is evident that complaints and demands by local residents are one of the main catalysts for traffic problems to be put on the agenda of the City Engineer's Department. In seven cases it was GIA residents' committees which demanded traffic management as part of their environmental improvement schemes. In several neighbourhood proposals involving one-way streets, prohibition and restriction of parking, and road closures were demanded and agreed by residents' committees in consultation with councillors and officers. Elsewhere, groups of residents organised petitions, public meetings and working parties, and wrote letters to try to persuade those in authority to take action.

Though many traffic problems were placed on the agenda as a result of complaints and demands on the part of the residents, this was no guarantee that they would be converted into draft orders for approval by the Transportation Committee. Certainly, responses were made to all written complaints made by individuals and demands made by neighbourhood organisations or substantial groups of residents were normally thoroughly investigated by traffic engineers. It was usual for those problems which affected several streets to be 'processed' by way of traffic surveys, working parties (comprising councillors, residents, local traders, the police etc.) and site visits and informal discussion with ward councillors and those who had brought the issue to the attention of the City Engineer's Department. In addition consultations were carried out with the AA and RAC as well as other public and interested bodies. At this stage the principal traffic engineer and his colleagues decided whether or not they should make a recommendation to the Transportation Committee that a draft order be made. This decision was based on the perceived seriousness of the problem as indicated by consultations, and the feasibility and likely acceptability to residents of an order, as well as the officially perceived need for the proposal in terms of traffic management. Questions of timing and cost were also taken into account as were the attitudes of ward councillors. For example, during 1978, a petition was received from residents in Chesterfield Road requesting that a one-way scheme be introduced to reduce congestion, noise and danger. Following this demand, a survey of traffic movements in this and surrounding roads was undertaken and the city engineer concluded — 'The roads are not heavily trafficked and are already covered by a prohibition of commercial vehicles over 3 tons . . . a one-way system would be costly and unnecessary in view of the inconvenience likely to be caused to residents in other roads, it may also encourage drivers to increase speeds . . . on balance it is considered that existing conditions in Chesterfield Road are not sufficiently dangerous to warrant a traffic management scheme' (Transportation Committee Minutes). (The Committee subsequently recorded that no action be taken). The initial report and recommendation of the City Engineer is a crucial factor in determining if and how demands by local residents and others become draft orders. The officials involved, however, do take the consultative process seriously. In part this is due to the nature of the issue itself, and the need for smooth implementation of the schemes. Unlike plans for development, or renovation of the built environment, traffic orders can be revoked or changed relatively easily. If councillors, or committees, were faced with a succession of protests after the schemes had been put into practice, this would create real problems for traffic engineers and other officials. Adequate consultation was in a sense then a prerequisite, for the programme of work in the City Engineer's Department.

The Preparation of a Proposal and Decision by the Transportation Committee. A detailed report was prepared following investigation and consideration within the department and consultations with the police and county surveyor. By this stage in the process local residents and ward councillors would also have been sounded out if the proposed scheme was a major one involving significant changes in the regulation of traffic movement, parking and loading and unloading. Following this proposals were presented to the six-weekly meetings of the Transportation (Passenger Transport and Traffic Management) Committee, together with detailed reports setting out their background and aims. To avoid proposals being 'suddenly' rejected by councillors, soundings were made by officers of the city engineer's department at pre-agenda meetings with their chairman and vice chairman. If they were found to be acceptable they were then placed on the agenda of the Committee. The recommendations of officers were rarely rejected and proposals then become draft orders. Very occasionally ward councillors intervened and halted the progress of a proposal because they thought it was unnecessary or unlikely to be unacceptable. For example, during 1978 a proposal had been made to control parking on two roads, following complaints, made by local residents of danger created by indiscriminate parking especially when Portsmouth Football Club were playing at home at nearby Fratton Park. However ward councillors spoke at the Committee indicating that in their view the proposal was too expensive for a problem which occurred only once a fortnight. The Committee resolved that the city Engineers should reappraise the situation in the light of the comments of ward councillors and eventually the proposal was deleted.

Other traffic issues were included on the agenda of the Committee for comment and a decision taken as to what action to take, e.g. a traffic regulation order or some alternative solution. For example, a petition was received from the parents of children at a first school demanding that through traffic should be restricted on adjoining roads. The City Engineer was asked to investigate and report back at a future meeting. Another petition for a prohibition of waiting outside a school in Southsea was deferred until a GIA residents' committee had been set up in the locality.

In general, therefore, the Transportation Committee agreed to the making of a draft order if recommended to do so by Departmental officers although to state that the committee was simply a rubber stamp is misleading. As outlined, such recommendations were primarily based on research and technical considerations together with comments from those bodies consulted at this stage of the procedure. None the less, the reasons for a proposal were frequently discussed at length by councillors before a decision was taken.

Objecting to Draft Orders. Having thus far been initially and marginally involved in the formulation of a draft order the public now have a chance to submit written objections. Under the statutory procedures outlined in Table 6.1. the draft order must by law be advertised in the press and in the roads affected by the order. These public notices include precise details of the order itself and where, when and to whom to object. These procedures of course are scrupulously observed because failure to do so would leave the City Council open to an appeal to the High Court or complaint to the local Ombudsman. This dual method of publicity seem to have been reasonably effective as an information system as the local newspaper is widely read even if the public notices section is not the first part to which readers turn!

Although Portsmouth City Council only allow three weeks for objections they did not rule out those which were received marginally late. In addition, individuals telephoning, writing or calling at the Guildhall Civic Offices in person (to see the detailed plans and maps) were provided with clarification, explanation and justification by officials. Some potential and actual objections were withdrawn following these discussions. No formal public hearings or indeed public inquiries were held during the two-year period 1977–8 but on a number of occasions city engineers did attend public meetings or GIA residents' committee meetings to explain draft orders.

While a substantial number of draft orders (31 orders covering a total of 67 roads) were the subject of no objections or indeed support, a majority (60 per cent) of draft orders were opposed by some local residents, trades, businesses and other organisations. There were few or no objections to certain types of draft orders notably the eight temporary traffic regulations and orders affecting roads in non-residential locations. The traders and businesses adjoining these roads did not feel their interests threatened by restrictions of parking and commercial and private users felt likewise or did not have an opportunity to see or at least clearly read the site notices. The other kind of draft order that was clearly welcomed was the prohibition of commercial vehicles over 3 tons in the north east of the city where residents in these suburban districts felt that such regulations would enhance their amenity by lessening noise and vibration and pressure on parking. Indeed the only objection to one order affecting no less than 48 roads in the north east of the city was a petition for inclusion from two roads which had been excluded from the order.

The analysis of objections shows that groups of residents and local traders and businesses who were directly affected by the schemes were the major sources of opposition to draft orders. 23 orders were opposed by commercial interests and 31 by groups of residents living in the roads to be affected by the proposals. In one case a petition was submitted but only ten of the signatures were of local residents the great majority being non-local patrons of two public houses objecting to the parking restrictions. Very few organisations previously consulted at the statutory consultation stage, for example the AA or RHA, objected. 'Reservations' were expressed by such bodies on only two occasions. In 12 cases petitions were submitted with varying numbers of signatures attached. In the case of the one way traffic scheme for Baffins and Milton Roads a petition with 85 signatures was presented by objectors even before the draft order had been officially published.

Reasons for Objecting. From the letters and petitions submitted to the City Council some of the probable motives as well as stated reasons for objection on the part of those in business, working or living in roads and streets concerned can be seen. As far as commercial organisations were concerned, objections were primarily based on 'loss of trade' resulting from the implementation of an order. In particular shop-keepers, publicans and hoteliers saw prohibition or restriction of parking outside and nearby their premises as likely to deter their potential customers, particularly those passing by rather than living locally. Graphic portrayals of trade being 'crippled' by parking restrictions were commonplace in the letters sent by shop-keepers in Southsea. Some representations were more restrained in their style — 'there would be a deleterious effect on the operation of retailing'. Publicans and club managers also feared that their regulars and members would be inconvenienced. (The solicitor representing Mr Ho in Kingston Road stated that his main anxiety was the effect the proposals would have on his carry-out premises. Captain Bateman, Secretary of the Royal Naval Club and Royal Albert Yacht Club (who incidentally was one of the few objectors to appear in person at a Committee meeting) pointed out that in his view 'the general city interests would be best served 'by abandonment of the parking limitation outside his club in Old Portsmouth, as some of his members were disabled'.)

Objections were also raised by businesses whose activities would be adversely affected by restrictions on loading and unloading. Some stores vigorously (and successfully) opposed a bus clearway which would have affected their operations. Many of these commercial organisations objected to the fact that although they claimed to be highly rated, their businesses were being penalised by the City Council. They deemed such draft orders to be costly and unnecessary. The timing of one particular order reducing parking in streets near a major shopping centre was deplored, since it occurred 'just before Christmas — our busiest period'. In a few cases employers clearly felt they were protecting their workforce in objecting. For example, Whitbreads Ltd. in Portsea objected to a 'residents only' parking scheme in neighbouring streets because it took no account of those working in the area. They already permanently rented 87 spaces in a car park and resented losing a further 72 spaces close to the brewery. Likewise when prohibition of waiting was suggested for two roads in a council estate in the north-east of the city it was not only the local branch of the trade union representing 53 workers at a city depot nearby who objected, but also the Director of Housing who protested on behalf of the management and maintenance staff of the estate's housing office. Finally objections were received from the matron of a children's home in Southsea because of the inconvenience that parking prohibitions would cause to social workers, parents and residential staff.

Objections from residents were mainly based on amenity considerations. Letters were replete with references to the inconvenience and possible increase in vandalism which would occur if parking spaces outside or near their houses were removed by the order. They referred to 'the possible unpleasantness which would be caused by having to park in front of other people's houses, the inconvenience of having to travel increased distances to go around a one-way system to get home'. Other residents feared that whoever might benefit from the draft order being implemented they (and their street) would suffer. Thus householders in several road, pleaded that they might be included in the zone in which heavy vehicles were to be barred to avoid 'heavy traffic, noise, pollution, danger to property and school children'. Other residents were afraid that a one-way traffic scheme on the Bailey's Road area of Southsea would increase 'congestion accidents and environmental stress'. Several objectors pointed out that in their view the effect of the order would be merely to cascade the problem to other areas. As for parking, difficulties would be compounded, not eased, by some of the orders proposed.

Other objections revolved around the need for the draft order or the right of those who supported it to speak for local people. The right of GIA residents' committees to represent the views of local residents and traders was questioned in several instances. Support for a prohibition of parking in Hamilton Road by the Residents Association was deemed to represent 'merely the whims of a few individuals' by a local garage proprietor who objected to the proposal. Some objectors cited the fact that no traffic accidents had occurred in the recent past as evidence that there was no need for an order to be made. Others claimed not that there was no need for action but that what was proposed was not the right one. In general, the tenor of comments ranged from constructive to outraged.

The Evaluation of Objections by Traffic Engineers and Their Rec-ommendations to the Transportation Committee. Before the Transportation Committee met to recommend whether or not a draft order should be made or amended in part, or its implementation delayed, each councillor was provided with a report setting out the original reasons for the draft order, a summary of the main points of objection with copies of actual letters and petitions, an 'answer' to these points stating their merits and demerits, and finally, a recommendation. The crucial questions to be answered in relation to this vital stage in the process are (1) were amendments, delays and deletions eventually made by the Committee wholly or partly in line with the recommendations of the officials and (2) what were the criteria which influenced traffic engineers in drawing up their recommendations; in particular were the number and nature of objections (and support) significant?

The first question is easily answered for, with only two exceptions, the changes which were made in the draft orders were all in line with the views expressed by traffic engineers in their reports to the Committee. In other words when an amendment to a draft order was recommended, for whatever reason, the Committee decided to approve the order to be made accordingly, and the full Council with only two exceptions decided likewise. This is not to say of course that elected representatives slavishly followed every suggestion made by their officers but that they, as members of the committee, and, in some cases also as ward councillors, were satisfied that the draft order was beneficial and acceptable. While their views may indeed have been influenced by other pressures or information none the less the detailed official evidence and recommendation constituted the most significant factor in influencing their decision making.

How and why did traffic engineers make their recommendations? The first point to be made is that, given the number of draft orders which were amended (22 out of 78) then the considered opinions and arguments of objectors were important in the process, even though in many of these 22 draft orders the concessions were relatively minor, involving the spatial or temporal extent of parking restrictions and prohibitions at the behest of businesses and groups of residents who strongly opposed them. Compromises were therefore accepted provided that the basic traffic aims and objectives of the order were maintained. For example, in relation to a scheme to prohibit waiting, it was stated that 'no waiting on Locksway Road though desirable is not essential at the current time for, as objectors point out, little obstruction is caused to buses . . . therefore we recommend that this part of the order be not implemented yet (but if the Passenger Transport Department or the Police report difficulties then the Committee if it thinks fit may approve a date for implementation'). This reflected the views of local residents. The expressed views of firms also were on occasions accepted — 'We thought that the firm would have welcomed a prohibition of waiting outside their premises to prevent obstruction but as this is not so the City Engineer considers that the order could be amended except where this would permit parking on both sides of the road'. In relation to the Baffins Road area one-way system the report cited the strong reaction from Baffins Road residents despite the fact that they may be at risk because of the problem. Thus whatever their misgivings officials were prepared to concede that objections of some local residents were strongly felt if not entirely valid, and made recommendations accordingly. The same point is apposite in relation to occasions when ward councillors intervened in support of objections, for example the deletion of parking prohibitions for part of Albert Road, and the concession made to the Royal Yacht Club after the personal intervention of its secretary.

As a corollary of this major finding there is evidence that some objections were overruled because they clashed with either (1) the basic aim of the order and what were considered sound traffic principles and (2) evidence of a well established body of support for the proposal. Thus in the case of a 1978 order to prohibit waiting on various roads engineers 'considered that although there may be drawbacks to this proposal it is on balance, justified because of the overriding need to improve road safety'. Similarly in relation to a draft order banning parking from the junctions of roads off Winter Road in central Southsea the City Engineer recommended making the order because — 'although it is acknowledged that some reduction of street parking for residents is entailed it has been kept to a minimum and standards of access, visibility and safety should take priority over the needs of parking'. (A working party comprising local councillors, traders and police etc. had also supported the scheme.)

All draft orders which had the support of GIA residents' committees were backed by officials, apart from a traffic management scheme supported in 1977 by only one of 3 GIAs in Fratton and actively opposed by residents and traders ('in view of the large number of objections it is recommended that the draft order is deferred to enable further discussions to take place with residents' committees) and not by the Residents' Committee of GIA 7. Thus in GIA 4 (King Street area) despite a petition with 522 signatures (10 local) and an animated public meeting the original scheme was recommended because since the GIA Committee represented the people living in the area 'it was assumed that those residents (who did not sign the petition) did not wish to sign or were not canvassed'. Later in 1978 the revised scheme for Fratton was approved because of 'the overwhelming support of the GIA committees'. Objections were overruled because 'a great deal of time has been spent on ensuring that the wishes of local residents have been taken into account when drawing up the scheme for this area'.

In yet other cases conflicting criteria for traffic regulation and apparently incompatible interests of residents, bus users and traders clearly made for difficulties in recommending a particular course of action. (Thus in the case of the Clarendon Road bus clearway, reservations expressed by the police and 'some inconvenience in loading and unloading was outweighed by the need to protect the interests of pedestrians and bus passengers'.) In some cases further consultation was felt to be necessary but more frequently officials indicated that they felt confident that discussions with residents had resolved outstanding dificulties.

Finally there were instances when however much they would have wished to acquiesce to the demands of objectors the city engineers maintained that they were unable to do so. For example, they argued that Old Manor Road and Grove Road in Drayton could not be included in the prohibition of commercial vehicles of over 3 tons zone until after alternative measures of access to the industrial estate had been provided.

Cases where 'residents were clearly divided' presented particular difficulties. In one case, it was recommended that the one-way system proposed for Auckland Road be taken out of the draft order and that the prohibition of waiting should remain. A second case involving a similar scheme in Villiers Road nearby was also to be amended but at the Committee meeting a second petition was received and, with the support of a ward councillor, the original draft order was reinstated.

Decisions by Transportation Committee, City Council and Hampshire County Council

As intimated earlier, very few recommendations of the City Engineer to the Transportation Committee were not agreed and likewise only a single example of the Committee recommendations being thrown out by the full council occurred during 1977 and 1978. In a sense therefore these two bodies as well as Hampshire County Council were merely rubber-stamping the recommendations of their officers. But this interpretation is misplaced: first, because officials had already entered into consultation and members were reassured that the schemes would be viable; second, because some issues at least generated lengthy discussion on the merits of draft orders and their desirability and political acceptability. At the end of the day though, on only a few occasions did councillors decide *not* to follow the advice of their officials.

An important element was that the views of ward councillors were actively sought and readily given to the Transportation Committee members. For example in the exclusion of Dorking Road and Magdala Road from a draft order to prohibit waiting it was local councillors who urged that 'inconvenience to residents should be minimised and unnecessary hardship avoided' and that these proposals for these two roads should be relaxed. Likewise ward councillors expressed concern on the adverse effects on the trade of a fancy-dress hire shop in Albert Road, Southsea, if parking restrictions were implemented. In the case of the one-way system in Milton it was ward councillors who reported that extensive enquiries in the area had indicated that the majority of residents in Milton Road were in favour of the scheme but not those in Baffins Road. Similarly in the debate over parking in Landport 'the committee considered all points raised and listened to the views of ward councillors who had reminded members of the conflicting interests of residents and traders'. In this case 'after a full debate' the draft order was agreed. Local representatives thus played a major role in the process.

The City Council only twice overturned its Committee's decisions. On the first occasion when the one way system in Southsea was deleted it reinstated that part of the order following the intervention of a senior majority party ward councillor who, on the basis of a counter-petition, convinced his colleagues to vote for the original order. In the second case businesses in the North End shopping centre persuaded the Council to throw out the proposal to designate a bus clearway at peak hours and thereby restrict loading and unloading and waiting. This decision followed a vociferous and well publicised campaign in the local newspaper and the plea that their custom and operation would be jeopardised by such action. The businesses were able to act in a concerted and public way and gain public support.

Despite being consulted at an early and late stage in the process of making of all orders there is no evidence that county officials or councillors intervened in any significant way. The County Secretary certainly did not issue a 'stop notice' on a single draft order.

Implementation of Orders. After the Transportation Committee recommends an order to be made objectors are notified in writing of the decision and reasons for overruling their objections. As has been seen, few objectors attempt to persuade or succeed in persuading the City Council to overturn earlier recommendations. Over the period 1977–8, actual implementation of three orders was delayed to fit into future developments. Parking restrictions surrounding both the Commercial Road and Palmerston Road shopping centres were delayed until major car park schemes had been completed and were opened to shoppers. Apart from these few cases, yellow lines and signs appeared on the designated roads within a matter of weeks as personnel and resources were available. In a few cases there seem to have been minor hiccups in the physical act of implementing orders. In Fratton, temporary barriers caused a stir amongst residents and certainly traders who had never been in favour of road closures. In Landport, local residents expressed their doubts as to the efficiency of the yellow lines. However the opportunity to change the order had long since passed. No members of the public availed themselves of the opportunity to appeal to the High Court against an order. There was one half-hearted attempt to take the City Council to the local Ombudsman because a very belated objection had been over-ruled. In this case a resident of Fratton felt that insufficient detail had been included on the site notice to indicate which parts of his road were forbidden for parking. In the end on the advice of a ward councillor no formal complaint was made.

Portsmouth Traffic Regulation Orders in Perspective

In the making of traffic regulation orders the public have a statutory right to be consulted. The lengthy process affords organisations such as the police as well as potentially affected residents and businessmen several opportunities to express their views. During 1977–8 the initiative for traffic management orders (in the first instance) came from either the City Engineer's Department or from groups of residents, in particular GIA residents committees. In cases where few or no residents were potentially affected by potential public action that is, in roads located outside residential areas, initial consultation with the County Council and the police was pursued as a matter of course. In cases which were significant in their potential impact, where there were likely to be beneficiaries as well as those negatively affected, informal investigations were made at an early stage with residents by way of public meetings, working parties and by means of traffic surveys. Some demands for action were not acceded to by City Engineers but a substantial number eventually became traffic orders. Because many traffic orders had the backing of groups of residents, especially GIA residents, they were made with sensitivity in the first place, though subsequent opposition was limited in all but a few cases.

The traffic engineers were prepared to compromise over minor details of orders, amend sections of them, delay their implementation, or monitor their effect in response to objections. Nevertheless, they rarely recommended that an order should be deleted in its entirety. Members of the Transportation Committee who were well informed of any objections and grounds for objection almost invariably took the advice of their (professional) officials. Only in cases where there was substantial opposition with grounds which were conceived of as being valid did engineers and councillors alter draft orders at Committee or Council stages. Some changes were made, however, despite the fact that officers clearly perceived the draft order as intrinsically well conceived and necessary. It was those draft orders over which residents were divided in their opinions which were opposed by a sizeable number of *local* people (as expressed in letters of objection, a petition or representation by ward councillors) which were amended or deleted. As a corollary, proposals to tackle traffic and parking problems to which any solution, e.g. one-way traffic or restrictions on parking, generated opposition (as well as support) were not initiated.

In objecting to draft regulation orders residents were motivated by fear that their access and amenity would be threatened. Stated grounds for objection in many cases included loss of parking outside or near the objector's house, and increase in the volume and speed of traffic in the objector's road. Although city traffic engineers were not always sympathetic to the need for on-street parking when it threatened the flow of traffic or road safety, they did place a high premium on amenity considerations. Indeed several orders (especially in GIAs) were aimed at reducing through traffic with its associated problems. In the half-dozen or so cases where traffic schemes supported by residents were opposed by traders and businesses it was the interests and views of residents which prevailed. Councillors and engineers also took seriously the fears expressed by businesses and commercial interests that their trade would be adversely affected by prohibition or restrictions on parking. In several cases draft orders were modified to meet some if not all of these objections.

In summary, few if any traffic regulation orders which affected residential areas were made (1) without the support of some residents and (2) in face of substantial opposition by local people. Whilst many orders were amended in minor ways in response to objections which were either substantial in number or deemed to have special merit (e.g. demand for spaces reserved for doctors) they were rarely altered in such a way as to defeat the overall purpose of the proposal. It is difficult to see how the process as statutorily required, and as actually operated in the city, could be improved in terms of public consultation. Despite the not inconsiderable efforts of officers to inform and explain proposals it was apparent that on occasions the potentially affected had not seen site notices and reacted when yellow lines started to be painted near their businesses or houses, or routes were closed which affected their journeys. But as has been seen, objectors did in many cases make their views known during 1977–8 and had their grounds for objection amply brought to the attention of officials and City Councillors at various stages of the process. It seems that traffic regulation orders are made in Portsmouth with the apparent consent of at least the majority of those affected.

Conclusion

A few years ago, an eminent professor of sociology likened geographers to draughts players watching a chess game. His unflattering comment was that while they were more than capable of observing the moves they had not the slightest idea of the rules of the game, and therefore were incapable of making any valid analysis. Clearly this uncharitable and obviously tongue-in-cheek remark is not true now, even if it was so before human geographers began to digest and apply Marxist and managerial theory to urban political topics. It is certainly the case that the aggregate-areal studies by geographers cited in the first sections of this chapter are more impressive in overcoming the technical problems of analysing spatial variation in resource allocation than probing the political processes behind them.

In the future the search for explanations of inter-city and intra-city distributions of public spending and provision, is likely to be more eclectic than in the past. It seems unlikely that a full understanding of who gets what, where and *how* by way of local authority grants, or capital expenditure on new facilities, can be gained if only one pair of theoretical spectacles are worn. Several paradigms — behavioural, ecological or political economy — provide insights (Burnett, 1984). Major budgetary allocations and minor distributional decisions are not made (or influenced) by the same people and are not subject to the same sort of constraints. There are enormous differences in the way that allocative and regulative outputs are arrived at in different national settings and, despite central government efforts to encourage uniformity, between cities in different countries.

Here it has been suggested — and illustrated — how on the basis of participant observation, scrutiny of public documents (minutes, agendas, reports and files) and interviews with key decision makers, data can be gathered on the mechanisms by which resources are allocated by those in authority in cities. Of course observing what is done, and reading about and listening to what is said, do not tell the whole story. Urban public authorities in western capitalist societies are far from being free agents in deciding how much they spend on what and where. None the less they still do retain some degree of autonomy and discretion over policies and plans which affect the quality of life of their citizens.

In has been shown in the City of Portsmouth that in the lengthy and complicated process of making traffic regulation orders, the public played a significant role. None the less it was mainly officers who guided and adjudicated in the case of conflicts of interest and opinion. For their part, councillors were more peripherally involved. Professional judgement together with acceptance on the part of at least a majority of those affected were influential factors in the series of decisions by which orders were made.

What is not known is whether or not the allocations involved such orders are made in the same way in other British cities, or is central government legislation and guidance interpreted differently elsewhere.

Further research is also needed to explore the relationship between and amongst councillors and senior officers in annual budget making and the myriad of allocation decisions which are made by all local authorities. Such explanatory models as bureaucratic decision rules, pork barrelling and incrementalism can be investigated from a spatial perspective. Detailed process-orientated case studies of the spatial variation in the expenditure and urban service provision are of intrinsic value and in addition neatly complement alternative approaches. In so doing they will make a contribution to creating a more political and pluralist subdiscipline.

References

Adams, J.S. (1976) *Urban Policy Making and Metropolitan Dynamics*, Ballinger, Cambridge, Massachusetts

Adler, M. and Asquith, S. (1981) *Discretion and Welfare*, Heinemann, London

Adrian, C. (1983) 'Analysing Service Equity. Fire Services in Sydney', *Environment and Planning A, 15*, 1083–100.

Antunes, G. and Mladenka, K. (1976) 'The Politics of Local Services and Service Distribution' in L. Massotti and R. Lineberry (eds.), *The New Politics*, Ballinger, Cambridge, Massachusetts

Ashford, D. (1975) 'Resources, Spending and Party Politics in British Local Government', *Administration and Society, 7*, 286–311

Bailey, S. (1982) 'Central City Decline and the Provision of Education Services', *Urban Studies, 19*, 263–79.

Barlow, I. (1981) *Spatial Dimensions of Urban Government*, Research Studies Press, Chichester

Beaumont, J. (1984) *The Location of Public Facilities: a Geographical Perspective*, Croom Helm, London

Benyon, J. (1982) 'Dual Loyalty of Planners and Councillors — the Case of Beverley Hills', *Local Government Studies 8*, 53–63

Boaden, N. (1971) *Urban Policy Making*, Cambridge University Press, London

Boyle, J. and Jacobs D. (1982) 'The Intra-city Distribution of Services: a Multivariate Analysis', *American Political Science Review, 76*, 371–9.

Bristow, A. (1982) 'Rates and Votes — the 1980 District Council Elections', *Policy and Politics, 10*, 163–80

Burnett, A. (1984) 'The Application of Alternative Theories in Political Geography: the Case of Political Participation' in P. Taylor and J. House (eds.), *Political Geography: Recent Advances and Future Directions*, Croom Helm, London

—— and Moon, G. (1983) 'Community Opposition to Hostels for Single Homeless Men', *Area, 15*, 161–6

—— and Hill, D. (1981) 'Neighbourhood Organisations and Local Political Outputs in British Cities' in R. Rich (ed.), *The Politics of Urban Public Services*,

Lexington Books, Lexington, Massachusetts
—— Cole, K. and Moon, G. (1983) 'Political Participation and Resource Allocation' in M. Bustead (ed.), *Developments in Political Geography*, Academic Press, London
Burnett, A.D. (1981) 'The Distribution of Local Political Outputs and Outcomes in British and North American Cities: a Review and Research Agenda' in A. Burnett and P. Taylor (eds.), *Political Studies from Spatial Perspectives*, John Wiley, Chichester
Bustead M.A. (1983) *Developments in Political Geography*, Academic Press, London
Clarke, G. and Dear, M. (1984) *State Apparatus: The Structure and Language of Legitimacy*, Allen and Unwin, Boston, Massachusetts
Coulter, P. (1980) 'Measuring the Inequity of Urban Public Services', *Policy Studies Journal*, *8*, 692–706
Cox, K. and McCarthy, J. (1980) 'Neighbourhood Activism in the American City', *Urban Geography*, *1*, 22–38
—— and Johnston, R. (1982) *Conflict, Politics and the Urban Scene*, Longman, London
Danziger, J. (1976) 'Assessing Incrementalism in British Municipal Budgeting', *British Journal of Political Science*, *6*, 335–50
—— (1978) *Making Budgets: Public Resource Allocation*, Sage, Beverly Hills
Davidson, J.L. (1979) *Political Partnership: Neighbourhood Residents and their Council Members*, Sage, Beverly Hills
Dear, M. and Taylor, S.M. (1983) *Not on Our Street*, Pion, London
Dearlove, J. (1973) *The Politics of Policy in Local Government*, Cambridge University Press, Cambridge
Fincher, R. (1981) 'Local Implementation Strategies in the Urban Built Environment, *Environment and Planning*, *A 13*, 1233–52
Friedland, R. (1982) *Power and Crisis in the City*, Macmillan, London
Gifford, J. (1977) *Local Politics in Britain*, Croom Helm, London
Glassberg, A. (1973) 'The Linkage between Urban Policy Outputs and Voting Behaviour, New York and London', *British Journal of Political Science*, *3*, 341–61
Goldsmith, M. (1982) 'Urban Politics', *Teaching Politics, 11*, 345–61
Göschel, A. *et al.* (1982) 'Infrastructural Inequality and Segregation: Theory, Methods, and Results of an Empirical Research Project Carried out in 12 Large Towns in Germany', *International Journal of Urban and Regional Research*, *6*, 503–32
Halford, R. (1983) 'Contracting Out in the Early Eighties', *Local Government Studies*, *9*, 51–7
Hardingham, S. (1983) 'LGC Surveys, Privatisation over the Last Year', *Local Government Chronicle*, No. 6055, 655–8
Hicks, C. (1982) 'Town Hall Goes Local', *Social Work Today*, *14*, 7–9.
Hoare, A. (1983) 'Pork Barrelling in Britain: a Review', *Environment and Planning C, 1* 413–38
Hoggart, K., (1983) 'Explaining Policy Outputs: English County Boroughs 1949–1974', *Local Government Studies*, *9*, no. 6, 57–68
—— (1984) 'Political Parties and Local Authority Capital Investment in English Cities 1966–1971', *Political Geography Quarterly*, *3*, 5–32
Honey, R. and Sorenson, D. (1984) 'Jurisdictional Benefits and Local Costs: the Politics of School Closing' in A. Kirby, P. Knox and S. Pinch (eds.) *Public Service Provision and Urban Politics*, Croom Helm, London, pp. 114–30
Humphreys, D., Mason, C. and Pinch, S. (1984) 'The Externality Fields of Football Grounds: a Case Study of The Dell, Southampton', *Geoforum 14*, 401–11
Jennings, R. (1982) 'The Changing Representative Role of Local Councillors in England', *Local Government Studies*, *8*, no. 5, 67–86

Johnston W.C. (1984) 'Citizen Participation in Local Planning: a Comparison of U.S. and British Experience', *Environment and Planning C* (2) 1–14.

Jones, B. (1980) *Service Delivery in the City: Citizen Demand and Bureaucratic Rules*, Longman, New York

—— (1983) *Governing Urban America: A Policy Focus*, Little Brown, Boston, Massachusetts

Jones, K. and Kirby, A. (1982) 'Provision and Wellbeing: an Agenda for Public Resources Research', *Environment and Planning A, 14*, 297–310

Kirby, A. and Jones, K. (1983) 'The Case of Primary Medical Facilities in Urban Areas: the Case of Vaccination Clinics in London', *Papers in Regulatory Science*, 13 Clarke (ed.), Pion, London

Kirby, A., Knox, P., and Pinch, S. (1983a) Developments in public provision and urban politics: an overview and agenda, *Area* 15 (4), 295–300

—— (eds.) (1983b) *Public Service Provision and Urban Politics*, Croom Helm, London

Knox, P. (1982) 'Residential Structure, Facility Location and Patterns of Crossibility' in K. Cox and R. Johnston (eds.), *Conflict, Politics and the Urban Scene*, Longman, London

—— and Cullen, J. (1981) 'Planners as Urban Managers: an Exploration of the Attitudes and Self-image of Senior British Planners', *Environment and Planning A, 13*, 885–98

Lineberry, R.L. (1977) *Equality and Public Policy*, Sage, Beverley Hills

Levy, F., Meltsner, A. and Wildavsky, A. (1974) *Urban Outcomes: Schools, Streets and Libraries*, University of California Press, Berkeley, California

Masotti, L. and Lineberry, R. (1976) (eds.), *The New Urban Politics*, Ballinger, Cambridge, Massachusetts

Massam, B.H. (1983) 'Spatial Structure of the State: the Local State', Paper Presented to the International Conference of Political Geographers, Oxford University

McLafferty, S. (1982) 'Urban Structure and Geographical Access to Public Services', *Annals, Association of American Geographers*, 72, 347–54

Merkl, P. (1970) *Modern Comparative Politics*, Holt Rinehart and Winston, New York

Mladenka, K. (1980) 'The Urban Bureaucracy at the Chicago Political Machine: Who get What and the Limits of Political Control', *American Political Science Review*, 74, 991–8

—— and Hill, K. (1977) 'The Distribution of Benefits in an Urban Environment Parks and Libraries in Houston', *Urban Affairs Quarterly 13*, 73–94

Moon, G. (1983) 'Political Geography and Public Services: a Case Study of a Suburban Borough', Ph.D. Thesis, Portsmouth Polytechnic

—— and Burnett, A. (1983) 'Conflict and Externality: the Case of the Residential Hostel', Paper given to the Conference on Public Provision and Urban Politics, University of Reading

Moulden, M. and Bradford, M. (1984) 'Influences on Educational Attainment; the Importance of the Local Residential Environment', *Environment and Planning A, 16*, 49–66

Newton, A. (1983) *The Government and Administration of Metropolitan Areas in Western Democracies*, Institute of Local Government Studies, University of Birmingham, Birmingham

Newton, K. (1976) *Second City Policies*, Oxford University Press, Oxford

—— (1981) (ed.), *Urban Political Economy*, Frances Pinter, London

—— and Sharpe, L. (1977) 'Local Outputs Research: Some Rejections and Proposals', *Policy and Politics*, 5, no. 3, 61–82

Noble, D. (1981) 'From Rules to Discretion: The Housing Corporation', in M. Adler and S. Asquith (eds.), *Discretion and Welfare*, Heinemann, London, pp. 171–84

Norton, A. (1983) *The Government and Administration of Metropolitan Areas in Western Democracies*, Institute of Local Government Studies, University of Birmingham

Ossenbrugge, J. (1983) 'Socio-spatial Relations, Local State, Collective Identity and Conflict Behaviour', Paper given to International Conference on Political Geography, Oxford University

Paddison, R. (1983) *The Fragmented State: the Political Geography of Power*, Chapters 5 and 6, Blackwell, London

Pahl, R. (1979) 'Socio-Political Factors in Resource Allocation' in D. Herbert and D. Smith (eds.), *Social Problem and the City*, Oxford University Press, Oxford

Peterson, P. (1979) 'Redistributive Policies and Patterns of Citizen Population in Local Politics in the USA' in L.J. Sharpe (ed.), *Decentralist Trends in Western Democracies*, Sage, Beverly Hills

Pinch, S. (1980) 'Local Authority Provision for the Elderly: an Overview and Case Study of London' in D.T. Herbert and R. Johnston (eds.) *Geography and the Urban Environment*, III, John Wiley, Chichester, pp. 295–343

—— (1982) 'Inequality in Pre-school Provision — a Geographical Perspective', in Kirby P. Knox and S. Pinch (eds.) *Public Service Provision and Urban Politics*, Croom Helm, London, pp. 231–82

Prentice, R.C. (1984) 'Stability and Change in the Views of Representatives: From Evidence from England' *Environment and Planning C.*, *29*, 79–92

Prottas, J.M. (1981) 'The Cost of Free Services: Organisational Impediments to Access to Public Services', *Public Administration Review, 5*, 526–34

Queenspark Rates Book Group (1983) *Brighton on the Rocks: Monetarism and the Local State*, Queenspark, New Series 1, Brighton

Rich, R. (1980) 'The Complex Web of Urban Governance', *American Behavioural Scientist, 24*, 277–98

Rich, R.C. (1979) 'Neglected Issues in the Study of Urban Service Distributions', *Urban Studies, 16*, 143–56

Richardson, A. (1983) *Participation: Concepts in Social Policy 1*, Routledge and Kegan Paul, London

Robertson, C. (1983) *Geographical Perspectives on the Personal Social Services: The Case of the Home Help Service*. Geography Department, Kings College London Occasional Paper No. 16

Schumaker, P. and Getter, R. (1983) 'Structural Sources of Unequal Responsiveness to Group Demands in American Cities', *Western Political Quarterly, 36*, 7–29

Sharpe, L. and Newton, K. (1984) *Does Politics Matter? The Determinants of Public Policy*, Clarendon Press, Oxford

Short, J.R. (1982) *An Introduction to Political Geography*, Routledge and Kegan Paul, London

Simmie, J. and Lovatt, D. (1983) *Marxism and Cities*, Macmillan, London

Spencer, K. (1983) 'Decentralisation and Neighbourhood Management — Is the Mood Changing? *Local Government Studies 9*, no. 4, 38–41

Taylor, P.J. (1982) 'A Materialism Framework for Political Geography', *Transactions, Institute of British Geographers*, *7*, 15–34

—— and House, J. (1984) (eds.) *Political Geography: Recent Advances and Future Direction*, Croom Helm, Beckenham

Walker, S. (1979) 'Educational Services in Sydney: Some Spatial Variations' *Australian Geographical Studies*, *17*, 175–92

Webster, B. *et al.* (1982) *The Impact of Local Authority Services on the Inner City*; Final Report to the D.O.E. *INLOGOV* University of Birmingham, Birmingham

Whitehead, P. (1983) 'Intra-urban Spatial Variation in Local Government Service Provision', *Environment and Planning C, 1*, 73–85; 229–48

Wolch, J. (1980) 'Residential Location and the Service Dependent Poor', *Annals, Association of American Geographers, 70*, 330–41

Wetherfield, M. (1980) 'The Politics of School Closing: Contextual Effects and Community Polarization', *Journal of Politics, 42*, 747–65

7   LOCAL DEMOCRACY IN THE CITY

R. Paddison

The idea (and ideal) of local democracy in the city, though by no means a new concept, has gained widespread popular currency within recent decades. During the 1960s citizen participation became something of a political catch-phrase, to its advocates the means by which greater, and more truly local, democracy could be achieved. Local democracy in the city can be taken to mean the way in which the separate localities making up the urban area, and the individual citizens living within these, are able to express their demands effectively, within the political and administrative decision-making processes. Within this framework, however it is clear that not only do the methods by which demand-making is channelled cover a broad spectrum, but that in practice a considerable variety of administrative solutions have been introduced in the cities of the advanced industrial nations. Such innovations give expression to the development of political activism at the neighbourhood level, reflecting in turn a heightened awareness of the importance of influencing political decision-making as it affects the local turf.

Few concepts can have generated so much debate amongst political scientists as has that of democracy. A quick glance at the literature will reveal a bewildering variety of alternative definitions and criteria by which democracy is to be assessed: it means majority rule, government for the people by the people, government in the public interest, or by common consent and so forth. Conceptually, the idea of democracy has suffered from definitional vagueness (Pickles, 1970; Pennock, 1979), though if there is consensus as to its meaning it is rooted in the ideal of rule by the people for the people. Democracy is to be associated, then, with the means by which the outputs of the political process are determined by popular will. If such a definition leans heavily towards the liberal interpretation of democracy, it need hardly be said that, put in these absolute terms, it remains an ideal, and that democracy in practice falls short of intentions.

Part of the mismatch between theory and practice particularly in the liberal democracies of the economically advanced world, can be attributed to the problem of scale. Political theorists since Classical times have been concerned with the likely effects of scale on democracy (Dahl and Tufte, 1973), by which they have more usually meant population mass rather than the geographer's factor of space. A common argument found within the writings of many of the early political theorists was that the chances of democracy thriving were enhanced when the population of the polity was 'small'. While some of the detail of their argument seems hardly relevant to the modern society, the virtues of small government, linked with the notion of political decentralisation, are still values to which political parties spanning the left-right spectrum subscribe, albeit with varying enthusiasm.

The city epitomises the contradictions between democracy and scale that are characteristic of the industrial society at large. The universal problem of government in a mass urbanised society is the reconciliation of the need for effective administration with the need for maximum accountability. The city confronts similar problems to those of the state, in which administrative effectiveness brings into play increasingly centralist tendencies, while the dictat of accountability argues for greater decentralisation. Direct forms of democracy within Western cities are the exception — cities are usually governed by administrations made up of elected and appointed officials. For the city, as for the state, democracy is indirect, considerable emphasis being placed on the accountability of the elected politician to his electorate, and to the regular (in some cities, annual) holding of elections.

Attempts at fostering local democracy within the city have sought to decentralise the decision-making process, so that as one element of this the separate communities making up the city have a greater role within policy-making. Not unexpectedly, actual achievement in this respect varies, related both to the objectives sought by city administrators in fostering local participation, and to the degree of political activism and mobilisation which the local communities have been able to harness. Not only are there differences between cities (as, for example, in the extent to which community participation has been implemented and encouraged by city administrations) but also within them. As Janelle and Millward (1976) have shown the urban ecological framework gives rise to spatially differentiated forms of conflict within the city. It follows that the extent to which neighbourhood activism influences policy-making will vary within different parts of the city. Thus in the inner city local activism is as likely to be directed to some redevelopment proposal as it is in more peripheral areas to the status-maintenance of a suburb.

While such differences are of interest, at the outset it is the fact that the neighbourhood has become increasingly politicised that should be recognised. Much of this action is directed towards the defence of the neighbourhood, the inspiration for which in American cities was greatly influenced by Jane Jacobs' book *The Death and Life of Great American Cities* published in 1961. To Jacobs maintaining the quality of the neighbourhood was an important contributory measure to maintaining the quality of living within cities. Neighbourhood and participation become inter-linked. Thus

The importance of the neighbourhood begins with the importance of citizenship. To be a citizen is to participate in civic affairs. 'Participate' is the key concept. To simply live in a place, and not participate in its civic affairs, is to be merely a resident, not a citizen (Morris and Hess, 1975 p. 7).

Political geographers interested in local democracy within the city need to address themselves to several basic questions relating to its origins, its implementation and its impacts. In this chapter local democracy within the city is taken to be associated with the emergence of neighbourhood political movements and citizen participation. The reasons why such movements have emerged as a more important political force raise questions about the nature of democracy in general, and about the interactions between the development of the city in the advanced capitalist state and its system of government in particular. Implementation focuses on the types of administrative and political machinery aimed at meeting the objective of incorporating citizen participation, and how this is linked to the socio-spatial organisation of the city. Finally, the question of impact raises the issue of achievement, the extent to which local action alters the urban fabric and contributes to the solving of conflicts. In so far as the channels for local participation have frequently been imposed 'from above', a key factor is the objectives which are sought for urban local democracy, goals which can (and do) vary between the city administrators and the local community. Thus neighbourhood participation might be seen as merely an informing and consultation device by city administrators, while at grassroots level it is seen as affording real opportunity in influencing decision-making processes. A key factor, then, is whether attempts at encouraging neighbourhood democracy are associated with attempts to redistribute power within the city. Before discussing these three elements it is important to clarify the nature of urban local democracy, which is best done through examining the different types of local political action characteristically found within Western cities.

Types of Local Democratic Action

In recognising different types of local democratic action within the city based on the urban neighbourhood a useful distinction (if not always clear-cut,) is whether such bodies have been generated spontaneously 'from below', or whether they have been deliberately fostered 'from above', by an urban or a higher level of government. In some respects such a distinction might be more apparent than real — the type of issues over which the locality becomes mobilised (anti-freeway movements or the improvement of public services, for example) may be similar for the two types, as can be their membership and the types of obstacles, bureaucratic or otherwise, encountered by the activist group in prosecuting its objectives. Nevertheless, in terms of the objectives sought for, and by, community participation, the militancy with which the local groups are willing to press their case and the degree of their formal incorporation within the machinery of urban government — imposed forms will enjoy greater automatic legitimacy — there are substantive differences between movements belonging to the two types.

In any city, local protest groups arise naturally from the conflicts and contradictions which capitalist urban development brings in its wake. Often such protest is directed towards specific issues; common examples would include groups established to fight urban freeway and other transportation proposals, developments involving a change of land-use which involve perceived negative externality effects, and demand-making over the wide range of public services for which the municipal jurisdictions are responsible (Burnett and Hill, 1982). In those cases in which such action groups arise from locational conflict Janelle and Millward (1976) have suggested a spatial model of where, within the city, conflicts of different types are likely to arise. Thus land-use planning issues, and particularly those of redevelopment and conservation, are more dominant in the central area and the transitional zone, demands for improved public services and conflicts arising from public and private housing are more characteristic of the transitional zone and newly expanding areas on the urban fringe, while certain issues, such as education, surface politically city-wide.

Analyses of the referenda held in Swiss municipalities illustrate the types of issue over which local conflict arises. In Swiss municipalities the referendum is a relatively well used instrument of 'semi-direct democracy', though the conditions under which it can be invoked vary between cantons. In the Vaud canton the right to hold a referendum is established once it is requested by 20 per cent of the electorate. Between 1950 and 1980 referenda were held increasingly more frequently, covering a diverse range of issues, but particularly those concerned with land-use conflict (Table 7.1).

Local protest groups established to fight a particular issue may only be temporary organisations; once the issue around which the group was formed has been resolved, successfully or otherwise, the need for the group's continuation will have been reduced. At least by design, experiments at fostering local democracy through the establishment of neighbourhood participation are more permanent, and intended to cover the broad range of issues affecting the local area. Prime examples include the community and neighbourhood councils established widely throughout West European cities (Kjellberg, 1979). The benefits of municipal decentralisation to the neighbourhood councils are viewed as not only flowing to the localities (in the sense of their greater formal incorporation within the decision-making process) but also to the higher order city governments in helping to bolster the legitimation of their actions.

The contrasts between the spontaneously formed local protest group and the formal, institutionalised modes of citizen participation, represented by the neighbourhood/community council movement, are more profound than their probable longevity and the range of responsibilities over which they are concerned. While the second type are organised from above by a local city, or possibly national, government, the first are generated at the grass-roots level. Coit (1978) terms the grass-roots organisation a local action group which, because of its mode of formation, implying the lack of any formal ties with the institutional machinery of government, has a greater chance of resulting in meaningful social change. Formal methods of establishing citizen participation are within Arnstein's (1969) terminology more likely to be 'tokenistic' gestures, involving only exceptionally a redistribution of power in favour of the local community. To Coit, projects such as the US Community Action

Program, and Model Cities Program institutionalised participation within a dominantly conservative ideology, that is, where the outcomes of participation were not to substantially alter the *status quo*. The local action group, by contrast, is more able to raise class consciousness, and, by focusing on particular issues around which protest can be organised, is able to develop an awareness of the contradictions of capitalist urban development.

Table 7.1: Referenda Requests in the Vaud Municipalities

Period	No. of referenda	Subjects				
		Local taxes/ fiscal issues	Demolition/ construction of buildings	Infrastructure projects	Land use policies	Other devt. proposals
1951–55	5	–	3	1	–	1
1956–60	18	2	5	4	–	7
1961–65	17	–	8	–	1	8
1966–70	23	1	10	2	1	9
1971–75	24	5	7	4	1	7
1976–80	47	12	5	7	11	12

Source: Adapted from Meylan (1981)

According to Kilmartin and Thorns (1978) the question of consciousness can be used to define different 'levels' of local political action in the city. In terms of its potential in effecting substantial social change, the 'highest-order' forms of urban action are those which are able to harness a revolutionary class consciousness. Such groups fall within Castell's (1977) definition of the urban social movement which adopts contestatory strategies aimed at a radical, if localised, transformation of the urban fabric. Such movements were represented by the various struggles against urban renewal and property speculation in the Cité du Peuple, Paris. The attempt to raise class consciousness using the vehicle of the local environmental pressure group was addressed directly by the Australian Green Ban Movement (Camina, 1975). Alliances were formed between local resident action groups and the trade union movement to halt the progress of what were considered unnecessary urban developments. As far as the trade union leadership was concerned local action was being used deliberately to heighten class consciousness and awareness of the conflicts between the objective interests of capital and the wider concept of social need.

More common than the urban social movement *sensu stricto* is the protest movement directed perhaps towards a particular conflict, but attempting problem resolution within a reformist framework rather than a more radical one. The level of consciousness in this 'intermediate' level of action is conflict rather than revolutionary-oriented (Giddens, 1973), seeking locally more sympathetic forms of change. In most cases such action groups are formed within territorially specific areas, characteristically in response to a proposal or change perceived as generating negative spillover effects. In other cases such action groups can be organised city-wide, e.g with principal interest groups such as an urban conservation society ready to contest specific local area proposals as part of their general policing role. Equally, protest over 'undesirable' urban change can involve local action by nationally organised interest groups.

A third form of local action is associated more closely with the urban community itself. As Bell and Newby (1976) argue, the community, where it represents a coherent socio-spatial entity, helps fashion a communion form of consciousness. Where the urban citizen is inevitably incorporated into some locality-based association — though the impact of being a member of a residential community varies between citizens — the community has become a major organisational basis for struggle. Urban communities, however, are fragile social structures and it may prove difficult to sustain within them high levels of political activism. It is only when the community is under threat that activism is likely to be high, even if this only involves some low level form of participation on the part of the individual such as petition-signing. At other times community action will be more latent than real, though latent power, the threat of confrontation, can act as an effective brake on the city politician and urban administrator. Harnessing local support is a politically judicious step, particularly for the elected politician where the local area represents his electoral power base. It is, in part, precisely for this reason that the urban community has become a major focus of attention within attempts to foster local participation.

In his more recent work on urban grassroots movements Castells (1983) argues that these can be subdivided on the basis of three different types of objective, though any particular movement is likely to combine more than one of these and, indeed, its success may be dependent on this. Local political mobilisation tends to focus around three issues: conflicts over collective consumption, over the cultural identity of the community and over the demand for local self-management. Conflicts over collective consumption arise because under capitalism the city is structured in exchange-value rather than use-value terms, so that the conditions of urban living and the provision of public services are considered as commodities. Thus protest centres on the provision of better housing, public transport and issues such as more open space. A second objective centres on the quest by the community to retain its cultural identity which might be ethnically or historically based. Finally, a third focus is represented by the demand by the local community for greater political control, and for a redistribution of power downwards from the establish organs of local government. The latter is fundamental; where there is a redistribution of power in favour of the local community the other types of objective are likely to be the more attainable. Tracing out the reasons why neighbourhood control has become a politically important issue is, therefore, of considerable significance.

Why Neighbourhood Democracy?

The reasons why neighbourhood democracy, the call for greater local political control, has become a common demand in Western cities are complex. While in recent decades it has enjoyed considerable vogue, the idea of neighbourhood democracy has been discussed for a long time; the relative merits of centralised city-wide government as opposed to more decentralised forms was debated in the nineteenth century as the Victorian city grew (Toulmin-Smith, 1851; Magnusson, 1979). Writing of American cities Kaufman (1969) has argued that the idea of power to the neighbourhoods has been a cyclical demand, the most recent phase being a reaction to 'executive dominance' and a call for greater representativeness in urban government. Even if there are some signs that, like the environment movement (Sandbach, 1980), the demand for neighbourhood participation has waned somewhat in recent years, there is no doubt that in the post World War II period, and particularly during the 1960s, the call for more local participation was a politically important issue. This raises two questions, the one more general as to why neighbourhood democracy, the other more historically specific as to its emergence particularly in the 1960s and 1970s. In part, these two questions can be answered simultaneously.

According to Yates (1973) there are several main reasons why urban decentralisation — by which he means the delegation of administrative and/or political power from City Hall to the neighbourhood — has become an important item on the political agenda in the United States. These include processes which have built up over the longer term and have served to underline the increasing degree of political centralisation, and those which have developed more recently exposing the contradictions between centralisation and the demands for greater political participation. Two events led to the more immediate demands for greater decentralisation, the failure to establish racial integration in the city stimulating in its wake more widespread community protest and involvement. When, during the 1960s, attempts by civil rights activists to achieve fuller integration, particularly of education, were slow to bring results, largely because of the intransigence of the city authorities, as in New York, protest switched from demands for integration to the demand for community control. Such protest became extended to cover the general range of services delivered locally, while simultaneously the community was being politically mobilised and fostered through Federally inspired programmes, such as the War on Poverty. The demand for greater community participation was contagious; while the call for community control had been spearheaded by the black neighbourhoods, white communities were quick to follow suit, both arguing that city governments had become unresponsive to meeting local needs.

The unresponsiveness of city government had resulted from longer-term changes in the organisation of urban political institutions. Machine politics had all but disappeared from the American city (Harrigan, 1976). Whatever claims had been made by its critics, machine politics had been an effective method of channelling citizen demand-making and of helping to ensure the local responsiveness of city administrations. Classically, the machines had controlled both the inputs and the outputs of city politics; through the local, decentralised party structure they provided access to government, while acting as the major distributor of rewards. Reform-style city governments, particularly those based on the strong mayor form, were more centralist, and though old machine politics was also founded on a high degree of centralisation, it incorporated too a strong decentralist element within the city's electoral wards. The move in the reform cities towards the at-large election, replacing the system of wards, removed one of the mainstays by which the citizen could gain access to the administration.

While city governments had tended to become more centralised, many of the services for which they were responsible were characteristically highly divisible, so that how they were provided in the separate neighbourhoods making up the city was all the more obvious. Services such as street-lighting, the provision of public parks, refuse collection, and police surveillance are all spatially-specific, mapping out fields of community advantage and disadvantage. Precisely because of their divisibility 'citizens do not care how well the city is collecting garbage, in general, but whether garbage is being collected on their block' (Yates, 1973, p. 5). Indeed, it is unlikely that the citizen has sufficient information to have much knowledge of the city-wide picture,but he is acutely aware of the conditions in his own territory. Public services, therefore, by their nature have politically centrifugal effects and through their perceived maldistribution provide the staple items of the micropolitics of the city.

It is clear from these arguments that while neighbourhood action and the demand for greater local participation is a response to local problems, in a broader context it is related to the dominant thrust towards centralisation characterising the modern state (Paddison, 1983). Many observers have suggested that increasing centralisation accompanies increasing alienation for the individual — neighbourhood democracy represents a collective reaction, then, to the general trend.

Centralisation has characterised much of the state apparatus, though its impact within local government has probably been of more immediate importance to the emergence of the demand for local area participation. That is, to the community power advocate local government — in particular, city-wide government — is no longer sufficiently local. In Britain the problem was given considerable airing during the debates preceding the reform of the local government structure in the late 1960s and early 1970s (Wood, 1974). Within Europe, excepting the Scandinavian countries, local government reform, as in Britain, was to result in a more dramatic reduction in the number of jurisdictions. Using 1950 as the base year (index = 100), the index of the number of local governments by the early to mid-1970s was in England 29, Denmark, 17, Sweden 10, the Federal Republic of Germany 37, Austria 74, Netherlands 88, Belgium 94 and France 98 (Council of Europe, 1980). However, changes in the number of jurisdictions alone give a misleading impression of the relationship between local government and the population served, in which as Sharpe (1978) has shown, the British position is markedly different from elsewhere in Europe. Thus within the countries listed above the median population of the basic unit of local government (the commune, or in West Germany, the *gemeinden*), was 16,170, whereas in England the average population of the newly formed districts was more than six times this figure.

While it is easy to make too much of these differences — neighbourhood participation has been widely introduced throughout Western Europe — the effect of local government reform generally has been to extend the distance between the citizen and the political process. As decentralisation within the city can be considered as an attempt to increase proximity, fostering in some cases participatory forms of democracy, it directly counters the twin problems which trends within local government have emphasised, the increasing physical distance between the citizen and City Hall, and the attenuation of the representative/electorate ratio. Innovations such as the little city halls in American cities, although their role is restricted to one of providing information, reduce the distance between the citizen and the service-delivery agencies (Yin, Hearn and Shapiro, 1974). The argument that remoteness is increased with worsening elected representative/citizen ratios is more intuitively — than empirically — based. Nevertheless, in English local government reorganisation council memberships were not increased proportionately to the increase in population served, so that in many urban jurisdictions the population/councillor ratio was doubled.

If the basic thrust of structural reorganisation leading to larger basic units of local government has been to centralise power in a smaller number of loci, other trends in local government have also accentuated centralisation. Within the present century local government has become increasingly bureaucratised and professionalised. Though it has lost functions to higher levels of government, in Britain many new services have been added to local government, notably housing, public transport and land-use planning. In an attempt to counter the administrative fragmentation surrounding the provision of these services corporate management techniques have been introduced accentuating the bureaucratic centralism, though attempts to establish a variant of it at sub-city level in some English and Scottish cities, through area management, have sought to act as a decentralist counter.

The professionalisation of the local government service has also had its centralising effects. Professionalism, it is argued, is antithetical to citizen participation and though in the case of some services, such as land-use planning and housing management, there have been conscious attempts to incorporate citizen participation, professionalisation has lent itself more towards elitist rather than participatory forms of democracy at the local level. Not only do such professionals have important gatekeeping roles, but where administrative decentralisations has given the urban street-level bureaucrat discretionary powers professionalism surfaces to produce a 'them and us' gap (Lipsky, 1976).

Pluralists root their argument for greater local democracy in the need to counter the growing centralisation of local government and to open up alternative, more localised centres of decision-making. Proposals as to how best to reorganise local government illustrate the arguments. Thus in the US the influential Committee for Economic Development has urged the consolidation of metropolitan units of local government, but recognised the need for a mechanism to ensure that the urban neighbourhood had an influence on policy-making. While recommending an 80 per cent reduction in the number of local government units, the Committee favoured the establishment of neighbourhood districts which would act as the representative organs for channelling local demands. Similarly, in Scotland the germ of the community council idea was developed in the submission to the Royal Commission by the Border Burghs Convention. While accepting that the revised map was likely to consist of a smaller number of larger local jurisdictions, it was argued that

> the smaller compact units of population within their areas may well develop a feeling of non-participation in their own local government affairs by reason of their remoteness from the centre of the local government of their area. To combat this the Convention suggests that there should be reserved to each compact community . . . the right, if it wishes to appoint a local committee . . . (Royal Commission on Local Government, Scotland, 1969, p. 206).

While the Convention represented small urban areas, with populations of less than 20,000, the proposal was even more attractive applied to the large cities. Such proposals tend to leave unsaid what the duties and rights of the community council should be, to their critics evidence of the power of non-decision making.

While the establishment of community forms of participation can

be interpreted in pluralist terms, in opening up political accessibility
and dispersing power, a structuralist's understanding of why neighbourhood committees/community councils have become widespread
would emphasise different factors (Coit, 1978; Cockburn, 1977).
Fostering the appearance of local democracy through such bodies
can be useful as a method of social control, that is, of containing
political protest. This is apparent not only because of the relatively
weak powers given to these institutionalised forms of participation,
but also because of their common association of developing political
involvement within territorial communities, which has the effect of
diverting attention from the real class conflict. Through its organisation on a community basis participation is structured within
'grounds prepared by the state'. The local ward-elected politician
and the area field office community worker are 'ready' for the local
community group, giving the impression to the activist, as Cockburn
argues, that problems (over service provision or urban restructuring)
arise within 'officialdom' rather than being products of wider
societal forces.

Equally, where within the 1960s and 1970s, and particularly
within the United States, there was widespread spontaneous protest
within the city, formal recognition of the need to incorporate citizen
participation within the political machinery had its advantages so
long as this was within constraints set from above. Coit (1978)
argues that citizen participation has been used conservatively; look-
ing at programmes such as the US War on Poverty 'one of the
prime goals was to give the lower classes, and particularly the ethnic
minorities, a middle class mentality rather than middle class
resources . . . which is a bad thing in that the poor become less
rather than more effective' (p. 300). As with the criticism made of
the British Community Development Programmes encouraging the
poor to participate was misleading.

Implementing Local Democracy and Mobilising the Community

Much of the criticism levelled against attempts at fostering community participation from above within American and British urban
aid programmes is founded on how it was implemented. As Arnstein
(1969) showed participation can be given different meanings. To
Arnstein citizen participation was equated with citizen power, the
ability to influence plans or policies — in other words, participation

should address itself to the key issue of power, and the ability of the local group to alter or stop proposals advocated by a higher agency.

The eight rungs of Arnstein's ladder are divided into three broad types:

(1) non-participation, divided into manipulation and therapy. Participatory forms of local democracy engineered at this level are in a real sense dishonest in that their likely effect on outcomes is minimal. They give the illusion of local power.

(2) 'degrees of tokenism', divided into the three rungs of informing, consultation and placation. Many experiments with citizen participation fall into one of these three categories. In the fourth rung consultation will be pursued by politicians and professional officers so as to obtain feedback on a proposal, which will help bolster the legitimacy of their actions. In this sense, participation is being used as an elitist mechanism, underlining that there is no redistribution of power, in contrast with the last part of the ladder.

(3) 'degrees of citizen power', subdivided into partnership, delegated power and the final rung, citizen control.

As devised by Arnstein the ladder concept encounters a number of problems. The division itself into eight rungs is too dogmatic and limited, and Arnstein herself agreed that 'in the real world of people and programmes there might be 150 rungs with less sharp and "pure" distinctions among them' (Arnstein, 1969, 217). The ladder was constructed on the basis of Arnstein's interpretation of the US social welfare programmes aimed at urban renewal, anti-poverty and model cities. Taking a broader look at US social welfare activity Moguluf (1970) devised a different framework. In spite of these drawbacks, Arnstein's model does provide a valuable guide to the broad practice of participation.

Among the more useful distinctions in the ladder is that between participation aimed at different degrees of tokenism and those more radical experiments including some element of local decision-making. Examining a variety of European experiments with neighbourhood decentralisation, a Council of Europe study classified the resulting institutions into those which had a purely information and consultation role, and those which had independent decision-making powers. In general the report concluded that European city governments have shown 'a conspicuous restraint when it comes to investing local bodies with independent decision-making powers. It is invariably advisory and information duties that occupy the forefront' (Council of Europe, 1981, p. 7). The common pattern is for the neighbourhood body to be used as a channel of information between the citizen and the decision-makers, and as an element of this the local bodies become the legitimate vehicles for participation and are routinely consulted. Thus in West Germany, Sweden, Italy and the UK neighbourhood councils usually have the right of being informed of plans affecting their area, and, in some cases, the duty of advising officials of local attitudes towards proposals.

In some European cities neighbourhood councils exist alongside other forms of intra-urban administrative decentralisation. A number of British cities have experimented with area management, an administrative device aimed at ensuring the matching of policies with local needs. Though uniformity of service provision within the city can be argued on anti-discrimination grounds or on the grounds of 'good administration' (Stewart, 1982), it is equally arguable that as local service needs vary within a city so a policy of absolute uniformity will have inequitable results. Besides catering for intra-urban variations in service need, area management has also given explicit recognition to the need to coordinate policies at the local level. In those cities where management has been introduced the geographical subunits are considerably larger than would normally be equated with the urban neighbourhood, populations in some cases exceeding 100,000. Furthermore, with few exceptions, area management teams rarely have executive power and, in particular, tend not to have the power to spend budgets of any significance, or to have formal powers of approval. Though experiments in area management have had their teething problems, it is clear as Webster (1982) has argued that the teams have been responsive to local needs in the way intended. They remain, however, administrative institutions, staffed mainly by elected politicians and officers of the city council. Neighbourhood groups, providing the local participatory element, are minority members, and in some cases are excluded.

Within Arnstein's typology most of the attempts at establishing neighbourhood councils are to be seen as token participation. Credited with the right to be consulted over questions which concern their turf, the neighbourhood council's main importance to the city council is in providing local feedback on its proposals. Typically such bodies are dependent on the higher jurisdiction, particularly on its willingness to incorporate the local bodies within the decision-making process. In Scotland the reluctance of the Edinburgh city councillors even to help establish community councils underlined the power imbalance, and the dependence of the urban localities on the city's willingness to play the participation game.

More radical attempts at establishing community power have begun from a recognition of this power imbalance. In the United States the move to radicalising the community, and to adopting militant tactics to win concessions from City Hall, is widely associated with the groups initiated by Saul Alinksy (1969). Having watched the tactics used to mobilise the coal-miners of southern Illinois, Alinsky recognised that were poor urban neighbourhoods to be similarly mobilised it would be possible to confront the city administrations on a more equal footing. His first experience in organizing the community was within the Chicago stockyard area — the Back of the Yards Community Council — made up of a coalition of workers, union leaders, small merchants and the church. A mixture of boycotts, marches and pickets was used to gain concessions for the community, the effect of such action also being to generate a strong community consciousness.

Alinsky groups are prime examples of local political communities built from below. Typically they consist of a single, large community organisation composed of member organisations who send representatives — membership is not open to local residents, but to all organisations. Block clubs dominate the membership (Table 7.2), through which residents channel their complaints. Initiating the group is a crucial step, and, somewhat controversially, Alinsky organisations are formed by a paid community organiser who must, however, be invited by the community. The organiser's task is to galvanise the community around some local issue, and subsequently to oversee the protest tactics to be employed.

Table 7.2: Member Organisations in an Alinsky Movement: the Organisation for a Better Austin (Chicago)

Organisation Type	%
Block Clubs	56.5
Church groups	22.5
Public education/youth	5.6
Association of Block Clubs	3.2
Others	12.2

Source: Bailey (1974)

The Alinsky movement, aiming at improving the local environment of the urban poor, has generated considerable controversy. Though Alinsky described himself as an urban radical his ideological commitment was to those elements — local autonomy, pluralism and political accountability — espoused by the Founding Fathers. Urban government had become over-centralised and insensitive to local needs, and community activism was a means of redressing the balance. Clearly, his approach was not radical in any revolutionary sense, though Alinsky recognised the importance of adopting militant tactics. Though an effective tool, it was the militancy of the movements which raised the greatest controversy, particularly as it was being orchestrated by a paid outsider. As Castells argues, in spite of some important differences, 'Alinsky, a fervent anti-Communist, would probably be outraged by the close resemblance of his organiser's profile to the one of the professional revolutionary depicted by Lenin in *What is to be done*?' (Castells, 1983, 62).

Whether community organisations are fostered by urban administrations or are generated as grassroots populist movements, one of the key issues to which their functioning is directed is the extent to which the community can be mobilised politically. As Alinsky was aware, it is the effectively mobilised community that will be the more successful in winning concessions for the local area. Mobilising the community is far from easy, however; contrary to the expectations of those who have advocated citizen participation, the image of a mass citizenry eager to participate is a myth (Allison, 1975). Ideally, community mobilisation requires the emergence of an issue which is specific, associated with possible threat or some other form of disadvantage and which is seen to be capable of 'solution' probably by a higher agency of government.

Apart from the issue itself around which community protest can be mobilised the other conditions upon which mobilisation depends relate to the characteristics of the local population, the definition of the community and the influences of the mode of participation used to channel local protest and action. It has long been recognised that citizens differ in their willingness (and ability) to participate politically. Within a hierarchical framework Milbrath (1965) has outlined a progression of political involvement, ranging from the non-voter to those willing to be involved marginally, such as through voting, through to the 'gladiator', a political activist who might even stand for office. It is in Milbrath's 'transitional activities' that local activisim is focused, either through attending a meeting or rally, or in contacting a public official, or at a somewhat lower level, in signing a petition.

In so far as local participation reflects, for the individual participant, the objective of meeting self-interests expressed jointly through collective action, the 'positional' characteristics of the individual are important in understanding how mobilisation operates. By positional characteristics is meant the attributes defining the participant, including factors such as socio-economic status, occupation, life-cycle position and household structure, housing tenure and gender. In their survey in Columbus (Ohio) Cox and McCarthy (1982) show that housing tenure, and in particular home-ownership, is strongly related to activism, as is household structure where the nuclear family had greater stakes in the community. Once the type of issue upon which conflict focuses is included, the biases as to who participates are more explicable. Whether the issues are zoning issues or proposals aimed at highway improvement/street widening, as in Columbus, their impact is likely to vary in relation to the investment the individual has in his neighbourhood. Not only was this greater for the homeowner in the Columbus survey, as opposed to those in other tenure positions, but also in zoning issues likely to affect the social composition of the neighbourhood, impacting on property prices and schooling, articulate middle class reaction will be aroused.

A second set of questions upon which mobilising the community will depend centres on the definition of the community itself. The assumption underlying neighbourhood participation and the formation of neighbourhood councils within cities is that it is possible to identify spatial communities of interest, and that such entities are the appropriate ones through which to channel participation. Apart from the argument that in the high-mobility society the local, spatially discrete community has little foundation (Webber, 1963), evidence does exist to support the idea that citizens commonly identify with their local area (Royal Commission on Local Government in England, 1969). Identifying such communities, however, and establishing boundaries is a major problem (Paddison, 1981; Pacione, 1984) and is a process, which judged from the variations in the population size and social composition of the resulting community bodies, defies the making of generalisations. The expectation would be that from the viewpoint of mobilisation the more tightly knit and socially coherent the community the easier the task of mobilising, though there has been no research to test the hypothesis.

On the other hand, there is evidence to illustrate the dangers of considering the spatial community in politically unitary terms. The assumption underlying the functioning of the intra-urban political community, that it reflects a commonality of interest, may belie the existence of within-community differences, those belonging either to the interests of individuals or to separate class fractions living within the area. Many of the issues generating conflict impact differently on households; proposals (for example) which have very restricted spatial negative externality fields will tend to divide the community, particularly where a counter-proposal introduces an alternative set of gains and losses within the local area.

Besides dividing the community such conflicts will illustrate differing power capabilities. Ferris's (1972) study of Barnsbury, an inner-city, gentrified suburb of London, demonstrates the conflicts which can arise and the general argument that working class groups are less effective participators than their middle class counterparts. During the mid-1960s the Barnsbury Association was formed by the newly arrived middle class occupants to oppose the local council's proposal to redevelop the area. The Association fought the plan because of its perceived impacts on the amenity of the area and, also, on property prices. The interests of the existing working class population were to halt the process of gentrification and to favour redevelopment, which would offer the opportunity of local rehousing in higher standard dwellings. An alternative plan was suggested by the Association, involving a traffic management scheme and the rehabilitation of older housing, ideas which within planning circles generally were becoming fashionable and which were adopted, after lobbying and after the Association had managed to secure the election of three of its members to the local council. Belated action by the more working class Barnsbury Action Group failed to reverse the policy. What the Barnsbury case illustrates is that giving the opportunities for more participation can favour the more easily mobilised and perpetuate power differences between class groups.

The channels through which community participation is structured, the types of administrative body, its functions and powers and relationships to local and other levels of government, also influence community mobilisation. As has been suggested earlier in the case of neighbourhood participation which has been socially engineered from above, the conditions under which participation is to be conducted and the powers of the local body are conditioned by extra-local agencies. The influence of the external, initiating authority extends over other aspects of community participation; frequently there are controls over the membership of the local committees and over other aspects of their constitution. In the Council of Europe (1981) study cited previously a common pattern was for the neighbourhood council to be made up of local, possibly elected, representatives, as well as members from local organisations. The effect of having at community level another layer of representation can be to produce a local elite; certainly one common result of neighbourhood decentralisation is the emergence of local political leadership, whose ability to mobilise the community is critical. The existence of the local elite, however, may lead to a gap between the neighbourhood committee and the residents (Yates, 1973).

Impacts

The question of the impacts of community-based participation, though a field in which political geographers have been conspicuously silent, can be studied in a number of ways. Being primarily interested in the spatial outcomes of participation, the political geographer's attention to the impact of neighbourhood decentralisation will differ from the primary interests of the political scientist. The latters' interest will centre around the extent to which neighbourhood decentralisation reduces feelings of powerlessness and increases political representativeness and accountability. While these are of obvious significance to the political geographer they need to be considered as means rather than as ends. In other words, it is as a result of the greater accountability and representativeness introduced by neighbourhood decentralisation that tangible effects within the community can be traced.

The impact of neighbourhood activism can be assessed in three ways:

(1) service impacts — the ability of local activism to secure the provision of public services in line with collective (or individual) demand, including the resolution of zoning conflicts successfully in relation to locally expressed wishes;
(2) community impacts — the extent to which decentralisation has fostered the development of local political communities;

(3) redistributive impacts — the extent to which local activism
has led to redistributive outcomes. Redistribution, in this sense,
has two main elements measuring political and economic variables. Politically, a key question concerns the impact of neighbourhood decentralisation on the redistribution of power downwards in favour of the local community. In economic terms
redistribution is to be assessed in the extent to which neighbourhood decentralisation has been able to favour the poor.

The conditions underwriting the success (or otherwise) of neighbourhood activism in altering the urban fabric in any one or more of
these ways are variable and defy generalisation. The types of
decentralisation (in terms of, for example, Arnstein's typology), the
behaviour of the actors involved, the impress of extra-local influences and the historical conditions against which local activism is
enacted produce unique sets of conditions under which neighbourhood action takes place. Based on a series of cross-cultural grassroots
movements Castells (1983) concluded that the Citizen Movements in
Madrid had had the greatest effect in altering urban conditions and
argued that this was because of four main reasons:

(1) the movements had been able to articulate their objectives in
terms of each of the three goals of collective consumption
demands, community culture and political self-management;
(2) the movements were conscious of their role as the agents of
possible urban change;
(3) the movements had correctly harnessed vital extralocal
agents, notably the media, professional administrators and the
political parties; and
(4) while the movements were connected to the political system,
they had remained organisationally and ideologically separate
from any political party.

The first of these reasons is the most critical.
While the political thrust of the Citizen Movements in Madrid was
sufficient for the city authorities to be forced to accept them as the
legitimate ('official') bodies through which neighbourhood participation was to be structured, initially their development was
generated from the grassroots. In terms of examining impacts it
might be useful at this juncture to reintroduce the simple dichotomy
outlined earlier, neighbourhood activism developed from below and

above, and, through two case-studies, demonstrate the outcomes of participation.

Though relatively short-lived the Australian Green Ban Movement provides an important example of the effects of local activism developed from below and of the effects on the power structure once alliances are struck between local residents and a powerful extra-local actor such as a trade union. The tactic adopted was simple — resident action groups who were contesting some development proposal would ask the Builders Labourers Federation to black it and possibly other sites in which the development company had an interest.

The union's first involvement brought an unlikely alliance between the BLF, which within its New South Wales branch was noted for its militancy, and middle class residents anxious to retain the sole remaining example of natural bush within the inner part of Sydney. While the movement spread to other parts of Australia, notably to Victoria and Tasmania, Sydney remained the main area affected, within which the bans were imposed on a wide variety of proposed developments (Table 7.3).

Table 7.3: Types of Development Affected by Green Bans

Types of Project	Number
Preservation of historic buildings, hotels	10
Bans on developments in inner city	7
Housing standards — refusal to build flats	6
Retention of parkland/open space	5
No demolition for expressways	5
No demolition of homes for car parks	3
Inadequate compensation for property	3
Miscellaneous social	4

Source: Camina (1975)

Several conclusions may be drawn from the episode. First, it is highly improbable that resident action groups working by themselves would have been able to halt the developments with anything like the effectiveness that was achieved. As Castells argues, the Green Ban Movements showed the importance of forging links with sympathetic, powerful extra-local agents, in this case the unions and the media. (While the press traditionally opposed union militancy, in the Green Ban Movements they gave their support.) Second, and of more lasting importance than the halting of developments, the Movements recast power relations, even if only to a limited extent. By itself the action had shown that both developers and professional planners would have to take greater account of local opinion. To this end the formal means for incorporating participation were extended, where within the planning legislation these had been minimal. Third, the episode was to underline the potential of direct action tactics by the community as opposed to more passive means.

The Priority Areas Project, initiated in 1975 by the city council of Newcastle upon Tyne (England), represents a very different form of citizen participation. The project was an attempt by the city authorities to work in liaison with local groups with a view to reducing the effects of multiple deprivation within those areas identified as subject to the greatest stress. Through a policy of positive discrimination the aim of the council was to alleviate the worst symptoms of stress; recognising that it would be unable to attack the root causes of stress, it could reduce its worst effects. To this end Priority Area Teams were established in each 'stress area', composed of a mix of elected ward politicians, field officers from the service departments representing housing, education, planning, recreation and social services, a Team Leader (a city official appointed part-time to the area project) and local action groups, notably community associations, tenants and residents' groups. Each Priority Area Team was made responsible for identifying local needs, devising plans to meet these and framing them within a budgeted programme, and for acting as a feedback channel through which community attitudes could be conveyed back to the council.

Among the more tangible products which have resulted from the Team's efforts are the community facilities which have been established as part of the locally decided budgets. Though the size of the budget at the discretion of the Teams is only a fraction of the total expenditure outlay of the service departments within each of the areas, the projects which have been funded have been, as a review of the initiative argued, of local importance (Newcastle upon Tyne, 1981). However, the review also revealed that attitudes varied as to whether as an exercise in participation the experiment had been successful. Here it is important to emphasise that there are at least two basic points of view, representing the different objectives sought for in the experiment by the city council and the participating local groups. The Inner City Forum, a collection of community and voluntary agencies participating in the Priority Area Teams, were critical of the experiment arguing that community participation *sensu stricto* had been minimal and that because the city councillors and other officials controlled the agenda the Teams had barely debated issues which were crucial to the areas, such as housing replacement policies and public expenditure cutbacks. While being realistic enough to accept that conflict between the city council and its citizens will always occur, the Forum made the salutary point that 'The question is whether (the council) can set up structures which make it *worthwhile* for community groups to influence the decision-making process from the inside' (Inner City Forum, 1981, p. 2).

Table 7.4: Types of Community Spending by Priority Area Teams — Newcastle upon Tyne, 1976–83

Types of expenditure field	Outlay (£000s)	
1. *Leisure and Recreation*		
Children's playgrounds etc	567	(21)a
Provision/upgrading of community meeting place	677	(25)
General community support	529	(20)
2. *Personal Social Services*		
Projects for elderly people	126	(5)
Special needs	48	(2)
3. *Housing/Environmental*		
Improvements to housing stock	137	(5)
Environmental improvements	554	(21)
4. *Other*	37	(1)

Note: a Figure in brackets represents percentage of total
Source: Adapted from City of Newcastle upon Tyne Report, 1984.

Clearly, these two case-studies do not bear direct comparison nor is it possible to draw any general conclusions from such a limited sample. Though a more transient form of participation the Green Ban Movement had the greater impact in redistributing power. To the extent that the Priority Area Team initiative is typical of top down forms of local participation the intention to redistribute power to the advantage of the localities was a less important objective than were other more administrative ones. To their critics the value of the Teams was reduced because the committee agendas were determined outside the local community.

240   *Local Democracy in the City*

Conclusions

Most advanced states occupy some intermediate position along the democracy continuum whose end points are the fully representative and participatory forms of democracy. In some countries the tradition of participatory democracy is more fully entrenched; the case of Switzerland is among the better known examples. But where local community participation has become an international phenomenon, it has meant that in many countries there has been a move, however modest, towards participatory forms of democracy.

Just as the state has become omnipresent in affecting the life-chances of its citizens, so participation, or the demand for greater control by the individual and the local community, has affected an ever wider set of issues. Evidently, public participation can have different meanings and its impacts correspondingly vary. Many of the conflicts on which participation within the city focuses are transient. In terms of Downs' (1972) issue-attention model it might be argued that the demand for community participation itself is likely to be a transient phenomena; that is, having realised the costs of community participation there is a gradual decline of public interest in the issue. There are several reasons for doubting such a development. Many of the issues on which participation centres have high visibility and in so far as they affect real income, have pronounced patterns of advantage and disadvantage. In short, the stakes are too high for the demand for community participation to be transient.

References

Alinsky, S. (1969) *Reveille for Radicals*, Vintage Books, New York
Allison, L. (1975) *Environmental Planning*, George Allen and Unwin, London
Arnstein, S. (1969) 'A Ladder of Citizen Participation', *Journal of the American Institute of Planners*, 35, 216–24
Bailey, R. Jr. (1974) *Radicals in Urban Politics*, University of Chicago Press, Chicago
Bell, C. and Newby, H. (1976) 'Community, Communion, Class and Community Action' in D. Herbert and R.J. Johnston (eds.), *Social Areas in Cities*, Wiley, London
Burnett, A.D. and Hill, D.M. (1982) 'Neighbourhood Organizations and the Distribution of Public Service Outputs in Britain' in Rich, R.C. (ed.), *The Politics of Urban Public Services*, Lexington Books, Lexington, Massachusetts, pp. 189–205
Camina, M.M. (1975) 'Public Participation — an Australian Dimension', *Planner*, 61, 232–5
Castells, M. (1977) *The Urban Question*, Edward Arnold, London

—— (1983) *The City and the Grassroots*, Edward Arnold, London

Cockburn, C. (1977) *The Local State*, Pluto Press, London

Coit, K. (1978) 'Local Action, not Citizen Participation' in W.K. Tabb and L. Sawers (eds.), *Marxism and the Metropolis*, Oxford University Press, New York, pp. 297–311

Council of Europe (1980) *Strengthening and Amalgamation of Local Authorities*, Council of Europe, Strasbourg

Council of Europe (1981) *Decentralisation of Local Government at Neighbourhood Level*, Council of Europe, Strasbourg

Cox, K.R. and McCarthy, J.J. (1982) 'Neighbourhood Activism as a Politics of Turf: a Critical Analysis' in K.R. Cox and R.J. Johnston (eds.), *Conflict, Politics and the Urban Scene*, Longman, London, pp. 196–219

Dahl, R.A. and Tufte, E. (1973) *Size and Democracy*, Stanford University Press, Stanford

Downs, A. (1972) 'Up and Down with Ecology — the "Issue–Attention Cycle" ', *The Public Interest*, 28, 38–50

Fagence, M. (1977) *Citizen Participation in Planning*, Pergamon, Oxford

Ferris, J. (1972) *Participation in Urban Planning: The Barnsbury Case*, G. Bell, London

Giddens, A. (1973) *The Class Structure of the Advanced Societies*, Hutchinson, London

Harrigan, J. (1976) *Political Change in the Metropolis*, Little Brown and Co, Boston, Massachusetts

Inner City Forum (1981) *Report on Priority Areas Project*, City of Newcastle upon Tyne

Jacobs, J. (1961) *The Death and Life of Great American Cities*, Random House, New York

Janelle, D.G. and Millward, H.A. (1976) 'Locational Conflict Patterns and Urban Ecological Structure', *Tijdschrift voor Economische en Sociale Geografie*, 67, 102–13

Jones, B.D. (1980) *Service Delivery in the City*, Longman, New York

Kilmartin, L. and Thorns, D.C. (1978) *Cities Unlimited*, George Allen and Unwin, Sydney

Kjellberg, F. (1979) 'A Comparative View of Municipal Decentralisation: Neighbourhood Democracy in Oslo and Bologna' in L.J. Sharpe (ed.), *Decentralist Trends in Western Democracies*, Sage, London, pp. 81–118

Lipsky, M. (1976) 'Towards a Theory of Street-level Bureaucracy' in W.D. Hawley et. al., *Theoretical Perspectives on Urban Politics*. Prentice Hall, Englewood Cliffs, New Jersey, pp. 100–45

Magnusson, W. (1979) 'The New Neighbourhood Democracy: Anglo-American Experience in Historical Perspective' in L.J. Sharpe (ed.), *Decentralist Trends in Western Democracies*, Sage, London, pp. 119–56

Meylan, J. (1981) Participation through the Local Referendum, Report to International Seminar on Public Participation in Urban Renaissance and the Action of Local Authorities, Vienna. Council of Europe, Strasbourg

Milbrath, L.W. (1965) *Political Participation*, Rand McNally, Chicago

Moguluf, M.B. (1970) *Citizen Participation*. Urban Institute, Washington, DC

Morris, D. and Hess, K. (1975) *Neighbourhood Power: The New Localism*, Beacon Press, Boston, Massachusetts

Newcastle upon Tyne (1981) Priority Areas Project

Pacione, M. (1984) 'Local Areas in the City' in D.T. Herbert and R.J. Johnston (eds.), *Geography and the Urban Environment: Progression Research and Applications*, vol. 6, John Wiley, Chichester, pp. 349–82

Paddison, R. (1981) 'Identifying the Local Political Community: a Case-study of

Glasgow' in A.D. Burnett and P.J. Taylor (eds.), *Political Studies from Spatial Perspectives*, John Wiley; Chichester, pp. 341–55
—— (1983) *The Fragmented State*, Basil Blackwell, Oxford
Pennock, J.R. (1979) *Democratic Political Theory*, Princeton University Press, Princeton, New Jersey
Pickles, D. (1970) *Democracy*, B.T. Batsford, London
Royal Commission on Local Government in England (1969) *Report*, vols. I and II, HMSO, London
Royal Commission on Local Government in Scotland (1969) 2 vols. HMSO, Edinburgh
Sandbach, F. (1980) *Environment, Ideology and Policy*, Basil Blackwell, Oxford
Sharpe, L.J. (1978) 'Reforming the Grass Roots: an Alternative Analysis' in D. Butler and A.H. Halsey (eds.), *Policy and Politics*, Macmillan, London, pp. 82–110
Stewart, J.Q. (1982) 'Area Administration' in R. Allen (ed.), *Making the City Work*, City of Glasgow, Glasgow
Toulmin-Smith, J. (1951) *Local Self-Government and Centralisation*, John Chapman, London
Webber, M.M. (1963) 'Order in Diversity: Community without Propinquity' in L. Wingo (ed.), *Cities and Space*, Johns Hopkins University Press, Baltimore, pp. 23–56
Webster, B. (1982) 'Area Management' in J.Q. Stewart (ed.), *Public Policy and Local Government*, George Allen and Unwin, London
Wood, B. (1974) *The Process of Local Government Reform 1966-74*, George Allen and Unwin, London
Yates, D. (1973) *Neighbourhood Democracy*, Lexington Books, Lexington, Massachusetts
Yin, R.K. (1982) *Conserving America's Neighbourhoods*, Plenum Press, New York
—— Hearn, R.W. and Shapiro, P. (1974) 'Administrative Decentralisation of Municipal Services', *Policy Sciences*, 5, 57–70

8 THE GEOGRAPHY OF ELECTIONS

P.J. Taylor

Quantitative electoral geography was a major growth area in political geography in the 1970s. It can justifiably claim to have made an important contribution to the modern resurgence of the subdiscipline. This research growth and substantive contribution were documented in *Geography of Elections* (Taylor and Johnston, 1979) which attempted to provide a 'state of the art' for the 1970s. Since this publication, research in electoral geography has maintained its popularity in political geography. Unlike other growth area of the recent past, electoral geography has gone from strength to strength as new techniques and methodologies have been applied to old problems. Hence even in the short period since 1979 there have been four further reviews of particular research themes in electoral geography (Woolstencroft, 1980; Taylor and Gudgin, 1982; Johnston, 1983b; and Taylor, Gudgin and Johnston, 1984).

The first purpose of this chapter is to go beyond these reviews of particular parts of electoral geography and provide a comprehensive up-date of *Geography of Elections*. This involves description and discussion of researches since 1978 when the above book was written. The size of the bibliography at the end of the chapter alone indicates the need for a new review. In order to maintain consistency the review uses the same framework as *Geography of Elections* so that the first section of the chapter is divided into 'Geography of Voting', 'Geographical Influences in Voting' and 'Geography of Representation'. This continuity of organisation should not be taken as indicating that recent researches in electoral geography have merely added to the quantitative stock of studies in this field, however. Under each of the above headings are to be found research themes either missing from, or only weakly developed in, *Geography of Elections*. This fact more than the mere size of the up-dated bibliography justifies this new review.

Quantitative research in all areas of geography is currently being reassessed and evaluated in the light of changes in the nature of the discipline. Quantitative electoral geography has not escaped such rethinking. Any attempt at a comprehensive review of recent electoral geography must ask questions to do with the relations between the three parts identified above and, more importantly, relations between electoral geography, political geography and geography in general. The second purpose of this chapter is to attempt to answer these two questions, which form separate parts of the second section of the chapter. What question is asked and how it is answered depends upon how fundamental a reassessment is sought. This in turn depends upon the nature of the geography underpinning the research and behind that the world-view of the person doing the research. The second section of this paper will inevitably lead us towards considerations beyond elections *per se* but I will argue that these are necessary excursions in order to place elections in a broader context than that usually addressed in quantitative electoral geography.

Research Themes: Continuity and Innovation

Although this section is organised along the same lines as *Geography of Elections*, within each part the topics discussed and the problems raised are distinctive to this review. This reflects both new developments in the elections themselves and research innovations which extend previous analyses.

Geography of Voting

This has always been the major theme in electoral geography and this continues to be the case. Since 1979 the focus of such studies has been electoral change which has involved the use of relatively sophisticated quantitative methods — factor analysis to study long-term change and entropy maximising procedures to estimate short-term changes. But before we describe this work we will briefly review some recent more traditional cross-sectional studies.

(i) Cross-sectional Analyses. One of the attractions of geography of voting is that new and interesting themes arise with every election that takes place. Hence there has developed a tradition of studies of major elections as they occur. This has continued in recent years with analyses of voting in US presidential elections for 1976 and 1980 (Swauger, 1980; Archer, 1982), the French presidential election of 1981 (Johnston, 1982d) and the general election in Britain and Northern Ireland in 1979 (Taylor, 1979; Johnston, 1979e; Pringle, 1979). Most of such studies are cross-sectional

analyses which concentrate upon the pattern of votes at that particular election. Their main interest from a geographical viewpoint is their identification of regional patterns in voting returns. Swauger and Archer, in particular, investigate the modern sectionalism of American politics and Johnston introduces a regionalisation procedure for multi-party systems in his French study.

Regional patterns are interesting but electoral geography is ultimately about much more than patterns *per se*. The processes producing the patterns continue to be investigated using a variety of techniques. Such studies inevitably reach beyond political geography for their hypotheses. Two such studies will be briefly described here.

The decline of political parties in American politics has become a major theme in political science. This was taken up and evaluated for elections and referenda in Massachusetts in 1978 by Downing *et al.* (1980). Votes for Democratic candidates for a range of offices plus referenda returns were collected for a sample of electoral areas. A factor analysis was applied to this data to find common patterns in the votes. In a party-dominated system a single-factor solution would be expected. In fact four distinctive patterns were found. The most important pattern did relate to party voting especially for candidates for minor offices. For the major offices (US Senator and Governor), however, aspects of alternative non-party criteria could be found in other factor patterns. This analysis illustrated the fact that the decline of party thesis is not as simple as the term implies. Party voting continues alongside non-party voting in a complex manner.

Reasons for the decline of Labour voting have fascinated observers of British elections. One commonly held hypothesis is the idea that as working people become more affluent they begin to behave in middle class ways which include voting Conservative. This 'embourgeoisement thesis' has been tested by Johnston (1981e, 1981f). He notes that the 1971 census provides a cross-classification of occupation and car-ownership which was not available in the 1966 census used by previous researchers. He is thus able to devise a test of the embourgeoisement hypothesis by identifying the proportion of car-owning (i.e. affluent) working class and middle class persons in every constituency. By adding these variables to his ecological model of party voting in the February 1974 general election results for England he is able to estimate the differential effect of car-ownership between working class and middle class vote proportions. He finds that car-ownership is more than seven times as effective as an explanatory criterion for working class as opposed to middle class constituency proportions. Hence he is able to provide some statistical backing for the embourgeoisement thesis.

There are some other interesting studies which come under this heading, Lemon (1981) on recent South African elections, Rumley (1981a) on participation and Johnston (1980c) on Swiss referenda, for example, but the major thrust of recent research has been towards longitudinal studies covering both long-term and short-term electoral change. O'Loughlin (1980), for example, shows how there has been a decline in block voting against black candidates in mayoral elections in four major US cities since 1969. Ingalls and Brunn (1979) show how the growth of Republican support in the American South since 1948 has been urban-based. Bodman (1982) has considered the problem of how electoral change is measured. In this review, however, I will concentrate upon just two technical procedures for analysing change.

(ii) Defining Normal Vote Patterns using Factor Analysis. If the proportion of the vote for a given party is available over a set of constant areal units for a number of elections this constitutes a data set amenable to T-mode factor analysis. If the vote proportions for different elections are correlated, factors are extracted which define common patterns of party voting (Taylor, 1981b). For instance between 1918 and 1974 just one factor (common pattern) accounts for over 84 per cent of the variation of Labour vote proportions in 17 general elections in England (Johnston, 1983b). Such common patterns may be referred to as normal votes signifying as they do stable patterns of support for a party.

The most ambitious project using this methodology is Archer and Taylor's (1981) attempt to investigate sectionalism in US presidential elections from 1828 to 1980 using vote percentages by states for Democratic party candidates. Two factor analyses covering 1828 to 1920 and 1872 to 1980 respectively reveal just two normal votes through this long period — a non-sectional normal vote in the Democrat versus Whig party system (1836–52) and the more familiar sectional normal vote between the civil war/reconstruction and World War II (1876–1944). This analysis suggests an alternative periodisation of American politics which differs significantly from that derived from the study of party systems. A geographical perspective emphasising sectionalism suggests just three periods —

sectional compromise to the civil war, sectional dominance to World War II, and sectional volatility in the post-war era.

This methodology has been applied to major parties in countries of the European Community (e.g. Johnston, O'Neill and Taylor, 1982) and to Indian and Ghanaian elections. The latter two analyses will be discussed in the final part of this chapter. Johnston (1982b) has considered gubernatorial and senate elections as well as presidential elections for US states from 1946 to 1980 and has been able to contribute to the decline of party debate by showing where the coat-tails effect (presidential candidates helping other candidates of the same party) has declined in what he terms 'the geography of de-alignment'.

Finally mention should be made of using this approach to define electoral regions. By correlating states in terms of their vote profiles over time, factors can be extracted which identify patterns of common state vote profiles. In the Archer and Taylor (1981) study just three factors were found which measured 'northernness', 'southernness' and 'westernness'. Each state could then be described in terms of these three measures. Whereas Vermont, Alabama and Idaho were dominated by one factor — northern, southern and western respectively — other states showed interesting mixtures of the three factors. In particular in the centre of the country overlapping patterns occurred and these have been further investigated by Shelley and Archer (1983). They have applied this methodology to 372 counties in Missouri, Kansas, Oklahoma and Arkansas using Democratic presidential vote proportions from 1912 to 1980. Not surprisingly the simple national pattern is reflected in a more complex six-region pattern at the county scale which they are able to interpret in terms of local and regional political cultures. Despite its decline in other areas of geography, factor analysis has an important role to play in modern electoral geography (Taylor, 1981a).

(iii) Estimating Intra-Constituency Vote Changes using Entropy Maximising. Although one of the reasons for electoral geography's popularity has been the easy availability of areal-based data (Taylor, 1978), such data bases are deficient in one important respect. For any two elections we can measure the *net* change in vote for a particular party in a constituency but we do not know how such net change relates to individual changes in voting preferences. Individual voting returns are confidential and most survey analyses are

not large enough to throw light on changes *within* constituencies. Hence we have no direct evidence for, say, larger voter defections among former Labour party supporters in one constituency as compared with another. All we have is the net change in the level of Labour support in the two constituencies which could, of course, be produced by very different processes.

Let us define what we require for a comprehensive analysis of short-term electoral change. For every constituency we would need the following matrix of information — notional figures have been included to facilitate discussion:

		Election I		
		Party A	Party B	Total
	Party A	80	20	100
Election II				
	Party B	40	60	100
	Total	120	80	200

In the first election (defined by the column *totals*) Party A wins easily but in the second election (defined by the row *totals*) Party B pulls up to produce a dead heat. How this occurs is shown in the inner *cells* of the matrix. Of the 120 Party A voters in the first election 40 defect to Party B in the second election. The reverse defection, B to A, is only half that number hence the net flow of 20 votes from A to B. Notice that this net flow is the result of 60 voters (i.e. 40 A voters and 20 B voters) changing their minds. The problem is that we do not normally have information on the cells within the matrix; we have only column and row totals in published returns. Hence we can only deal with the net changes not the total pattern of change.

Fortunately we do have information for the cells of the matrix at a national scale from survey data. Opinion polls are able to find out proportions of people switching their vote for the *country as a whole*. Using this information, estimates can be derived for constituency matrices using the entropy maximising approach. This is a commonly used method in geography where flows are estimated — usually traffic or migration flows — using overall patterns with constraints on total flows in and out of local areas. This transport problem is essentially the same as the vote change problem outlined above (Johnston and Hay, 1983). In a series of papers Johnston has applied the method to short-term changes in New Zealand and British general elections; we describe some of his findings here and others below when we discuss the neighbourhood effect.

In a study of voting changes in New Zealand between the 1972 and 1975 general elections Johnston (1982a) used a national survey of 2682 electors to produce a 6 × 5 national voter transition matrix between parties and abstentions. This was applied to 83 constituencies to produce 30 cell estimates of flows of votes for each constituency. The constituencies were then divided into 18 sectional categories in terms of combinations of regional (island), urban/rural and metropolitan differences. Each sectional category's estimated 30 flows of votes were compared to the national flows of votes to find sectional differences in voting behaviour. In a similar analysis for the two 1974 elections in Britain Johnston and Hay (1983) use a 4 × 4 national transition for England to provide estimates of flows of votes between the three main parties and abstentions. Constituencies were then divided into four categories: super-marginal, marginal, semi-marginal and safe. Johnston and Hay were then able to show that the more marginal the constituency the more loyal were Labour and Conservative voters and conversely the more marginal the constituency the less likely that Labour or Conservative voters would convert to Liberal voting. This analysis confirms earlier hypotheses that 'tactical' voting was important in the second 1974 general election. Johnston (1983f) has applied this same methodology to predict the vote flows between the 1972 and 1976 US presidential elections for individual states. The result is a set of four very interesting maps on the spatial variation in the sources of Carter's vote from those in 1972 who voted for Nixon, McGovern, other candidates or who were abstainers.

It should be emphasized that these applications involve testing hypotheses using *estimates* of vote flows. In transport studies such estimates have been compared with actual flows and been found to be acceptably accurate. This is not usually possible in voting studies as we have previously indicated. However using a sample of 4,574 electors for just ten constituencies in Western Australia, Johnston, Hay and Rumley (1983) have been able to apply these estimating procedures to flows of votes where the actual flows are known. The results are very encouraging and suggest that estimates using entropy maximisation in electoral geography do provide a new and powerful tool for studying the detailed geography of short-term electoral changes.

Geographical Influences in Voting

For some geographers this aspect of electoral geography represents

their unique contribution to voting studies since it involves particular spatial influences on voting distinct from the socio-economic
explanations offered by political scientists and political sociologists.
Here we consider recent studies on structural effects (neighbourhood effect), candidate voting (friends and neighbours effect) and
campaign effects before returning to the entropy maximising
approach to evaluate these effects as alternative determinants of
electoral change.

(*i*) *The Neighbourhood Effect and the Polarisation Model.* The
neighbourhood effect on voting is a spatial structural process
whereby the partisan nature of a person's home district influences
his or her voting decision. For instance a working class person living
in a working class district is *more* likely to vote Labour than a working class person living in a middle class district. Hence neighbourhood effects reinforce the voter segregation beyond socioeconomic
segregation. Rumley (1979, 1981b) has provided two useful discussions of this process in human geography in general and in voting
studies in particular.

The problem with this process has always been that it is difficult to
measure. The original approach was to treat the neighbourhood
effect as a residual after socio-economic variables had been
accounted for. This approach has been adopted by O'Loughlin
(1981) in a comprehensive and rigorous statistical evaluation of the
neighbourhood effect. He considered elections in Indianapolis,
Detroit, Winnipeg and Dusseldorf. A wide-range of socio-economic
variables were regressed against voting returns in each city and
residuals from the analysis mapped. An autocorrelation analysis of
these residuals showed very significant 'clustering' in all four cases.
This indicates that the variation in voting not explained by the socio-
economic variables is *not* spatially random. From this it is inferred
that some form of neighbourhood effect is operating in addition to
the socio-economic determinants of voting.

Johnston (1979e) has devised another method of inferring neighbourhood effects. If a national voter transition matrix is applied
separately to each individual constituency's first election results, an
estimate of a new voting pattern is produced which assumes every
constituency changes in exactly the same way as the country as a
whole. This predicted voting pattern can be compared to the actual
voting pattern in the second election. Differences between the actual
and predicted are direct measures of how each constituency differs

from the national trend. As such they can be used to evaluate the neighbourhood effect.

If the neighbourhood effect operated we would expect constituency differences from national trends to be positively correlated to level of party voting at the first election. For instance where Labour was initially strong, the actual level of its vote in the second election should be larger than that predicted from the national voter transition matrix. This polarisation model has been tested by Johnston using both British and New Zealand general elections. Johnston (1981c) applies it to English constituencies and regions for 1974–9 changes, and Johnston (1981a) to changes between consecutive pairs of elections from 1966 to 1979 for a set of 17 regions. The model was generally successful, particularly for the Labour Party. Hence we can conclude that in England deviations from national trends do reflect prior party strength from which we can infer the operation of a neighbourhood effect. Tests of this model for New Zealand (Johnston, 1981d) were less successful but after allowance is made for minor party effects and sectional patterns the model does become moderately successful.

Finally reference should be made to Dunleavy's (1979) criticism of the neighbourhood effect as being without adequate theoretical foundation. He suggests that his consumption model of the voting process should be able to account for the deviations from class voting reported earlier. In fact Johnston (1983c) has shown that addition of consumption variables does not eradicate the empirical evidence from which neighbourhood effects can be inferred. As he so aptly puts it 'The neighbourhood effect won't go away'. The theoretical point has been addressed by Taylor (1984a) who suggests that the process has been viewed too narrowly at an inter-personal level over relatively short periods. Instead it is proposed to integrate the neighbourhood effect into a much broader process of 'mass indoctrination' in the ideological sphere of the modern state.

(*ii*) *Candidate Voting and Campaign Effects.* Two other local influences on election results have been of recent concern of geographers. The particular process of 'friends and neighbours' voting and the more general campaign effects have both been further researched in recent years.

The friends and neighbours model postulates additional voting for a candidate in his or her home area. The process involved relates to a candidate's supposed special knowledge of the area and the constituents' special knowledge of the candidate. This process is particularly evident in multi-member constituencies where electors can vote for the party of their choice and express a preference for candidates within that party's slate. This is precisely the situation in Ireland using the single transferable vote and Parker (1982, 1983) has investigated friends and neighbours voting in this context. Galway West constituency has four representatives and the main parties (Fianna Fail and Fine Gael) each put up four candidates. Mapping the first preference votes for each set of party candidates shows distinctive local biases within the constituency. Parker (1982) suggests that this reflects party strategies whereby the constituency is divided into zones and 'local' party candidates are provided for each zone. Each party, in effect, attempts to enhance its electoral position by adding a friends and neighbours component to its vote. The success of this strategy is indicated by the significant correlations between votes for each candidate and distance from the candidate's home. For two of the candidates this correlation is disappointing and in both cases it is former homes which distort the correlation. Friends and neighbours voting is alive and well and flourishing in Ireland.

More general campaign strategies have been discussed for other countries. The most comprehensive analysis is that of Minghi and Rumley (1978) who provide details of the spatial campaign strategies of the parties in Vancouver, BC in the 1972 provincial election. Patterns of expenditure, local issues raised in campaign literature and canvassing allow for assessment of differential campaign intensity by parties. At a much broader scale Archer (1982) discussed the different sectional bases of the Democrat and Republican US presidential campaigns in 1980. Finally Johnston (1979b, 1981b, 1983a) has continued his investigation of the effects of campaign expenditure in Britain. Generally speaking his findings have been most disappointing. A prime example is the influence of expenditure by all parties on turnout in the 1979 European elections. As the first election of its kind and with relatively little public interest it would seem to be an ideal test of the efficacy of political advertising. Johnston (1983a) however, finds no relationship between the combined campaign expenditure by the three main parties and the subsequent turnout. As Minghi and Rumley (1978) prudently conclude, the relationships in this field are 'highly complex' and are not uncovered as simple effects.

(*iii*) *Entropy Maximisation and the Components of Electoral Change.* The entropy maximisation estimates of vote flows within constituencies provide a new form of information to test some of the local effects described above. For 452 constituencies in England which all three parties fought in both 1974 general elections, Johnston (1982a) has computed all sixteen possible flows of vote from Conservative, Labour, Liberal or abstention in February to one of the above in October. These sixteen types of flow for all 452 constituencies are then used as dependent variables to be explained by independent variables measuring neighbourhood effect (the February level of a party's vote), campaign spending for all three parties and a typology of 26 constituency classes. Sixteen regression equations allow the effects of these variables on different flows of votes to be assessed. Once again neighbourhood effect comes out as consistently significant, campaign spending is somewhat contradictory and the typology is generally significant.

A more ambitious accounting framework has been employed in Johnston, Hay and Taylor (1982) which considers all flows of votes and actual migration in and out of constituencies as well as changes in voter preferences. This enables the following categories of voter to be identified for each party: loyal stayers who neither move nor change their vote, loyal movers who move but do not change their vote, switching stayers who change their vote but who do not move and switching movers who change both vote and district or region. With both electoral and migration data these categories can be estimated using the entropy approach. From such estimates the following hypotheses can be tested. The neighbourhood effect hypothesis that a party will attract more switching stayers the higher its initial vote. The differential migration hypothesis that a party will attract more loyal movers the higher its initial vote. The migration-conversion hypothesis that a party will attract more switching movers the higher its initial vote. Data demands to test these hypotheses are very severe and to date only one such analysis has been carried out for a six-region division of New Zealand for the 1972–75 inter-election period. Johnston (1983b) was able to show that the strongest hypothesis was for migration-conversion which was important for Labour, Values and Social Credit parties but not for the National party. Differential migration was important for Values and National parties and the neighbourhood effect for Values and Labour parties. Of course the latter finding no doubt reflects the use of just six relatively large regions. Nevertheless these results show the potential of this approach where suitable data is available.

Geography of Representation

Geographical interest in representation has centred upon electoral districting and the twin abuses of malapportionment and gerrymandering. This is still the case although the means of study have evolved from reporting abuses to relatively sophisticated analysis and evaluation of districting solutions and electoral systems in general (Taylor, Gudgin and Johnston, 1984). Some of this work has been brought together in an Association of American Geographers Resource Publication (Morrill, 1981).

(*i*) *Malapportionment beyond USA*. Malapportionment was the major districting issue in the USA in the 1960s in what came to be known as the reapportionment revolution. Since this period the concern of US reformers has moved on to other issues (Grofman, 1982; Morrill, 1982). Current research on malapportionment, therefore, has been on areas outside the USA where strict population equality has not been achieved. The major study in this respect is O'Loughlin's (1980b) analysis of sixteen countries in which district size is related to effects on political parties. More typical of earlier studies is Burdess's (1980) case study of municipal electorates in New South Wales and Douglas and Osborne (1981) and Osborne's (1979a) concern for the malapportionment of Northern Ireland's parliamentary districts. The latter author has also written on Northern Ireland local government areas (Osborne, 1979b). Knowles (1981) has analysed malapportionment in the Norwegian proportional representation system and has shown that on three occasions — 1961, 1969 and 1977 — malapportionment directly affected party control of parliament and hence government.

Two recent studies report on political attempts to change electoral systems taking due regard to malapportionment. Johnston (1983d) describes the court case in Britain in 1982–3 whereby the English Boundary Commissioners' proposed constituencies were challenged on the grounds of inequality of electorates. Johnston terms this a reapportionment revolution that failed. For Israel, Waterman (1980) explores the effects of a proposal to divide the country into districts for its proportional representation list system. Currently the whole country is treated as one district by the electoral law and Waterman uses equal population districting algorithms developed in the USA in the 1960s to divide the country into a proposed set of electoral districts.

(*ii*) *Gerrymandering and Grouping Algorithms.* Gerrymandering has traditionally been associated with unusually shaped districts. Erwin (1979) continues this spatial concern by studying the actual shape of Mississippi districts and inferring gerrymandering. Most recent studies, however, do not concentrate on the one particular districting solution that is in operation, rather they attempt to set the actual solution within the context of all possible solutions (Gudgin and Taylor, 1979). The required grouping algorithms have been developed and documented by Johnston and Rossiter (1981a).

This methodology has been applied by Johnston and Hughes (1978), Johnston and Rossiter (1980, 1981b, 1981c and 1982) and O'Loughlin (1982; O'Loughlin and Taylor, 1982). Both Johnston and Rossiter (1981) and O'Loughlin and Taylor (1982) have added evaluation of the shapes of districts in all solutions on the grounds that, although not always a legal requirement, many districting agencies do apply this criterion. Johnston and Rossiter (1981a, 1981b) show that this is definitely the case with the English Boundary Commissioners. In twelve separate problems (cities and London boroughs), the Boundary Commission chose the most compact solution on five occasions and the second or third most compact on another three occasions. For each problem there were several hundred feasible solutions from which the Boundary Commissions could choose.

In practice nearly all gerrymandering legal challenges have been and continue to be related to racial or ethnic representation. O'Loughlin's work is particularly interesting, therefore, because he addresses directly the issue of racial gerrymandering and uses the all-feasible-solutions method to evaluate past and current legal challenges. In the 1964 *Wright* v. *Rockefeller* case concerning congressional districts on Manhattan, for example, O'Loughlin (1982) is able to generate 59 feasible solutions which show that the most common solution has no black majority district. This tends to support the judicial conclusion of no racial discrimination. Other litigation concerning New Orleans city council districts, Mississippi congressional districts and Mobile City Commission districts is evaluated for black representation prospects in a similar manner. O'Loughlin clearly demonstrates the utility of this approach as a tool for combatants in such litigation.

(*iii*) *Components of Electoral Bias.* In any election the vote proportion and seat proportion that a party obtains will not normally coincide. The difference between the two is termed electoral bias and this can be decomposed into several elements some of which we have dealt with above. There has been a small debate concerning these procedures (Chisholm *et al.*, 1981; Taylor and Gudgin, 1984) but the main findings are reported in Gudgin and Taylor (1981) for plurality elections.

The procedure consists of first dividing electoral bias (B) into two parts — a size effect and a distribution effect. The size effect is then in turn divided into malapportionment (M), turnout (T) and minor party (P) effects plus an interaction term (I) and the distribution effect into cube-law winner's bias (C), additional normal segregation (N) and a non-normality effect (R). The following equation is then derived

$$B = M + T + P + I + C + N + R.$$

An application to the 1979 British general election shows that the most important effect for the Conservative party was the cube law winner's bias (worth + 6.5 per cent additional seats) which was counteracted by a malapportionment effect (– 1.13 per cent), additional normal segregation (– 1.19 per cent) and a non-normality effect (– 2.24 per cent). With the other minor effects this resulted in an overall election bias of + 1.62 per cent. This clearly shows that in plurality elections it is not just the number of votes that a party receives which is important; where those votes occurred may have a vital impact on the election result.

(iv) The Question of Power. The reapportionment revolution in the USA was pursued under the slogan 'one man, one vote, one vote, one value'. This can be used to argue for more than equi-populous districts however. In Britain the debate has centred on proportional representation of parties in parliament. In particular, concern has been expressed at the treatment of the Liberal party whose evenly spread minority support means they lose in nearly all constituencies and hence suffer severe electoral bias. But proportional representation of parties does not ensure 'one vote, one value'.

The power that a party holds in a parliament is not the same as its representation. Power is wielded when the party can influence the decisions of the parliament. Since these are majority decisions they will often rely on coalitions of parties. Power can then be measured as the ability of a party to destroy a potential governing coalition by withdrawing from it (Laver, 1978; Johnston, 1978). The total power that a party holds is the number of coalitions it can destroy and this can be expressed as a proportion of majority coalition destruction by all parties. Johnston (1979a, 1982g) has conducted numerous experiments on the relationship between proportion of power and proportion of seats in a parliament. His two main findings are that there is no simple relation — extra seats do not ensure extra power — and the relation is highly unstable depending as it does on the particular configuration of party strengths — a small change in seats may produce a disproportionate change in power. Johnston (1983e) has used this methodology to evaluate the possibilities of providing fairer representation in the European parliament. The most interesting application, however, is in his challenging of the fairness assumptions of electoral reformers who aim for proportional representation (Johnston, 1984a; 1984b).

The proportional representation debate leads us into concern for electoral systems in general. Christopher (1983) and Johnston (1982f) have described the way in which boundary commissioners operate in South Africa and Britain respectively and Pringle (1980) has discussed the change in the electoral system in Northern Ireland in the 1920s. For the USA Clotfelter and Vavrichek (1980) discuss regional and campaigning implications of a reform of presidential elections by replacing the electoral college by a direct vote. Shelley (1982) employs a constitutional choice approach to justify use of bipartisan districting agencies. Clearly, discussion of electoral systems takes us beyond narrow conceptions of power as defined above to consideration of the relationships between elections and the political system in which they occur.

Reorientation: Reform or Revolution?

The main criticism of electoral geography is that elections are often studied as ends in themselves. In this second part of the chapter I will describe some attempts to develop an electoral geography that counters such criticism. Clearly this will involve treating elections as more than a vote-counting exercise. There have been some interesting recent studies which use analysis of election returns to throw light on more general political issues. Bennett and Earle (1983), for instance, analyse the distribution of the 1912 US presidential vote for the Socialist candidate as part of their explanation for the failure of socialism in America. Ley and Mercer (1980) use election results as part of their explanation of the sectoral bias in the geography of conflicts in Vancouver, BC. The most common use of elections for much wider issues are the studies which consider the distribution of 'nationalist' party votes as part of modern separatist ethnic movements. Three recent examples are Williams (1980) on Welsh nationalism, Williams (1981) on Quebec separatism and Agnew (1984) on Scottish nationalism. In our discussion below we will not consider further studies of elections as aspects of such wider themes. Instead we will continue to focus attention on the elections themselves, but not in isolation from their political context.

A Systems Framework

In the 1960s and 1970s there were several calls for the application of the systems approach to political geography. This was mostly only lip-service to current fashion with little substantive research to back up the methodological arguments (Burnett and Taylor, 1981). Nevertheless in the late 1970s it seemed that a systems framework might provide linkages between the three parts of electoral geography and show how electoral geography fitted into the broader political geography (Johnston, 1979a).

(i) Input, Throughput and Output: New Priorities. The simplest way of viewing any political system is as a sequence of input, throughput and output with a feedback loop from output to input. If this is applied to electoral studies in geography we can allocate geography of voting and geographical influences in voting to input, geography of representation to throughput and very little to output. This latter feature reflects the traditional concern for studying elections for their own sake. This simple framework was suggested by Taylor (1978) as a way of making electoral geography a more integrated and coherent subject. Subsequently Johnston (1980b) has extended the argument both backwards to the social system and forwards into the political system within which elections operate. Hence the input, geography of voting, depends upon political cleavages which reflect the socio-economic structure of society and the output, the geography of policy, links elections into the political system. In this way the study of electoral geography need no longer be the most isolated part of political geography.

The main lesson to be drawn from the above argument for research priorities centred on the dearth of studies on output. It was suggested that inputs had been over-emphasised at the expense of outputs. Hence a new research priority was identified in the field of outputs of the electoral sub-system, what may be termed a geography of policy. For Johnston (1980b) such study becomes part of a wider political geography but where the policy feeds back into the geography of voting it remains part of the electoral sub-system and hence will be treated here as a theme in electoral geography.

(*ii*) *Feedback: The Pork Barrel Process.* Although the geography of government expenditure has been sporadically studied by geographers this has been a weakly developed research theme. In contrast, in political science this topic appears in two contexts. First there are studies of representatives using their office to favour their own constituency and hence bolster their re-election chances. This is commonly referred to as pork barrel politics. Second there are more formal models which assume that governments' major interest is to obtain re-election and that they therefore pursue policies in line with majority opinion. This is the Downsian model which predicts that governments of right or left will pursue centre (= majority) policies. Both of these types of study view politics from the point of view of the politician and reduce politics to a vote-buying exercise. This simple feedback process has recently attracted some political geography interest in the work of Johnston (1979c, 1979d, 1980a) and Archer (1980) for USA expenditure patterns.

A comprehensive assessment of pork barrel politics is to be found in Johnston's (1980a) *The Geography of Federal Spending in the United States of America.* The most interesting feature of the work is its failure to sustain vote-buying hypotheses. Scores of tables, numerous regression and correlation analyses all fail to show any consistent relationship between expenditure patterns and political variables such as committee membership and seniority. This is therefore a very rare book built as it is around *negative* findings: 'What this book has achieved is the falsification of a simple hypothesis erected to account for the geography of public spending' (Johnston, 1980a, p. 165).

This does not mean that pork barrel politics do not occur, but simply that this effect is not important enough to influence the broad pattern of public expenditure. Johnston can only conclude that he has stumbled upon a 'complex subject' which cannot be modelled as a simple feedback loop in the electoral sub-system. Clearly this research theme requires some major rethinking.

(iii) Critique: The Real Geography of Elections. Johnston's (1980a) 'negative' manuscript is a breath of fresh air in electoral geography. Being forced to think anew we can not only reject the simple feed-back loop but can begin the task of rejecting the whole systems framework. The 'complexity' of government expenditure leads us to query the assumptions upon which the electoral sub-system and political system are built. In fact what we have been doing is treating liberal democracy uncritically at its own face value. We have assumed an ideal liberal democratic society where people vote to produce governments which are responsive to their needs. If govern-ment does not match up to the needs of the people then they have it in their hands to get rid of the government through the ballot box. This is an ideal type devoid of all history or geography. It is too good to be true. If the world really is this simple why was the system so difficult to set up in the first place? And, more crucially, why is it only used in a *minority* of countries throughout the world. In short if this self-adjusting political system is so good why is it so rare?

Liberal democracy is not randomly distributed over the world. It is highly concentrated in a particular type of country. It is the political system of the rich countries — the core of the world economy. This is the real *geography* of elections. Although at any one point in time elections can be found in third world countries they do not provide the same stability of government as enjoyed in the core countries. In the periphery, elections alternate with other forms of government creation — military coups, insurgency, foreign invasion — depending on the particular circumstances. Even in the peripheral countries with a relatively strong democratic tradition such as India and Jamaica, electoral politics are much more fragile than in the core. It is when we come to look at this geography of elections that we realise we need a completely new framework for our studies (Johnston, 1984a).

A Critical Perspective

The basic proposition of this final section of the chapter is that electoral geography will not advance by developing its technical equipment alone. Despite the real improvements in techniques in quantitative electoral geography described earlier, no amount of sophisticated statistical manipulation can prevent the unsatisfactory systems framework outlined above from hindering any real advance in our geographical understanding of elections. A revolution in thinking is required to take electoral geography beyond interesting case studies and simplistic adherence to the tenets of liberal democracy.

Some tentative steps in devising such a new electoral geography are outlined below. The argument is developed through three levels of analysis. First, we consider electoral geography and government formation with particular regard for the role of political parties. Second, at a more abstract level, the relationship between elections and theories of the state are explored and the dialectics of electoral geography are derived. Finally we return to a more concrete analysis but at the global scale: Electoral geographies are considered in the core and in the periphery of the world-economy to illustrate contrasting yet complementary political processes within the world-system.

(*i*) *Electoral Geography and Government Formation.* The first step in developing any new electoral geography is to ensure that it does not treat elections as ends in themselves. We shall assume that the first purpose of elections is to produce governments. Although parliaments originated as a means of providing representations to executives, the advent of popular elections has democratised both arms of government so that today elections are primarily about who formally controls government in both its executive and legislative functions. The overriding fact in all modern liberal democracies is that although this control may be derived from popular elections, it is mediated through political parties. Governments are dominated by parties. Liberal democracy implies alternative elected governments which in practice has meant electoral competition by political parties. Despite this crucial role of parties in electoral geography they have been relatively neglected as objects of interest.

Archer and Taylor (1981) have attempted to bring political parties to the centre of the electoral geography stage in their application of Schattschneider's conflict theory of politics. In this theory there are innumerable possible conflicts in any given society all of which divide that society into two or more parts. Each one of these cleavages may form the basis of the society's politics. But not all of them can. A coherent politics can only be developed along a restricted number of cleavages. Political parties organise politics around these few selected cleavages. All other conflicts are, as it were, organised out of politics. Hence at any election the voter is presented with just a small number of meaningful choices by his or her country's party system. Choice is severely constrained since you can vote for or against a party but not for or against a party system. This is what Schattschneider terms the great act of organisation. In the USA since the first popular election of 1828 there have been only three parties who have successfully had their nominee elected president — Democratic, Whig and Republican. Archer and Taylor (1981) relate this party dominance to the geographical division of the country into sections. The inter-weaving of these themes of party and section provides an initial framework for an electoral geography of the USA.

In the case of the USA there has been much discussion of the 'end of party' which we have previously noted has been investigated by Downing *et al.* (1980) and Johnston (1982b). The important point, however, is that party control of the presidency has certainly not weakened as John Anderson and other independent candidates found to their cost in 1980. Nevertheless there are genuine examples where party dominance has been eliminated. The classic case is the progressive reforms at the beginning of this century which aimed at eliminating machine politics from US urban government. This reform movement was anti-party and non-partisan elections were instituted for many city and some state elections. The political effect of these reforms was to curtail working class political advances (Taylor, 1984a). This process of 'taking the politics out of politics' can be found today in the proportional representation movement (Johnston, 1984b). An important motive of early PR reformers was to neutralise the increasingly popular socialist parties of Europe in the early part of this century. In today's debate reformers continue to emphasise representation at the expense of government formation. From the latter perspective it is proportional tenure of government office which is the proper measure of fairness. Taylor (1984b) has discussed this issue with respect to the British electoral system and has developed alternative measures of electoral bias based on government formation rather than representation (Taylor, 1984c).

(ii) Electoral Geography and Functions of the State. Identification of government formation as the purpose of elections is a first step in our critical argument, but it is only a first step. Elections do not just provide governments. Elections have an important legitimising function in liberal democracies as indicated by the term 'free world' to distinguish such forms of government from the opposing camp. In fact the 'free world' encompasses much more than the liberal-democratic world of the rich countries but even in the periphery

some governments have had to go through democratic electoral procedures to confirm foreign support and aid. Although more often 'free' in theory than in practice, the liberal theory remains an important prop of the modern world order. We explore this theme here.

Taylor (1984d) uses O'Connor's definition of state functions to relate electoral geography to theories of the state. This involves two separate functions which are fundamental to the purposes of all states. First there is the need to provide conditions conducive for capital accumulation. Any state is ultimately only as strong as the 'economy' upon which it is based. Second there is a need to legitimate the system within which the state operates. No state can survive for long by coercing its people into submission, it must produce conditions in which the people accept its authority with minimal resistance. The problem is that good conditions for accumulation are likely to be bad conditions for legitimation and vice versa. In practise therefore states exist in conditions of compromise between these two functions, the actual balance depending on the particular circumstances of the state. Nevertheless compromises turn out to be short-term strategies which only temporarily hide the fundamental crisis of the state — the accumulation-legitimation contradiction. Taylor (1984d) uses this logic to suggest that one way in which the crisis of the state is deflected is through its party system.

The dialectics of electoral geography derive directly from this theory. In any election there are *two* sets of processes underlying the geography. The first is the politics of support which is reflected in the geography of voting described previously. This depends upon the ability of parties to mobilise supporters for their candidates but in the process they integrate the population into the system. Potentially rebellious subjects become citizens, partners within the state. This contributes towards the legitimating function of the state. The second process is the politics of power. This is concerned with the accumulation function or how the state will facilitate capital expansion. It therefore relates to the interests supporting particular parties and the way in which that interest is translated into policy when the party forms a government. From these two processes we can describe *two* electoral geographies not one. The simple geography of voting needs to be supplemented with the much more subtle geography of power. Taylor (1984d) argues that it is the latter geography which should form the focus of future research.

This new model of electoral geography is best illustrated by way of examples. There are two classic party systems in the USA which show how support and power can produce contradictory geographies. The second party system of Whigs versus Democrats has been described by Archer and Taylor (1981) in terms of a non-sectional normal vote pattern in the period 1836 to 1852. This is the politics of support reflected in a particular geography of voting. The paradox is, of course, that the major conflict of this period was between north and south which is not reflected in the party system: Sectionalism was organised out of politics. The politics of power was only able to overcome this politics of support with the replacement of Whigs by Republicans in 1856. After the civil war the politics of power and support continued to be quite distinct although in a different way from the earlier contrast. The politics of power in this period centred on the tariff issue with Republicans representing the protectionist lobby and Democrats taking a more free trade stance. Hence the differences between parties at this policy level concerns a basic *economic* difference. In contrast studies of voting patterns for this period show that economic variables are poor predictors of party support, instead parties were mobilising electors along ethnocultural lines. The geography of voting, therefore, reflects racial, ethnic and religious distributions. And yet between the civil war and World War I no cultural issue became a major policy difference between the parties. Mobilising voters and running the government were clearly treated as two distinct and separate aspects of party activity.

We can also describe two similar classic contradictions between power and support in British elections. At the beginning of the century the Liberals were the party of free trade and the Conservatives the party of protection. And yet the geography of their support did not reflect the economic interests behind these tariff policies (Taylor, 1984d). 'Consumer England' (the south) was overwhelmingly Conservative despite the higher prices that protection offered whereas 'Producer England' (the north) was equally strong in its support for the Liberals despite their advocacy of no protection for vulnerable industry. A similar paradox exists today according to Sharpe (1982). He identifies as 'a puzzle' the contrast between the Labour party's geography of voting concentrated in northern England, Wales and Scotland and its failure to seriously tackle the dominance of London and the south-east. In terms of the politics of support Labour is 'the party of the periphery' whereas in terms of the politics of power Labour is as centrist as its Conservative rivals. Once again these two processes are separate and distinct:

we need two geographies of election to fully understand the situation.

It is much easier to call for more research on geographies of power than it is to actually carry this out. Whereas support for parties is directly expressed through the ballot box the power behind parties is much more difficult to assess. In some cases it may extend beyond the borders of a country as when the CIA funds parties or destabilises governments of unfriendly parties. One recent study has unmasked a geography of power behind one particularly dominant political party, the National Party of South Africa (Pirie *et al.*, 1980). Here we have a contrast between the rural-bias of the party's geography of voting (Lemon, 1981) and the influence of the urban-based secret society, the Broederbond. Such explicit descriptions of politics of power are likely to be rare, however. Taylor (1984d) has suggested five structural tendencies as a guide for helping identify politics of power within electoral geography.

(*iii*) *Electoral Geography in the World-Economy.* There are two aspects of electoral geography which have not yet been adequately covered in this critical perspective. First there is the question of change. How do elections relate to changes in politics? Such questions suggest that we search for the mechanism of change within the 'political system'. Below we present an alternative political-economy approach which locates all social change in the basic production process. Second there is the question of the geography of electoral geography. How do the elections that occur outside the stable liberal democracies relate to the processes discussed above? We will again propose a political-economy answer which suggests the existence of distinctive yet complementary politics in different sections of the world-economy.

The power that political parties have and use through their control of government is not absolute. It is relative to the position of their state within the world-order. And that position is ultimately derived from location within the capitalist world-economy (Wallerstein, 1979; Chase-Dunn, 1981; Taylor, 1984a). It is changes within the world-economy that govern the context of the politics within any state. Whether the world-economy is stagnating or growing changes the parameters of the politics of all states. Those parameters will vary state-by-state but all states will face varying opportunities as the world-economy stagnates and grows. These phases of the world-economy are now well documented as long-term production cycles the most well-known being the fifty-year Kondratieff cycles. We are currently experiencing the B-phase (stagnation) of the fourth Kondratieff cycle.

How do these long cycles affect electoral geography? Each phase of a cycle produces a new economic situation. This situation directly affects what can and what cannot be achieved by government. This is reflected in changes in the political agenda. Old assumptions are discarded and new ways of using control of government are devised. We shall term these phases of 'new politics' which coincide with or follow the changes in economic prospects (Taylor, 1982a).

These ideas may be illustrated by an example. British politics since World War I can be divided in six phases of new politics corresponding to the B phase of the third Kondratieff cycle and the A (growth) and B phases of the fourth Kondratieff cycle. Hence each production phases relates to two political phases (Taylor, 1982a, 1984a). Broadly speaking we can identify politics of crisis and national interest in the two B-phases corresponding to the 1920s (crisis I), 1930s (national interest I), the 1970s (crisis II) and 1980s (national interest II). In between in the A-phase there have been the politics of social democratic consensus starting in the 1940s and continuing through the 1950s followed by the technocratic politics of the 1960s. There are three important features of this typology. First, each new politics is not the invention of one party. Both parties are forced by circumstances to accept the new assumptions. Second, the new politics are not themselves an electoral issue. Elections do not normally occur in which voters are asked to choose between such alternative politics. Hence the key dates separating new politics are not election years. For instance the social democratic consensus evolved *before* Labour's 1945 election victory just as technocratic politics evolved *before* Labour's 1964 election victory even though in both cases it was those Labour governments that became most clearly associated with these two new politics (Taylor, 1982a). Third, the new politics are part of the politics of power; one of the primary tasks of political parties is to mobilise their supporters behind each successive new politics. Hence there will be continuity in the geography of support through different geographies of power. In Britain, for instance and as noted previously, Johnston (1983b) has shown that just one normal vote pattern describes the Labour Party's geography of votes from 1918 to October 1974 accounting for over 84 per cent of areal variation in seventeen elections. Here we have just one politics of support for five politics of power.

The consecutive new politics we have described for Britain were all translated into electoral politics. The same overall cycles of the world-economy affect peripheral states even more severely than core countries. In such situations alternative new politics may involve transfers of power from elected civilian governments to military or unelected civilian governments. The major political issue in these states is maintenance of order. This very basic politics of stability may involve a politics of support but normally revolves around the politics of power within the dominant classes of the state, both internal and external (Osei-Kwame and Taylor, 1984). Hence the separation of processes of power and support tends to be even more acute in this context. In Africa, for instance, the politics of support are based upon ethnic geographies whereas politics of power are very clearly economic in nature. This has been illustrated for Ghana, where alternative ethnic coalitions have been mobilised to out-vote the economically dominant Ashante cocoa-growers in order to use their foreign earnings to invest in urban-industrial infra-structure (Osei-Kwame and Taylor, 1984). Hence the ethnic map is used to create a new economic map. In this particular case continual economic failures have produced a politics of failure far more severe than either of Britain's politics of crisis and national interest.

There are of course fundamental differences between the politics of the core — liberal democracy — and the politics of the periphery. This is not a matter of those countries that hold regular elections and those that do not. Elections in the core are stable predictable events with no rival means of government formation. In the periphery elections are merely one of several methods of government formation. As such the electoral geography of peripheral countries should not proceed on the assumption that such elections are the equivalent of those in the stable liberal democracies. This is sometimes implied by Indian political geographers (e.g. Mehta and Sekhon, 1980) but such an assumption is highly misleading. In one Indian paper, however, we can find a clue to their distinctive electoral geography. Dikshit and Sharma (1982) have used factor analysis to describe the Congress Party vote patterns in the Punjab. Their results are completely different from the factor analysis results reported earlier which generated normal vote patterns. For the Congress in the Punjab there is simply no normal vote pattern. Dikshit and Sharma provide maps of Congress support for six elections which show no correspondence with one another. At each election Congress mobilised a different coalition of support. This finding has been repeated for Ghanaian elections where again the normal vote pattern is conspicuous by its absence to be replaced by alternative ethnic mobilisations (Osei-Kwame and Taylor, 1984).

These findings suggest that a new electoral geography can fit easily into the world-systems perspective on political geography (Taylor, 1981b; 1982b). The world-systems approach involves the identification of distinctive yet complementary processes operating in different sectors of the world economy. The best-known dichotomy is that between 'development' in the core and the 'development of underdevelopment' in the periphery. A major task of electoral geography is to investigate the equivalent core and peripheral processes that operate for elections. Distinctive yet complementary geographies of support and power underlying government formation in the core and parts of the periphery provide a most exciting research agenda for the future.

References

Agnew, J. (1984) 'Place and Political Behaviour: the Geography of Scottish Nationalism', *Political Geography Quarterly*, *3*, 191–206
Archer, J.C. (1980) 'Congressional Incumbent Re-election Success and Federal Outlays Distribution: a Test of the Electoral Connection Hypothesis', *Environment and Planning* A, *12*, 263–78
—— (1982) 'Some Geographical Aspects of the American Presidential Election of 1980', *Political Geography Quarterly*, *1*, 123–35
—— and Taylor, P.J. (1981) *Section and Party: A Political Geography of American Presidential Elections from Andrew Jackson to Ronald Reagan*, John Wiley, Chichester
Bennett, S. and Earle, C. (1983) 'Socialism in America: a Geographical Interpretation of Failure', *Political Geography Quarterly*, *2*, 31–56
Bodman, A.R. (1982) 'Measuring Political Change', *Environment and Planning* A, *14*, 33–48
Burdess, N. (1980) 'Variations in Municipal Electoral Size in New South Wales', *Australian Geographer*, *14*, 278–85
Burnett, A.D. and Taylor, P.J. (1981) 'Introduction' in A.D. Burnett and P.J. Taylor (eds.), *Political Studies from Spatial Perspectives*, John Wiley, Chichester, pp. 3–10
Chase-Dunn, C.K. (1981) 'Interstate System and Capitalist World-Economy: One Logic or Two' in W.L. Hollist and J.N. Rosenau (eds.), *World System Structure*, Sage, Beverly Hills, pp. 25–41
Chisholm, M., Devereaux, B. and Versey, R. (1981) 'The Myth of Non-Partisan Cartography: the Tale Continued', *Urban Studies*, *18*, 213–8
Christopher, A.J. (1983) 'Parliamentary Delimitation in South Africa, 1910–1980', *Political Geography Quarterly*, *2*, 205–18
Clotfelter, C.T. and Vavrichele, B. (1980) 'Campaign Resource Allocation and the Regional Impact of Electoral College Reform', *Journal of Regional Science*, *20*, 311–29

Dikshit, R.D. and Sharma, J.C. (1982) 'Electoral Performance of the Congress Party in Punjab (1952–1977): an Ecological Analysis', *Transactions, Institute of Indian Geographers*, *4*, 1–15

Douglas, J.N.H. and Osborne, R.D. (1981) 'Northern Ireland's Increased Representation in the Westminster Parliament', *Irish Geography*, *14*, 37–40

Downing, B., Hudson, T. Taylor, P.J. Bland, P. and Villanueva N. (1980) 'The Decline of Party Voting: a Geographical Analysis of the 1978 Massachusetts Election', *Professional Geographer*, *32*, 454–61

Dunleavy, P. (1979) 'The Urban Basis of Political Alignment: Social Class, Domestic Property Ownership and State Intervention in Consumption Processes', *British Journal of Political Science*, *9*, 409–43

Erwin, N. (1979) 'Unique Shapes in Mississippi's Political Districts and the Possibility of Gerrymandering', *Mississippi Geographer*, *7*, 20–34

Gudgin, G. and Taylor, P.J. (1979) *Seats, Votes and the Spatial Organization of Elections*, Pion, London

———— (1981) 'The Decomposition of Electoral Bias in a Plurality Election', *British Journal of Political* Science, *10*, 515–21

Ingalls, G.L. and Brunn, S.D. (1979) 'Electoral Change in the American South, 1948–1976: the Influence of Population Size', *Southeastern Geographer*, *19*, 80–90

Johnston, R.J. (1978) 'On the Measurement of Power: Some Reactions to Laver' *Environment and Planning* A, *10*, 907–14

—— (1979a) *Political, Electoral and Spatial Systems*, Oxford University Press, London

—— (1979b) 'Campaign Spending and Votes: a Reconsideration', *Public Choice*, *33*, 97–106

—— (1979c) 'Congressional Committees and Inter-State Distribution of Military Spending', *Geoforum*, *10*, 151–62

—— (1979d) 'Congressional Committees and Department Spending: the Political Influence on the Geography of Federal Expenditure in the United States', *Transactions, Institute of British Geographers*, NS, *4*, 373–84

—— (1979e) 'Regional Variations in the 1979 General Election Results for England', *Area*, *11*, 294–8

—— (1979f) 'Class, Conflict and Electoral Geography', *Antipode*, *11*, no. 3, 36–43

—— (1980a) *The Geography of Federal Spending in the United States of America*, Wiley, Chichester

—— (1980b) 'Electoral Geography and Political Geography', *Australian Geographical Studies*, *18*, 37–50

—— (1980c) 'Xenophobia and Referenda: an Example of the Exploratory Use of Ecological Regression', *L'Espace Geographique*, *9*, 73–80

—— (1981a) 'Regional Variations in British Voting Trends — 1966–1979: Tests of an Ecological Model', *Regional Studies*, *15*, 23–32

—— (1981b) 'Campaign Expenditure and the Efficacy of Advertising: a Response', *Political Studies*, *29*, 113–4

—— (1981c) 'Testing the Butler-Stokes Model of a Polarization Effect around the National Swing in Partisan Preferences: England, 1979', *British Journal of Political Science*, *11*, 113–7

—— (1981d) 'Changing Voter Preferences, Uniform Electoral Swing, and the Geography of Voting in New Zealand', *New Zealand Geographer*, *37*, 13–19

—— (1981e) 'Embourgeoisement, the Property Owning Democracy, and Ecological Models of Voting in England', *British Journal of Political Science*, *11*, 499–503

—— (1981f) 'Embourgeoisement and Voting: England 1974', *Area*, *13*, 345–51

—— (1981g) 'Short-term Electoral Change in England, 1974', *Geoforum*, *12*, 237–44

—— (1982a) 'The Geography of Electoral Change: an Illustration of an Estimating Procedure', *Geografiska Annaler*, B, *64*, 51–60

—— (1982b) 'The Changing Geography of Voting in the United States, 1946-1980', *Transactions, Institute of British Geographers*, NS 7, 187-204

—— (1982c) 'Short-term Electoral Change in England: Estimates of its Spatial Variation', *Political Geography Quarterly*, 1, 41-56

—— (1982d) 'The Definition of Voting Regions in Multi-Party Contests', *European Journal of Political Research*, 10, 293-304

—— (1982e) 'Uncovering Structural Effects in Ecological Data: an Entropy Maximising Approach', *Geographical Analysis*, 14, 355-65

—— (1982f) 'Redistricting by Independent Commissions: a Perspective from Britain', *Annals, Association of American Geographers*, 72, 457-70

—— (1982g) 'Political Geography and Political Power' in M.J. Holler (ed.), *Power, Voting and Voting Power*, Physica-Verlag, Wien, pp. 289-306

—— (1983a) 'Campaign Spending and Voting in England: Analyses of the Efficacy of Political Advertising', *Environment and Planning* C, 1, 117-26

—— (1983b) 'Spatial Continuity and Individual Variability', *Electoral Studies*, 2, 53-68

—— (1983c) 'The Neighbourhood Effect Won't Go Away: Observations on the Electoral Geography of England in the Light of Dunleavy's Critique', *Geoforum*, 14, 161-68

—— (1983d) 'The Reapportionment Revolution that Failed', *Political Geography Quarterly*, 2, 309-18

—— (1983e) 'Proportional Representation and Fair Representation in the European Parliament', *Area*, 15, 347-55

—— (1984a) 'The Political Geography of Electoral Geography' in P.J. Taylor and J.W. House (eds.), *Political Geography: Recent Advances and Future Directions*, Croom Helm, London

—— (1984b) 'People, Places, Parties and Parliaments: a Geographical Perspective on Electoral Reform in Great Britain', *Geographical Journal*, forthcoming

—— and Hay, A.M. (1982) 'On the Parameters of Uniform Swing in Single Member Constituency Electoral Systems', *Environment and Planning* A, 14, 61-74

—— (1983) 'Voter Transition Probability Estimates: an Entropy Maximising Approach', *European Journal of Political Research*, 11, 93-8

—— and Rumley, D. (1983) 'Entropy Maximising Method for Estimating Voting Data: a Critical Test', *Area*, 15, 35-41

—— and Taylor, P.J. (1982) 'Estimating the Sources of Spatial Change in Election Results: a Multiproportional Matrix Approach', *Environment and Planning* A, 14, 951-61

—— and Hughes, C.A. (1978) 'Constituency Delimitation and the Unintentional Gerrymander in Brisbane', *Australian Geographical Studies*, 16, 99-110

—— O'Neill A.B. and Taylor, P.J. (1983) 'The Changing Electoral Geography of the Netherlands: 1946-1981', *Tijdschrift voor Economische en Sociale Geografie*, 74, 185-95

—— and Rossiter, D.J. (1980) 'The Current Redistribution of Parliamentary Seats: Eight Greater London Boroughs', *Area*, 12, 223-8

—— (1981a) 'Program GROUP: the Identification of all Possible Solutions to a Constituency-delimitation Problem', *Environment and Planning* A, 13, 231-8

—— (1981b) 'Share and the Definition of Parliamentary Constituencies', *Urban Studies*, 18, 219-23

—— (1981c) 'An Approach to the Delimitation of Planning Regions', *Applied Geography*, 1, 55-70

—— (1982) 'Constituency Building, Political Representation and Electoral Bias in Urban England' in D.T. Herbert and R.J. Johnston (eds.), *Geography and the Urban Environment*, John Wiley, Chichester, pp. 113-55

Knowles, R.D. (1981) 'Malapportionment in Norway's Parliamentary Elections since 1921', *Norsk Geografiska Tidsskrift*, 35, 147-59

Laver, M. (1978) 'The Problem of Measuring Power in Europe', *Environment and Planning* A, *10*, 901–6

Lemon, A. (1981) 'The Geography of Voting Patterns in South African Elections, 1974–77' in A.D. Burnett and P.J. Taylor (eds.), *Political Studies from Spatial Perspectives*, John Wiley, Chichester, pp. 419–42

Ley, D. and Mercer, J. (1980) 'Locational Conflict and the Politics of Consumption', *Economic Geography*, *56*, 89–109

Mehta, S. and Sekhon, J.S. (1980) 'Patterns of Voting Participation in Himachal Pradesh: a Spatial Perspective', *Indian Journal of Political Science*, *41*, 79–90

Minghi, J.V. and Rumley, D. (1978) 'Toward a Geography of Campaigning: Some Evidence from a Provincial Election in Vancouver, British Columbia', *Canadian Geographer*, *22*, 145–62

Morrill, R.L. (1981) *Political Redistricting and Geographic Theory*, Association of American Geographers, Washington, D.C.

—— (1982) 'Redistricting Standards and Strategies after 20 years', *Political Geography Quarterly*, *1*, 361–70

O'Loughlin, J. (1980a) 'The Election of Black Mayors, 1977', *Annals, Association of American Geographers*, *70*, 353–70

—— (1980b) 'District Size and Party Electoral Strength: a Comparison of Sixteen Democracies, *Environment and Planning* A, *12*, 247–62

—— (1981) 'The Neighbourhood Effect on Urban Voting Surfaces: a Cross-national Analysis' in A.D. Burnett and P.J. Taylor (eds.), *Political Studies from Spatial Perspectives*, John Wiley, Chichester, pp. 357–88

—— (1982) 'The Identification and Evaluation of Racial Gerrymandering', *Annals, Association of American Geographers*, *72*, 165–84

—— and Taylor A.M., (1982) 'Choices in Redistricting and Electoral Outcomes: the Case of Mobile, Alabama', *Political Geography Quarterly*, *1*, 317–40

Osborne, R.D. (1979a) 'The Northern Ireland Parliamentary Electoral System: the 1979 Reapportionment', *Irish Geography*, *12*, 42–56

—— (1979b) 'Local Government Electoral Areas in Northern Ireland,' *Irish Geography*, *12*, 183–6

Osei-Kwame, P. and Taylor, P.J. (1984) 'The Politics of Failure: a Political Geography of Ghanaian Elections, 1954–79', *Annals, Association of American Geographers*, *74*, forthcoming

Parker, A.J. (1982) 'The "Friends and Neighbours" Voting Effect in the Galway West Constituency', *Political Geography Quarterly*, *1*, 243–62

—— (1983) 'Localism and Bailiwicks: the Galway West Constituency in the 1977 General Election', *Proceedings of the Royal Irish Academy*, *83* C, 17–36

Pirie, C.H., Rogerson, C.M. and Beavon, K.S.O. (1980) 'Covert Power in South Africa: the Geography of the Afrikaner Broederbond', *Area*, *12*, 97–104

Pringle, D.G. (1979) 'The Northern Ireland Westminster Elections, 1979', *Irish Geography*, *12*, 114–7

—— (1980) 'Electoral Systems and Political Manipulation: a Case Study of Northern Ireland in the 1920s', *Economic and Social Review*, *11*, 187–205

Rumley, D. (1979) 'The Study of Structural Effects in Human Geography', *Tidschrift voor Economische en Sociale Geografie*, *70*, 350–60

—— (1981a) 'Some Aspects of the Geography of Political Participation in Western Australia', *Environment and Planning* A, *12*, 671–84

—— (1981b) 'Spatial Structural Effects in Voting Behaviour: Description and Explanation', *Tidschrift voor Economische en Sociale Geografie*, *72*, 214–23

Sharpe, L.J. (1982) 'The Labour Party and the Geography of Inequality: a Puzzle' in D. Kavanagh (ed.), *The Politics of the Labour Party*, George Allen and Unwin, London, pp. 135–70

Shelley, F.M. (1982) 'A Constitutional Choice Approach to Electoral District Boundary Delimitation', *Political Geography Quarterly*, *1*, 341–50

—— and Archer, J.C. (1983) 'Political Habit, Political Culture and the Electoral Mosaic of a Border Region', Paper presented at the Conference of the South-West Division of the Association of American Geographers, Norman, Oklahoma

Swauger, J. (1980) 'Regionalism in the 1976 Presidential Election', *Geographical Review, 70,* 157–66

Taylor, P.J. (1978) 'Progress Report: Political Geography', *Progress in Human Geography, 2,* 153–62

—— (1979) 'The Changing Geography of Representation in Britain,' *Area, 11,* 289–94

—— (1981a) 'Factor Analysis in Geographical Research' in R.J. Bennett (ed.), *European Progress in Quantitative Geography,* Pion, London, pp. 251–67

—— (1981b) 'Political Geography and the World-Economy' in A.D. Burnett and P.J. Taylor (eds.), *Political Studies from Spatial Perspectives,* John Wiley, Chichester, pp. 157–74

—— (1982a) 'The Changing Political Map' in R.J. Johnston and J.C. Doornkamp (eds.), *The Changing Geography of the United Kingdom,* Methuen, London, pp. 275–90

—— (1982b) 'A Materialist Framework for Political Geography', *Transactions, Institute of British Geographers,* NS, 7, 15–34

—— (1984a) *Political Geography: World-Economy, Nation-State and Locality,* Longman, Harlow, Essex

—— (1984b) 'Accumulation, Legitimation and the Electoral Geographies within Liberal Democracies' in P.J. Taylor and J.W. House (eds.), *Political Geography: Recent Advances and Future Directions,* Croom Helm, London

—— (1984c) 'The Case for Proportional Tenure: a Defence of the British Electoral System' in B. Grofman and A. Lijphart (eds.), *Choosing an Electoral System: Issues and Alternatives,* Praeger

—— (1984d) ' "All Organisation is Bias": the Political Geography of Electoral Reform', *Geographical Journal,* forthcoming

—— and Gudgin, G. (1982) 'Geography of Elections' in N. Wrigley (ed.), *Quantitative Geography: A British View,* Routledge and Kegan Paul, London, pp. 382–6

—— (1984) 'The Myth of Non-partisan Cartography: Clarifications', *Urban Studies,* forthcoming

—— Gudgin G. and Johnston, R.J. (1984) 'The Geography of Representation: a Review of Recent Findings' in B. Grofman and A. Lijphart (eds.), *Electoral Laws and their Political Consequences,* Agathon

—— and Johnston, R.J. (1979) *Geography of Elections,* Penguin, London

Wallerstein, I. (1979) *The Capitalist World-Economy,* Cambridge University Press, Cambridge

Waterman, S. (1980) 'The Dilemma of Electoral Districting for Israel', *Tijdschrift voor Economische en Sociale Geografie, 71,* 88–97

Williams, C.H. (1980) 'Ethnic Separatism in Western Europe', *Tijdschrift voor Economische en Sociale Geografie, 71,* 142–58

—— (1981) 'Identity through Autonomy: Ethnic Separatism in Quebec' in A.D. Burnett and P.J. Taylor (eds.), *Political Studies from Spatial Perspectives,* John Wiley, Chichester, pp. 389–420

Woolstencroft, R.P. (1980) 'Electoral Geography: Retrospect and Prospect', *International Political Science Review, 1,* 540–60

NOTES ON CONTRIBUTORS

Dr. J.C. Archer	Department of Geography, University of Oklahoma, Norman, USA.
Professor S.D. Brunn	Department of Geography, University of Kentucky, Lexington, USA.
Mr. A. Burnett	Department of Geography, Portsmouth Polytechnic, England.
Dr. J.N.H. Douglas	Department of Geography, Queens University, Belfast, N. Ireland.
Professor R.J. Johnston	Department of Geography, University of Sheffield, England.
Dr. K.A. Mingst	Department of Political Science, University of Kentucky, Lexington, USA.
Dr. M. Pacione	Department of Geography, University of Strathclyde, Glasgow, Scotland.
Dr. R. Paddison	Department of Geography, University of Glasgow, Scotland.
Dr. F. Shelley	Department of Geography, University of Oklahoma, Norman, USA.
Dr. P.J. Taylor	Department of Geography, University of Newcastle upon Tyne, England.
Dr. C.H. Williams	Department of Geography and Recreation Studies, North Staffordshire Polytechnic, England.

INDEX